ANCHORING TO THE POWER OF THE CROSS

# SIX HOURS ONE FRIDAY

MAX LUCADO

Multnomah® Publishers *Sisters, Oregon*

SIX HOURS ONE FRIDAY
published by Multnomah Publishers, Inc.



*International Standard Book Number: 1-59052-233-8 (3-in-1 ABA)*

Cover image by Adobe Image Library
Cover design by Stephen Gardner

Printed in the United States of America



For information:
MULTNOMAH PUBLISHERS, INC.
POST OFFICE BOX 1720
SISTERS, OREGON 97759

Library of Congress Cataloging-in-Publication Data:
Lucado, Max.

Six hours one Friday: anchoring to the cross / Max Lucado.
p. cm.
ISBN 0-88070-793-3 hard
ISBN 0-88070-827-1 paper
ISBN 1-57673-600-8 hard
ISBN 1-57673-601-6 paper
1. Jesus Christ—Passion—Meditations. I Title.
BT431.L795 1989
232.96—dc20 89-9429
CIP

03 04 05 06 07 — 42 41 40 39 38

for

Jacquelyn, Joan, and Dee

from

your baby brother

# CONTENTS

STUDY GUIDE

ANCHORING DEEP

ACKNOWLEDGMENTS

This book was begun on one side of the equator and finished on the other. I've got people to thank in both places.

To the Christians in Rio de Janeiro, Brazil—Thanks for five thrilling years. Obrigado por tudo!

To the Christians at Oak Hills—Your faith and devotion are inspiring.

To Jim Toombs, Mike Cope, Rubel Shelly, Randy Mayeux, and Jim Woodroof—I appreciate the warm words and good advice.

To Ron Bailey—You gave the right counsel at the right time. Thanks.

To my relentless editor, Liz Heaney—I don't know how you do it, but you have a way of turning coal into diamonds.

To my secretary, Mary Stain—What would we do without you at the helm? Thanks for typing and typing and typing and...

To Marcelle Le Gallo and Kathleen McCleery—Thank you for doing Mary's work so she could do mine.

And a special thanks to my wife, Denalyn—You make coming home the highlight of my day.

CHAPTER 1

# HURRICANE WARNINGS

Labor Day weekend, 1979. Throughout the nation people were enjoying their last waltz with summertime. Weekend reunions, camping trips, picnics.

Except in Miami.

While the rest of the nation played, the Gold Coast of south Florida watched. Hurricane David was whirling through the Caribbean, leaving a trail of flooded islands and homeless people.

Floridians don't have to be told to duck when a hurricane is on the warpath. Windows were taped up, canned goods were bought, flashlights were tested. David was about to pounce.

On the Miami River a group of single guys was trying to figure out the best way to protect their houseboat. Not that it was much of a vessel. It was, at best, a rustic cabin on a leaky barge.

But it was home. And if they didn't do something, their home was going to be at the bottom of the river.

None of the fellows had ever lived on a boat before, much less weathered a hurricane. Any sailor worth his salt would have had a good laugh watching those landlubbers.

It was like a *McHale's Navy* rerun. They bought enough rope to tie up the *Queen Mary.* They had their boat tied to trees, tied to moorings, tied to herself. When they were through, the little craft looked as if she'd been caught in a spider's web. They were so busy tying her to everything, it's a wonder one of the guys didn't get tied up.

How was I privy to such a fiasco? You guessed it. The houseboat was mine.

Don't ask what I was doing with a houseboat. Part adventure and part bargain, I guess. But that Labor Day weekend was more adventure than I'd bargained for. I had owned the boat for three monthly payments, and now I was about to have to sacrifice her to the hurricane! I was desperate. *Tie her down!* was all I could think.

I was reaching the end of my rope, in more ways than one, when Phil showed up. Now Phil knew boats. He even looked boat-wise.

He was born wearing a suntan and dock-siders. He spoke the lingo and knew the knots. He also knew hurricanes. Word on the river had it that he had ridden one out for three days in a ten-foot sailboat. They made him a living legend.

He felt sorry for us, so he came to give some advice…and it was sailor-sound. "Tie her to land and you'll regret it. Those trees are gonna get eaten by the 'cane. Your only hope is to anchor deep," he said. "Place four anchors in four different locations, leave the rope slack, and pray for the best."

*Anchor deep.* Good advice. We took it and...well, before I tell you whether or not we handled the hurricane, let's talk about anchor points.

Chances are someone reading these words is about to get caught in a storm. The weather is brewing and the water is rising and you can see the trees beginning to bend.

> You've done everything possible, but your marriage still won't stand. It's just a matter of time.
>
> You bit off more than you could chew. You never should have agreed to take on an assignment like that. There is no way you can meet the deadline. And when that due date comes and you don't produce...
>
> You've been dreading this meeting all week. They've already laid off several men. Why else would the personnel director need to talk to you? And with a newborn at home.

Perhaps the winds have already reached gale force and you're holding on for your life.

> "Why our son?" are the only words you can muster. The funeral is over and the words of comfort have been politely said. Now it is just you, your memories, and your question, "Why me?"

"The tests were positive. The tumor is malignant." Just when you thought the biggest struggle was over. More surgery.

"They took the other bid." That sale was your last hope. To be outbid could mean you'll have to shut down the shop. That client would have been just enough to keep the business afloat for another quarter. But now?

Waves that suck our joy out to sea. Winds that rip out our hopes by their roots. Rising tides that seep under the doors of our lives and cover the floors of our hearts.

I got caught in a hurricane as this chapter was being completed. The warning came in a telephone call during a meeting. The forecaster with the grim news was my wife. "Max, your sister just called. Your mother is going to have quadruple bypass surgery at eight o'clock tomorrow morning." A few quick calls to the airlines. Clothes thrown in a bag. A race to the airport in time to grab the last seat on the last flight.

No time to develop a personal philosophy on pain and suffering. No time to analyze the mystery of death. No time to set anchors. Time only to sit tight and trust the anchor points.

Anchor points. Firm rocks sunk deeply in a solid foundation. Not casual opinions or negotiable hypotheses, but ironclad undeniables that will keep you afloat. How strong are yours? How sturdy is your life when faced with one of these three storms?

*Futility.* You're riding high and getting higher. You should be content. You should be pleased. You are doing what you set out to do. You have a house. You have a job. You have security. You have two cars in the garage and a CD in the bank. By everyone's estimations you should be pleased.

Then why are you so unhappy? Is it because you know that every tide that rises also falls? Is it because your degree and promotion don't answer the questions that keep you awake at night? "What's it for, anyway?" "Who will know what I did?" "Who cares who I am?" "What is the purpose of it all?"

*Failure.* You can't hide it anymore. You blew it. You were wrong. You let everyone down. Instead of standing tall, you fell short. Instead of stepping out, you stepped back. The very thing you swore you'd never do is exactly what you did.

Your anchors drag through sand, finding no rocks. Unless a solid point is found soon, the hull of your heart will be splintered.

*Finality.* The scene repeats itself thousands of times each day in America. Folding chairs on manicured grass. Nicely dressed people under a canvas canopy. Kleenexes. Tears. Words. Metal casket. Flowers. Dirt. Open grave.

It's the wave of finality.

Though it has slapped the beach countless times, you never considered it would hit you, but it did. Uninvited and unexpected, it hit with tidal force, washing away your youth, your innocence, your mate, your friend. And now you're soaked and shivering, wondering if you will be next.

Futility,

failure,

finality.

You don't have to face these monsters alone. Listen to Phil's advice. It's sailor-sound both in and out of the water: Anchor deep.

Got any hurricanes coming your way?

This book examines three anchor points. Three boulders which can stand against any storm. Three rocks that repel the tallest of waves. Three petrified ledges to which you can hook your anchors. Each anchor point was planted firmly in bedrock two thousand years ago by a carpenter who claimed to be the Christ. And it was all done in the course of a single day. A single Friday. All done during six hours, one Friday.

---

To the casual observer there was nothing unusual about these six hours. To the casual observer this Friday was a normal Friday. Six hours of routine. Six hours of the expected.

Six hours. One Friday.

Enough time for

a shepherd to examine his flocks,

a housewife to clean and organize her house,

a physician to receive a baby from a mother's womb

and cool the fever of one near death.

Six hours. From 9:00 A.M. to 3:00 P.M.

Six hours. One Friday.

Six hours filled with, as are all hours, the mystery of life.

---

The bright noonday sun casts a common shadow for the Judean countryside. It's the black silhouette of a shepherd standing near his fat-tailed flock. He stares at the clear sky, searching for clouds. There are none.

He looks back at his sheep. They graze lazily on the rocky hillside. An occasional sycamore provides shade. He sits on the slope and places a blade of grass in his mouth. He looks beyond the flock at the road below.

For the first time in days the traffic is thin. For over a week a river of pilgrims has streamed through this valley, bustling down the road with animals and loaded carts. For days he has watched them from his perch. Though he couldn't hear them, he knew they were speaking a dozen different dialects. And though he didn't talk to them, he knew where they were going and why.

They were going to Jerusalem. And they were going to sacrifice lambs in the temple.

The celebration strikes him as ironic. Streets jammed with people. Marketplaces full of the sounds of the bleating of goats and the selling of birds.

Endless observances.

The people relish the festivities. They awaken early and retire late. They find strange fulfillment in the pageantry.

Not him.

What kind of God would be appeased by the death of an animal?

Oh, the shepherd's doubts are never voiced anywhere except on the hillside. But on this day, they shout.

It isn't the slaughter of the animals that disturbs him. It is the endlessness of it all. How many years has he seen the people come and go? How many caravans? How many sacrifices? How many bloody carcasses?

Memories stalk him. Memories of uncontrolled anger… uncontrolled desire…uncontrolled anxiety. So many mistakes. So many stumbles. So much guilt. God seems so far away. *Lamb after lamb, Passover after Passover. Yet I still feel the same.*

He turns his head and looks again at the sky. Will the blood of yet another lamb really matter?

---

The wife sits in her house. It's Friday. She's alone. Her husband, a priest, is at the temple. It's time for lunch, but she has no appetite. Besides, it's hardly worth the trouble to prepare a meal for one. So, she sits and looks out the window.

The narrow street in front of her house is thick with people. Were she younger, she would be out there. Even if she had no reason to go on the streets, she would go. There was a time when she was energized by such activity. Not now. Now her hair is gray. Her face is wrinkled, and she is tired.

For years she has observed the holidays. For years she has watched the people. Many summers have passed, taking with them her youth and leaving only the perplexities that hound her.

As a young woman she was too busy to ponder. She had children to raise. Meals to prepare. Schedules to keep. She brushed away the riddles like she brushed back her hair. But now her home is empty. Those who needed her have others who need them. Now, the questions are relentless. Who am I? Where did I come from? Where am I going? Why is it all happening?

---

The house is alive with excitement. In one room a man paces. In another a woman pushes. Sweat beads glisten on her forehead. Her eyes close, then open. She laughs, then groans. The young doctor encourages her. "Not much more. Don't give up." With a deep breath she leans forward and exerts her last ounce of energy. Then she leans back, pale and spent.

"You have a son." She raises her head just enough to see the red infant cradled in the broad palms of the physician.

Delighted with his task, the doctor cleans the eyes and smiles as he watches them fight to open. The child, freshly welcomed from the womb, is returned to his mother.

The next house he visits is quiet. Outside the bedroom a white-haired wife sits. Inside is the frail frame of her husband, hot with fever. Nothing can be done. The doctor is helpless as the man takes his last breath. It's deep—his bony, bare chest rises. His mouth opens wide, so wide that his lips whiten. Then he dies.

The same hands that cleansed the eyes of the infant now close the eyes of the dead. All during a period of six hours on one Friday.

He fights off the questions. He hasn't time to hear them today. But they are stubborn and demand to be heard.

Why heal the sick only to postpone death?

Why give strength only to see it ebb away?

Why be born and then begin to die?

Who points the crooked finger at death's next victim?

Who is this one that with such regular randomness separates soul from body?

He shrugs and places the sheet over the ashening face.

Six hours, one Friday.

To the casual observer the six hours are mundane. A shepherd with his sheep, a housewife with her thoughts, a doctor with his patients. But to the handful of awestruck witnesses, the most maddening of miracles is occurring.

God is on a cross. The creator of the universe is being executed.

Spit and blood are caked to his cheeks, and his lips are cracked and swollen. Thorns rip his scalp. His lungs scream with pain. His legs knot with cramps. Taut nerves threaten to snap as pain twangs her morbid melody. Yet, death is not ready. And there is no one to save him, for he is sacrificing himself.

It is no normal six hours....it is no normal Friday.

Far worse than the breaking of his body is the shredding of his heart.

His own countrymen clamored for his death.

His own disciple planted the kiss of betrayal.

His own friends ran for cover.

And now his own father is beginning to turn his back on him, leaving him alone.

A witness could not help but ask: Jesus, do you give no thought to saving yourself? What keeps you there? What holds you to the cross? Nails don't hold gods to trees. What makes you stay?

---

The shepherd stands staring at the now blackened sky. Only seconds before he had stared at the sun. Now there is no sun.

The air is cool. The sky is black. No thunder. No lightning. No clouds. The sheep are restless. The feeling is eerie. The shepherd stands alone, wondering and listening.

What is this hellish darkness? What is this mysterious eclipse? What has happened to the light?

There is a scream in the distance. The shepherd turns toward Jerusalem.

A soldier, unaware that his impulse is part of a divine plan, plunges the spear into the side. The blood of the Lamb of God comes forth and cleanses.

The woman has scarcely lit the lamp when her husband rushes in the door. The reflection of the lamp's flame dances wildly in his wide eyes. "The temple curtain...," he begins breathlessly, "torn! Ripped in two from top to bottom!"

The black angel hovers over the one on the center cross.

No delegation for this death, no demon for this duty. Satan has reserved this task for himself. Gleefully he passes his hand of death over these eyes of life.

But just when the last breath escapes, the war begins.

The pit of the earth rumbles. The young physician nearly loses his balance.

It is an earthquake—a rock-splitting rumble. A stampedelike vibration, as if prison doors have been opened and the captives are thundering to freedom. The doctor fights to keep his balance as he hurries back to the room of the one who has just died.

The body is gone.

---

Six hours. One Friday.

Let me ask you a question: What do you do with that day in history? What do you do with its claims?

If it really happened...if God did commandeer his own crucifixion...if he did turn his back on his own son...if he did storm Satan's gate, then those six hours that Friday were packed with tragic triumph. If that was God on that cross, then the hill called Skull is granite studded with stakes to which you can anchor.

Those six hours were no normal six hours. They were the most critical hours in history. For during those six hours on that Friday, God embedded in the earth three anchor points sturdy enough to withstand any hurricane.

Anchor point #1—*My life is not futile.* This rock secures the hull of your heart. Its sole function is to give you something which you can grip when facing the surging tides of futility and relativism. It's a firm grasp on the conviction that there is truth.

Someone is in control and you have a purpose.

Anchor point #2—*My failures are not fatal.* It's not that he loves what you did, but he loves who you are. You are his. The one who has the right to condemn you provided the way to acquit you. You make mistakes. God doesn't. And he made you.

Anchor point #3—*My death is not final.* There is one more stone to which you should tie. It's large. It's round. And it's heavy. It blocked the door of a grave. It wasn't big enough, though. The tomb that it sealed was the tomb of a transient. He only went in to prove he could come out. And on the way out he took the stone with him and turned it into an anchor point. He dropped it deep into the uncharted waters of death. Tie to his rock and the typhoon of the tomb becomes a spring breeze on Easter Sunday.

There they are. Three anchor points. The anchor points of the cross.

Oh, by the way, Hurricane David never made it to Miami. Thirty minutes off the coast he decided to bear north. The worst damage my boat suffered were some rope burns inflicted by her overzealous crew.

I hope your hurricane misses you, too. But in case it doesn't, take the sailor's advice. "Anchor deep, say a prayer, and hold on." And don't be surprised if someone walks across the water to give you a hand.

ANCHOR POINT 1

# My Life Is Not Futile

CHAPTER 2

# GOD'S FORMULA FOR FATIGUE

It's late. It's past the bedtime hour. They think I'm studying. They think I think they're going to sleep. I know better. Too many giggles. Too many whispers. Too many trips to the closet to get another doll. Too many dashes in the dark to trade pillows.

It's late. It's time for little girls to be going to sleep. But for four-year-old Jenna and two-year-old Andrea, sleep is the last item on their list of things to do.

Here's the list.

> Andrea still needs to flip on her back and let her feet hang out the crib a bit.
>
> Jenna will fluff her pillow, then fluff her pillow and, well, it still needs a little fluffing.

Andrea will scoot from one side of the bed to the other.

Jenna has yet to count her fingers in a whisper and pump her make-believe bicycle.

And before sleep settles over them, more juice will be requested, another song will be sung, and a story will be told.

I love it. It's a game. The contestants? Childhood joy and sleepy eyes. The name of the game? Catch-me-if-you-can.

Sleep is determined to bring the day to a close, and joy is determined to stretch the day out as long as possible. One last enchanted kingdom. One last giggle. One last game.

Maybe you are like that. Maybe, if you had your way, your day would never end. Every moment demands to be savored. You resist sleep as long as possible because you love being awake so much. If you are like that, congratulations. If not, welcome to the majority.

Most of us have learned another way of going to bed, haven't we? It's called crash and burn. Life is so full of games that the last thing we want is another one as we are trying to sleep. So, for most of us, it's good-bye world, hello pillow. Sleep, for many, is not a robber but a refuge—eight hours of relief for our wounded souls.

And if you are kept awake, it's not by counting your fingers but by counting your debts, tasks, or even your tears.

You are tired.

You are weary.

Weary of being slapped by the waves of broken dreams.

Weary of being stepped on and run over in the endless marathon to the top.

Weary of trusting in someone only to have that trust returned in an envelope with no return address.

Weary of staring into the future and seeing only futility.

What steals our childhood zeal? For a child, the possibilities are limitless.

Then weariness finds us. Sesame Street gets traffic-jammed. Dreams of Peter Pan are buried with Grandpa. And Star Trek's endless horizon gets hidden behind smog and skyscrapers.

What is the source of such weariness? What are the names of these burdens?

In this book we are looking at three. Futility, failure, and finality. The three Fs on the human report card. The three burdens that are too big for any back, too heavy for any biceps. Three burdens that no man can carry alone.

Let's look at futility. Few things can weary you more than the fast pace of the human race. Too many sprints for success. Too many laps in the gray-flannel fast lane. Too many nine-to-five masquerade parties. Too many days of doing whatever it takes eventually take their toll. You are left gasping for air, holding your sides on the side of the track.

And it isn't the late night reports or countless airports that sap your strength as much as it is the question you dare not admit you are asking yourself. *Is it worth it? When I get what I want, will it be worth the price I paid?*

Perhaps those were the thoughts of a San Antonio lawyer I read about recently. Successful, well paid, with a new wife and a remodeled house. But apparently it wasn't enough. One day he came home, took a gun out of his vault, climbed into a sleeping bag, and took his life. His note to his bride read, "It's not that I don't love you. It's just that I'm tired and I want to rest."

It is this weariness that makes the words of the carpenter so compelling. Listen to them. "Come to me, all you who are weary and burdened, and I will give you rest."[1]

*Come to me....* The invitation is to come to him. Why him?

He offers the invitation as a penniless rabbi in an oppressed nation. He has no political office, no connections with the authorities in Rome. He hasn't written a best-seller or earned a diploma.

Yet, he dares to look into the leathery faces of farmers and tired faces of housewives and offer rest. He looks into the disillusioned eyes of a preacher or two from Jerusalem. He gazes into the cynical stare of a banker and the hungry eyes of a bartender and makes this paradoxical promise: "Take my yoke upon you and learn from me, for I am gentle and humble in heart, and you will find rest for your souls."[2]

The people came. They came out of the cul-de-sacs and office complexes of their day. They brought him the burdens of their existence, and he gave them not religion, not doctrine, not systems, but rest.

As a result, they called him Lord.

As a result, they called him Savior.

Not so much because of what he said, but because of what he did.

What he did on the cross during six hours, one Friday.

On the following pages you will see several people. They may be new to you, or they may be old acquaintances. They have one thing in common—they came to Jesus weary with the futility of life. A rejected woman. A confused patriarch. Disoriented disciples. A discouraged missionary.

They all found rest. They found anchor points for their storm-tossed souls. And they found that Jesus was the only man to walk God's earth who claimed to have an answer for man's burdens. "Come to me," he invited them.

My prayer is that you, too, will find rest. And that you will sleep like a baby.

1. Matthew 11:28   2. Matthew 11:29

CHAPTER 3

# TWO TOMBSTONES

I had driven by the place countless times. Daily I passed the small plot of land on the way to my office. Daily I told myself, *Someday I need to stop there.*

Today, that "someday" came. I convinced a tight-fisted schedule to give me thirty minutes, and I drove in.

The intersection appears no different from any other in San Antonio: a Burger King, a Rodeway Inn, a restaurant. But turn northwest, go under the cast-iron sign, and you will find yourself on an island of history that is holding its own against the river of progress.

The name on the sign? Locke Hill Cemetery.

As I parked, a darkened sky threatened rain. A lonely path invited me to walk through the two-hundred-plus tombstones.

The fatherly oak trees arched above me, providing a ceiling for the solemn chambers. Tall grass, still wet from the morning dew, brushed my ankles.

The tombstones, though weathered and chipped, were alive with yesterday.

*Ruhet in herrn* accents the markers that bear names like Schmidt, Faustman, Grundmeyer, and Eckert.

Ruth Lacey is buried there. Born in the days of Napoleon—1807. Died over a century ago—1877.

I stood on the same spot where a mother wept on a cold day some eight decades past. The tombstone read simply, "Baby Boldt—Born and died December 10, 1910."

Eighteen-year-old Harry Ferguson was laid to rest in 1883 under these words, "Sleep sweetly tired young pilgrim." I wondered what wearied him so.

Then I saw it. It was chiseled into a tombstone on the northern end of the cemetery. The stone marks the destination of the body of Grace Llewellen Smith. No date of birth is listed, no date of death. Just the names of her two husbands, and this epitaph:

*Sleeps, but rests not.*
*Loved, but was loved not.*
*Tried to please, but pleased not.*
*Died as she lived—alone.*

Words of futility.

I stared at the marker and wondered about Grace Llewellen

Smith. I wondered about her life. I wondered if she'd written the words…or just lived them. I wondered if she deserved the pain. I wondered if she was bitter or beaten. I wondered if she was plain. I wondered if she was beautiful. I wondered why some lives are so fruitful while others are so futile.

I caught myself wondering aloud, "Mrs. Smith, what broke your heart?"

Raindrops smudged my ink as I copied the words.

*Loved, but was loved not…*

Long nights. Empty beds. Silence. No response to messages left. No return to letters written. No love exchanged for love given.

*Tried to please, but pleased not…*

I could hear the hatchet of disappointment.

"How many times do I have to tell you?" Chop.

"You'll never amount to anything." Chop. Chop.

"Why can't you do anything right?" Chop, chop, chop.

*Died as she lived—alone.*

How many Grace Llewellen Smiths are there? How many people will die in the loneliness in which they are living? The homeless in Atlanta. The happy-hour hopper in L.A. A bag lady in Miami. The preacher in Nashville. Any person who doubts whether the world needs him. Any person who is convinced that no one really cares.

Any person who has been given a ring, but never a heart; criticism, but never a chance; a bed, but never rest.

These are the victims of futility.

And unless someone intervenes, unless something happens, the epitaph of Grace Smith will be theirs.

That's why the story you are about to read is significant. It's the story of another tombstone. This time, however, the tombstone doesn't mark the death of a person—it marks the birth.[1]

Her eyes squint against the noonday sun. Her shoulders stoop under the weight of the water jar. Her feet trudge, stirring dust on the path. She keeps her eyes down so she can dodge the stares of the others.

She is a Samaritan; she knows the sting of racism. She is a woman; she's bumped her head on the ceiling of sexism. She's been married to five men. Five. Five different marriages. Five different beds. Five different rejections. She knows the sound of slamming doors.

She knows what it means to love and receive no love in return. Her current mate won't even give her his name. He only gives her a place to sleep.

If there is a Grace Llewellen Smith in the New Testament, it is this woman. The epitaph of insignificance could have been hers. And it would have been, except for an encounter with a stranger.

On this particular day, she came to the well at noon. Why hadn't she gone in the early morning with the other women? Maybe she had. Maybe she just needed an extra draw of water on a hot day. Or maybe not. Maybe it was the other women she was avoiding. A walk in the hot sun was a small price to pay in order to escape their sharp tongues.

"Here she comes."

"Have you heard? She's got a new man!"

"They say she'll sleep with anyone."

"Shhh. There she is."

So she came to the well at noon. She expected silence. She expected solitude. Instead, she found one who knew her better than she knew herself.

He was seated on the ground: legs outstretched, hands folded, back resting against the well. His eyes were closed. She stopped and looked at him. She looked around. No one was near. She looked back at him. He was obviously Jewish. What was he doing here? His eyes opened and hers ducked in embarrassment. She went quickly about her task.

Sensing her discomfort, Jesus asked her for water. But she was too streetwise to think that all he wanted was a drink. "Since when does an uptown fellow like you ask a girl like me for water?" She wanted to know what he really had in mind. Her intuition was partly correct. He was interested in more than water. He was interested in her heart.

They talked. Who could remember the last time a man had spoken to her with respect?

He told her about a spring of water that would quench not the thirst of the throat, but of the soul.

That intrigued her. "Sir, give me this water so that I won't get thirsty and have to keep coming here to draw water."

"Go, call your husband and come back."

Her heart must have sunk. Here was a Jew who didn't care if she was a Samaritan. Here was a man who didn't look down on her as a woman. Here was the closest thing to gentleness she'd ever seen. And now he was asking her about...that.

Anything but that. Maybe she considered lying. "Oh, my husband? He's busy." Maybe she wanted to change the subject. Perhaps she wanted to leave—but she stayed. And she told the truth.

"I have no husband." (Kindness has a way of inviting honesty.)

You probably know the rest of the story. I wish you didn't. I wish you were hearing it for the first time. For if you were, you'd be wide eyed as you waited to see what Jesus would do next. Why? Because you've wanted to do the same thing.

You've wanted to take off your mask. You've wanted to stop pretending. You've wondered what God would do if you opened your cobweb-covered door of secret sin.

This woman wondered what Jesus would do. She must have wondered if the kindness would cease when the truth was revealed. *He will be angry. He will leave. He will think I'm worthless.*

If you've had the same anxieties, then get out your pencil. You'll want to underline Jesus' answer.

"You're right. You have had five husbands and the man you are with now won't even give you a name."

No criticism? No anger? No what-kind-of-mess-have-you-made-of-your-life lectures?

No. It wasn't perfection that Jesus was seeking, it was honesty.

The woman was amazed.

"I can see that you are a prophet." Translation? "There is something different about you. Do you mind if I ask you something?"

Then she asked the question that revealed the gaping hole in her soul.

"Where is God? My people say he is on the mountain. Your people say he is in Jerusalem. I don't know where he is."

I'd give a thousand sunsets to see the expression on Jesus' face as he heard those words. Did his eyes water? Did he smile? Did he look up into the clouds and wink at his father? Of all the places to find a hungry heart—Samaria?

Of all the Samaritans to be searching for God—a woman?

Of all the women to have an insatiable appetite for God—a five-time divorcée?

And of all the people to be chosen to personally receive the secret of the ages, an outcast among outcasts? The most "insignificant" person in the region?

Remarkable. Jesus didn't reveal the secret to King Herod. He didn't request an audience of the Sanhedrin and tell them the news. It wasn't within the colonnades of a Roman court that he announced his identity.

No, it was in the shade of a well in a rejected land to an ostracized woman. His eyes must have danced as he whispered the secret.

"I am the Messiah."

The most important phrase in the chapter is one easily overlooked. "Then, leaving her water jar, the woman went back to the town and said to the people, 'Come, see a man who told me everything I ever did. Could this be the Christ?'"[2]

Don't miss the drama of the moment. Look at her eyes, wide with amazement. Listen to her as she struggles for words. "Y-y-you a-a-a-are the M-m-m-messiah!" And watch as she scrambles to her feet, takes one last look at this grinning Nazarene, turns and runs right into the burly chest of Peter. She almost falls, regains her balance, and hotfoots it toward her hometown.

Did you notice what she forgot? She forgot her water jar. She left behind the jug that had caused the sag in her shoulders. She left behind the burden she brought.

Suddenly the shame of the tattered romances disappeared. Suddenly the insignificance of her life was swallowed by the significance of the moment. "God is here! God has come! God cares…for me!"

That is why she forgot her water jar. That is why she ran to the city. That is why she grabbed the first person she saw and announced her discovery, "I just talked to a man who knows everything I ever did…and he loves me anyway!"

The disciples offered Jesus some food. He refused it—he was too excited! He had just done what he does best. He had taken a life that was drifting and given it direction.

He was exuberant!

"Look!" he announced to disciples, pointing at the woman who was running to the village. "Vast fields of human souls are ripening all around us, and are ready now for the reaping."[3]

Who could eat at a time like this?

---

For some of you the story of these two women is touching but distant. You belong. You are needed and you know it. You've got more friends than you can visit and more tasks than you can accomplish.

Insignificance will not be chiseled on your tombstone.

Be thankful.

But others of you are different. You paused at the epitaph because it was yours. You see the face of Grace Smith when you look into the mirror. You know why the Samaritan woman was avoiding people. You do the same thing.

You know what it's like to have no one sit by you at the cafeteria. You've wondered what it would be like to have one good friend. You've been in love and you wonder if it is worth the pain to do it again.

And you, too, have wondered where in the world God is.

I have a friend named Joy who teaches underprivileged children in an inner city church. Her class is a lively group of nine-year-olds who love life and aren't afraid of God. There is one exception, however—a timid girl by the name of Barbara.

Her difficult home life had left her afraid and insecure. For the weeks that my friend was teaching the class, Barbara never spoke. Never. While the other children talked, she sat. While the others sang, she was silent. While the others giggled, she was quiet.

Always present. Always listening. Always speechless.

Until the day Joy gave a class on heaven. Joy talked about seeing God. She talked about tearless eyes and deathless lives.

Barbara was fascinated. She wouldn't release Joy from her stare.

She listened with hunger. Then she raised her hand. "Mrs. Joy?"

Joy was stunned. Barbara had never asked a question. "Yes, Barbara?"

"Is heaven for girls like me?"

Again, I would give a thousand sunsets to have seen Jesus' face as this tiny prayer reached his throne. For indeed that is what it was—a prayer.

An earnest prayer that a good God in heaven would remember a forgotten soul on earth. A prayer that God's grace would seep into the cracks and cover one the church let slip through. A prayer to take a life that no one else could use and use it as no one else could.

Not a prayer from a pulpit, but one from a bed in a convalescent home. Not a prayer prayed confidently by a black-robed seminarian, but one whispered fearfully by a recovering alcoholic.

A prayer to do what God does best: take the common and make it spectacular. To once again take the rod and divide the sea. To take a pebble and kill a Goliath. To take water and make sparkling wine. To take a peasant boy's lunch and feed a multitude. To take mud and restore sight. To take three spikes and a wooden beam and make them the hope of humanity. To take a rejected woman and make her a missionary.

---

There are two graves in this chapter. The first is the lonely one in the Locke Hill Cemetery. The grave of Grace Llewellen Smith. She knew not love. She knew not gratification. She knew only the pain of the chisel as it carved this epitaph into her life.

*Sleeps, but rests not.*
*Loved, but was loved not.*
*Tried to please, but pleased not.*
*Died as she lived—alone.*

That, however, is not the only grave in this story. The second is near a water well. The tombstone? A water jug. A forgotten water jug. It has no words, but has great significance—for it is the burial place of insignificance.

1. This story is found in John 4:1-42. 2. John 4:28, 29 3. John 4:35, Living Bible

CHAPTER 4

# Living Proof

"Jenna, wake up. It's time to go to school."

She will hear those words a thousand times in her life. But she heard them for the first time this morning.

I sat on the edge of her bed for a while before I said them to her. To tell the truth, I didn't want to say them. I didn't want to wake her. A queer hesitancy hung over me as I sat in the early morning blackness. As I sat in the silence, I realized that my words would awaken her to a new world.

For four lightning-fast years she'd been ours, and ours alone. And now that was all going to change.

We put her to bed last night as "our girl"—exclusive property of Mommy and Daddy. Mommy and Daddy read to her, taught her, listened to her. But beginning today, someone else would, too.

Until today, it was Mommy and Daddy who wiped away the tears and put on the Band-Aids. But beginning today, someone else would, too.

I didn't want to wake her.

Until today, her life was essentially us—Mom, Dad, and baby sister Andrea. Today that life would grow—new friends, a teacher. Her world was this house—her room, her toys, her swing set. Today her world would expand. She would enter the winding halls of education—painting, reading, calculating...becoming.

I didn't want to wake her. Not because of the school. It's a fine one. Not because I don't want her to learn. Heaven knows I want her to grow, to read, to mature. Not because she doesn't want to go. School has been all she could talk about for the last week!

No, I didn't want to wake her up because I didn't want to give her up.

But I woke her anyway. I interrupted her childhood with the inevitable proclamation, "Jenna, wake up.... It's time to go to school."

It took me forever to get dressed. Denalyn saw me moping around and heard me humming "Sunrise, Sunset" and said, "You'll never make it through her wedding." She's right.

We drove to school in two cars so I could go directly to work. I asked Jenna to ride with me. I thought I should give her a bit of fatherly assurance. As it turned out, I was the one needing assurance.

For one dedicated to the craft of words, I found very few to share with her. I told her to enjoy herself. I told her to obey her teacher. I told her, "If you get lonely or afraid, tell your teacher to call me and I'll come and get you." "Okay," she smiled. Then she asked if she could listen to a tape with kids' music. "Okay," I said.

So while she sang songs, I swallowed lumps. I watched her as she sang. She looked big. Her little neck stretched as high as it could to look over the dash. Her eyes were hungry and bright. Her hands were folded in her lap. Her feet, wearing brand new turquoise and pink tennis shoes, barely extended over the seat.

"Denalyn was right," I mumbled to myself. "I'll never make it through the wedding."

*What is she thinking?* I wondered. *Does she know how tall this ladder of education is that she will begin climbing this morning?*

No, she didn't. But I did. How many chalkboards will those eyes see? How many books will those hands hold? How many teachers will those feet follow and—gulp—imitate?

Were it within my power, I would have, at that very instant, assembled all the hundreds of teachers, instructors, coaches, and tutors she would have over the next eighteen years and announced, "This is no normal student. This is my child. Be careful with her!"

As I parked and turned off the engine, my big girl became small again. And it was a voice of a very little girl that broke the silence. "Daddy, I don't want to get out."

I looked at her. The eyes that had been bright were now fearful. The lips that had been singing were now trembling.

I fought a Herculean urge to grant her request. Everything

within me wanted to say, "Okay, let's forget it all and get out of here." For a brief, eternal moment I considered kidnapping my own daughters, grabbing my wife, and escaping these horrid paws of progress to live forever in the Himalayas.

But I knew better. I knew it was time. I knew it was right. And I knew she would be fine. But I never knew it would be so hard to say, "Honey, you'll be all right. Come on, I'll carry you."

And she was all right. One step into the classroom and the cat of curiosity pounced on her. And I walked away. I gave her up. Not much. And not as much as I will have to in the future. But I gave her up as much as I could today.

As I was walking back to my truck, a verse pounced on me. It was a passage I'd studied before. Today's events took it from black-and-white theology to Technicolor reality.

"What, then, shall we say in response to this? If God is for us, who can be against us? He who did not spare his own Son, but *gave him up for us all*—how will he not also, along with him, graciously give us all things?"[1]

Is that how you felt, God? Is what I felt this morning anything like what you felt when you gave up your son?

If so, it explains so much. It explains the proclamation of the angels to the shepherds outside Bethlehem. (A proud father was announcing the birth of a son.)

It explains the voice at Jesus' baptism, "This is my son...." (You did what I wanted to do, but couldn't.)

It explains the transfiguration of Moses and Elijah on the

mountaintop. (You sent them to encourage him.)

And it explains how your heart must have ached as you heard the cracking voice of your son, "Father, take this cup away."

I was releasing Jenna into a safe environment with a compassionate teacher who stood ready to wipe away any tears. You released Jesus into a hostile arena with a cruel soldier who turned the back of your son into raw meat.

I said good-bye to Jenna knowing she would make friends, laugh, and draw pictures. You said good-bye to Jesus knowing he would be spat upon, laughed at, and killed.

I gave up my child fully aware that were she to need me I would be at her side in a heartbeat. You said good-bye to your son fully aware that when he would need you the most, when his cry of despair would roar through the heavens, you would sit in silence. The angels, though positioned, would hear no command from you. Your son, though in anguish, would feel no comfort from your hands.

"He gave his best," Paul reasons. "Why should we doubt his love?"

Before the day was over, I sat in silence a second time. This time not beside my daughter, but before my Father. This time not sad over what I had to give, but grateful for what I'd already received—living proof that God does care.

1. Romans 8:31, 32 (emphasis mine)

CHAPTER 5

# Flaming Torches and Living Promises

Doubt. He's a nosy neighbor. He's an unwanted visitor. He's an obnoxious guest. Just when you were all prepared for a weekend of relaxation...just when you pulled off your work clothes and climbed into your Bermuda shorts...just when you unfolded the lawn chair and sat down with a magazine and a glass of iced tea...his voice interrupted your thoughts.

"Hey, Bob. Got a few minutes? I've got a few questions. I don't mean to be obnoxious, Bob, but how can you believe that a big God could ever give a hoot about you? Don't you think you are being presumptuous in thinking God wants you in heaven?

"You may assume you are on pretty good terms with the man upstairs, but haven't you forgotten that business trip in Atlanta? You think he won't call your cards on that one?

"How do you know God gives a flip about you anyway?"

Got a neighbor like this?

He'll pester you. He'll irritate you. He'll criticize your judgment. He'll kick the stool out from under you and refuse to help you up. He'll tell you not to believe in the invisible yet offer no answer for the inadequacy of the visible.

He's a mealy-mouthed, two-faced liar who deals from the bottom of the deck. His aim is not to convince you but to confuse you. He doesn't offer solutions, he only raises questions.

Don't let him fool you. Though he may speak the current jargon, he is no newcomer. His first seeds of doubt were sown in the Garden of Eden in the heart of Eve.

There she sat, enjoying the trees, sipping on a mint julep and catching a few rays when she noticed a pair of beady eyes peering over the shrubs.

After a little small talk, he positioned himself between Eve and the sun and cast his first shadow of a doubt. "Did God really say, 'You must not eat from any tree in the garden'?"[1]

No anger. No picket signs. No "God is dead" demonstrations. Just questions.

Had any visits from this fellow lately? If you find yourself going to church in order to be saved and not because you are saved, then you've been listening to him. If you find yourself doubting God could forgive you *again* for *that,* you've been sold some snake oil. If you are more cynical about Christians than sincere about Christ, then guess who came to dinner?

I suggest you put a lock on your gate. I suggest you post a "Do Not Enter" sign on your door. I also suggest you take a look at an encounter between a fitful doubter and a faithful God.

---

Abraham, or Abram as he was known at the time, was finding God's promises about as easy to swallow as a chicken bone. The promise? That his descendants would be as numerous as the stars. The problem? No son. "No problem," came God's response.

Abram looked over at his wife, Sarah, as she shuffled by in her gown and slippers with the aid of a walker. The chicken bone stuck for a few minutes but eventually slid down his throat.

Just as he was turning away to invite Sarah to a candlelight dinner, he heard promise number two.

"Abram."

"Yes, Lord?"

"All this land will be yours."

Imagine God telling you that your children will someday own Fifth Avenue, and you will understand Abram's hesitation.

"On that one, Father, I need a little help."

And a little help was given.

---

It's a curious scene.

Twilight. The sky is a soft blue ceiling with starry diamonds. The air is cool. The animals in the pasture are quiet. The trees are silhouettes. Abram dozes under a tree. His sleep is fitful.

It's as if God is allowing Abram's doubt to run its course. In his dreams Abram is forced to face the lunacy of it all. The voices of doubt speak convincingly.

*How do I know God is with me?*

*What if this is all a hoax?*

*How do you know that is God who is speaking?*

The thick and dreadful darkness of doubt.

The same darkness you feel when you sit on a polished pew in a funeral chapel and listen to the obituary of the one you love more than life.

The same darkness you feel when you hear the words, "The tumor is malignant. We have to operate."

The same darkness that falls upon you when you realize you just lost your temper…again.

The same darkness you feel when you realize the divorce you never wanted is final.

The same darkness into which Jesus screamed, "My God, my God, why have you forsaken me?"

Appropriate words. For when we doubt, God seems very far away.

Which is exactly why he chose to draw so near.

God had told Abram to take three animals, cut them in half, and arrange the halves facing each other. To us the command is mysterious. To Abram, it wasn't. He'd seen the ceremony before. He'd participated in it. He'd sealed many covenants by walking through the divided carcasses and stating, "May what has happened to these animals happen also to me if I fail to uphold my word."[2]

That is why his heart must have skipped a beat when he saw the lights in the darkness passing between the carcasses. The soft golden glow from the coals in the firepot and the courageous flames from the torch. What did they mean?

The invisible God had drawn near to make his immovable promise. "To your descendants I give this land."[3]

---

And though God's people often forgot their God, God didn't forget them. He kept his word. The land became theirs.

God didn't give up. He never gives up.

When Joseph was dropped into a pit by his own brothers, God didn't give up.

When Moses said, "Here I am, send Aaron," God didn't give up.

When the delivered Israelites wanted Egyptian slavery instead of milk and honey, God didn't give up.

When Aaron was making a false god at the very moment Moses was with the true God, God didn't give up.

When only two of the ten spies thought the Creator was powerful enough to deliver the created, God didn't give up.

When Samson whispered to Delilah, when Saul roared after David, when David schemed against Uriah, God didn't give up.

When God's word lay forgotten and man's idols stood glistening, God didn't give up.

When the children of Israel were taken into captivity, God didn't give up.

He could have given up. He could have turned his back. He could have walked away from the wretched mess, but he didn't.

He didn't give up.

When he became flesh and was the victim of an assassination attempt before he was two years old, he didn't give up.

When the people from his own hometown tried to push him over a cliff, he didn't give up.

When his brothers ridiculed him, he didn't give up.

When he was accused of blaspheming God by people who didn't fear God, he didn't give up.

When Peter worshiped him at the supper and cursed him at the fire, he didn't give up.

When people spat in his face, he didn't spit back. When the bystanders slapped him, he didn't slap them. When a whip ripped his sides, he didn't turn and command the awaiting angels to stuff that whip down that soldier's throat.

And when human hands fastened the divine hands to a cross with spikes, it wasn't the soldiers who held the hands of Jesus steady. It was God who held them steady. For those wounded hands were the same invisible hands that had carried the firepot and the torch two thousand years earlier. They were the same hands that had brought light into Abram's thick and dreadful darkness. They had come to do it again.

So, the next time that obnoxious neighbor walks in, escort him out. Out to the hill. Out to Calvary. Out to the cross where, with holy blood, the hand that carried the flame wrote the promise, "God would give up his only son before he'd give up on you."

1. Genesis 3:1 2. Jeremiah 34:18 3. Genesis 15:18

CHAPTER 6

# ANGELIC MESSAGES

I had every right to be angry. If you'd had a week like mine, you would have been angry, too.

My problems began on Sunday night. I was still living in Brazil and was taking some relatives to southern Brazil to see the Iguaçú Falls. A canceled flight left us stranded several hours in the Saõ Paulo airport. No warning. No explanation. Just a notification as we were landing that the plane we were going to catch was going nowhere. If we wanted, we could wait two hours and catch another one.

"If we wanted!" Grrrr.

When we got to our hotel, it was raining. It rained until the day we left.

Determined to record the falls, I carried my video camera for one mile through a rainstorm. I don't mean a drizzle or a sprinkle or a shower. I mean a blinding downpour. When I reached the falls, I realized I had left the camera turned on for the previous hour and filmed the inside of the camera bag and run down the battery.

When I got back to the hotel, I realized that the rain had ruined the camera. How much ruin? Three hundred dollars' worth of ruin. That was Wednesday. The week wasn't over yet.

When I got back to Rio, I found out Denalyn had told her family that we were going to spend the upcoming Christmas with them. I had already told my family that we were going to spend the holidays with them.

Thursday was the clincher. Denalyn called me at home. Our car had broken down. The car that the car dealer promised was in great shape. The car that the car dealer promised was worth the extra money. The car that the car dealer had sworn was trouble free. It broke down. Downtown. Again. On my day off.

I walked to the shopping center. I spoke to no one. No one dared to speak to me.

I sat in the car and tried to start it. No luck. When I turned the key in the ignition, all I could hear were the promises of the car dealer and the jingle of the mechanic's cash register. I spent an hour tinkering with a broken-down car in a parking lot.

Finally I called the mechanic. The tow truck was busy. Could I wait a few minutes? In Brazil, the word *minutes* can better be translated *years.* So I waited. And I waited. And I waited. My children grew up and had children of their own, and still I was waiting.

Finally, as the sun was setting, the truck appeared. "Put it in neutral," I was instructed. As I climbed in the car, I thought, *Might as well try it one more time.* I turned the key in the ignition. Guess what? You got it. It started.

That should have been good news. It was, until I saw the driver of the tow truck in no hurry to leave. He wanted to be paid. "For what?" I implored. "Was it my fault your car started?" he replied. It's a good thing I didn't know how to say "smart aleck" in Portuguese. So I paid him for watching me start my car.

I immediately drove the car to the mechanic. As I drove, two devils came and perched on my shoulders. The fact that I couldn't see them didn't make them any less real. I could hear them—they spoke the language of the Liar.

One was anger. If there was anything I wasn't mad at by this point, he took care of that. My list of offenses was long and ugly.

The other was self-pity. Boy, did he find a listening ear. Not only had I had a bad week, he reminded me that I had been plagued with a bad life! Born with the handicap of freckles and red hair. Always too slow for track. Never elected "most likely to succeed." And now, a missionary suffering on foreign soil.

Anger in one ear and self-pity in the other...if I hadn't seen him, who knows what I would have done.

He didn't look like an angel. In fact, he looked like anything but an angel. But I know he was an angel, for only angels bring that type of a message.

He knocked on my car window.

*"Trocadinho, Senhor?"* ("Do you have any spare change, sir?")

He was, at most, nine years old. Shirtless. Barefooted. Dirty. So dirty I couldn't tell if he was wearing shorts or not. His hair was matted. His skin was crusty. I rolled down the window. The voices on my shoulders became silent.

"What's your name?" I asked.

"José."

I looked over at the sidewalk. Two other street orphans were walking towards the cars behind me. They were naked except for ragged gym shorts.

"Are they your brothers?" I asked.

"No, just friends."

"Have you collected much money today?"

He opened a dirty hand full of coins. Enough money, perhaps, for a soft drink.

I reached in my wallet and pulled out the equivalent to a dollar. His eyes brightened. Mine watered. The light changed and the cars behind me honked. As I drove away, I saw him running to tell his friends what he had received.

The voices on my shoulders didn't dare say a word. Nor did I. The three of us drove in shameful silence.

I figured I had said enough. And God had heard every word.

What if God had responded to my grumblings? What if he'd heeded my complaints? He could have. He could have answered my carelessly mumbled prayers.

And had he chosen to do so, a prototype of the result had just appeared at my door.

"Don't want to mess with airlines? This boy doesn't have that problem. Frustrated with your video camera? That's one headache this boy doesn't have. He may have to worry about tonight's dinner, but he doesn't have to worry about video cameras. And family? I'm sure this orphan would gladly take one of your families if you are too busy to appreciate them. And cars? Yes, they are a hassle, aren't they? You should try this boy's mode of transportation—bare feet."

God sent the boy with a message. And the point the boy made was razor sharp.

"You cry over spilled champagne."

Ouch.

"Your complaints are not over the lack of necessities but the abundance of benefits. You bellyache over the frills, not the basics; over benefits, not essentials. The source of your problems is your blessings."

José gave me a lot for my dollar; he gave me a lesson on gratitude.

Gratitude. More aware of what you have than what you don't. Recognizing the treasure in the simple—a child's hug, fertile soil, a golden sunset. Relishing in the comfort of the common—a warm bed, a hot meal, a clean shirt.

And no one has more reason to be grateful than the one who has been reminded of God's gift by one of God's angels. I was. And so was Franciszek Gajowniczek. His story is moving.

It's difficult to find beauty in death. It's even more difficult to find beauty in a death camp. Especially Auschwitz. Four million Jews died there in World War II. A half-ton of human hair is still preserved. The showers that sprayed poison gas still stand.

But for all the ugly memories of Auschwitz there is one of beauty. It's the memory Gajowniczek has of Maximilian Kolbe.

In February 1941 Kolbe was incarcerated at Auschwitz. He was a Franciscan priest. In the harshness of the slaughterhouse he maintained the gentleness of Christ. He shared his food. He gave up his bunk. He prayed for his captors. One could call him the "Saint of Auschwitz."

In July of that same year there was an escape from the prison. It was the custom at Auschwitz to kill ten prisoners for every one who escaped. All the prisoners would be gathered in the courtyard, and the commandant would randomly select ten men from the ranks. These victims would be immediately taken to a cell where they would receive no food or water until they died.

The commandant begins his selection. At each selection another prisoner steps forward to fill the sinister quota. The tenth name he calls is Gajowniczek.

As the SS officers check the numbers of the condemned, one of the condemned begins to sob. "My wife and my children," he weeps.

The officers turn as they hear movement among the prisoners. The guards raise their rifles. The dogs tense, anticipating a command to attack. A prisoner has left his row and is pushing his way to the front.

It is Kolbe. No fear on his face. No hesitancy in his step. The capo shouts at him to stop or be shot. "I want to talk to the commander," he says calmly. For some reason the officer doesn't club or kill him. Kolbe stops a few paces from the commandant, removes his hat, and looks the German officer in the eye.

"Herr Commandant, I wish to make a request, please."

That no one shot him is a miracle.

"I want to die in the place of this prisoner." He points at the sobbing Gajowniczek. The audacious request is presented without stammer.

"I have no wife and children. Besides, I am old and not good for anything. He's in better condition." Kolbe knew well the Nazi mentality.

"Who are you?" the officer asks.

"A Catholic priest."

The block is stunned. The commandant, uncharacteristically speechless. After a moment, he barks, "Request granted."

Prisoners were never allowed to speak. Gajowniczek says, "I could only thank him with my eyes. I was stunned and could hardly grasp what was going on. The immensity of it: I, the condemned, am to live and someone else willingly and voluntarily offers his life for me—a stranger. Is this some dream?"

The Saint of Auschwitz outlived the other nine. In fact, he didn't die of thirst or starvation. He died only after carbolic acid was injected into his veins. It was August 14, 1941.

Gajowniczek survived the Holocaust. He made his way back

to his hometown. Every year, however, he goes back to Auschwitz. Every August 14 he goes back to say thank you to the man who died in his place.

In his backyard there is a plaque. A plaque he carved with his own hands. A tribute to Maximilian Kolbe—the man who died so he could live.[1]

There are times that it takes an angel to remind us about what we have.

There aren't very many similarities between Franciszek Gajowniczek and Max Lucado. We speak two different languages. We salute two different flags. We know two different homelands. But we do have three things in common.

We both had an angel set us free from a prison. We both had a Jewish teacher die in our place. And we both learned that what we already have is far greater than anything we might want.

1. This story is adapted from the book *A Man for Others* by Patricia Treece.

CHAPTER 7

# REMEMBER

*On the evening of that first day of the week,*
*when the disciples were together,*
*with the doors locked for fear of the Jews...*
*John 20:19*

The church of Jesus Christ began with a group of frightened men in a second-floor room in Jerusalem.

Though trained and taught, they didn't know what to say. Though they'd marched with him for three years, they now sat...afraid. They were timid soldiers, reluctant warriors, speechless messengers.

Their most courageous act was to get up and lock the door.

Some looked out the window, some looked at the wall, some looked at the floor, but all looked inside themselves.

And well they should, for it was an hour of self-examination. All their efforts seemed so futile. Nagging their memories were the promises they'd made but not kept. When the Roman soldiers took Jesus, Jesus' followers took off. With the very wine of the covenant on their breath and the bread of his sacrifice in their bellies, they fled.

All those boasts of bravado? All those declarations of devotion? They lay broken and shattered at the gate of Gethsemane's garden.

We don't know where the disciples went when they fled the garden, but we do know what they took: a memory. They took a heart-stopping memory of a man who called himself no less than God in the flesh. And they couldn't get him out of their minds. Try as they might to lose him in the crowd, they couldn't forget him. If they saw a leper, they thought of his compassion. If they heard a storm, they would remember the day he silenced one. If they saw a child, they would think of the day he held one. And if they saw a lamb being carried to the temple, they would remember his face streaked with blood and his eyes flooded with love.

No, they couldn't forget him. As a result, they came back. And, as a result, the church of our Lord began with a group of frightened men in an upper room.

---

Sound familiar? Things haven't changed much in two thousand years, have they? How many churches today find themselves paralyzed in the upper room?

How many congregations have just enough religion to come together, but not enough passion to go out? If the doors aren't locked, they might as well be.

Upper-room futility. A little bit of faith but very little fire.

> "Sure, we're doing our part to reach the world. Why, just last year we mailed ten correspondence courses. We're anticipating a response any day now."
>
> "You bet we care that the world is reached! We send $150 a month to…uh, well…ol' what's-his-name down there in…uh, well, oh, I forget the place, but…we pray for it often."
>
> "World hunger? Why, that's high on our priority list! In fact, we have plans to plan a planning session. At least, that is what we are planning to do."

Good people. Lots of ideas. Plenty of good intentions. Budgets. Meetings. Words. Promises. But while all this is going on, the door remains locked and the story stays a secret.

You don't turn your back on Christ, but you don't turn toward him either. You don't curse his name, but neither do you praise it. You know you should do something, but you're not sure what. You know you should come together, but you're not sure why.

Upper-room futility. Confused ambassadors behind locked doors. What will it take to unlock them? What will it take to ignite the fire? What will it take to restore the first-century passion? What will have to happen before the padlocks of futility tumble from our doors and are trampled under the feet of departing disciples?

More training? That's part of it. Better strategies? That would help. A greater world vision? Undoubtedly. More money? That's imperative. A greater dependence on the Holy Spirit? Absolutely.

But in the midst of these items there is one basic ingredient that cannot be overlooked. There is one element so vital that its absence ensures our failure. What is needed to get us out is exactly what got the apostles out.

Picture the scene. Peter, John, James. They came back. Banking on some zany possibility that the well of forgiveness still had a few drops, they came back. Daring to dream that the master had left them some word, some plan, some direction, they came back.

But little did they know their wildest dream wasn't wild enough. Just as someone mumbles, "It's no use," they hear a noise. They hear a voice.

"Peace be with you."[1]

Every head lifted. Every eye turned. Every mouth dropped open. Someone looked at the door.

It was still locked.

It was a moment the apostles would never forget, a story they would never cease to tell. The stone of the tomb was not enough to keep him in. The walls of the room were not enough to keep him out.

The one betrayed sought his betrayers. What did he say to them? Not "What a bunch of flops!" Not "I told you so." No "Where-were-you-when-I-needed-you?" speeches. But simply one phrase, "Peace be with you." The very thing they didn't have was the very thing he offered: peace.

It was too good to be true! So amazing was the appearance that some were saying, "Pinch me, I'm dreaming" even at the ascension.[2] No wonder they returned to Jerusalem with great joy![3] No wonder they were always in the temple praising God![4]

A transformed group stood beside a transformed Peter as he announced some weeks later: "Therefore let all Israel be assured of this: God has made this Jesus, whom you crucified, both Lord and Christ."[5]

No timidity in his words. No reluctance. About three thousand people believed his message.

The apostles sparked a movement. The people became followers of the death-conqueror. They couldn't hear enough or say enough about him. People began to call them "Christ-ians." Christ was their model, their message. They preached "Jesus Christ and him crucified," not for the lack of another topic, but because they couldn't exhaust this one.

What unlocked the doors of the apostles' hearts?

Simple. They saw Jesus. They encountered the Christ. Their sins collided with their Savior and their Savior won! What lit the boiler of the apostles was a red-hot conviction that the very one who should have sent them to hell, went to hell for them and came back to tell about it.

A lot of things would happen to them over the next few decades. Many nights would be spent away from home. Hunger would gnaw at their bellies. Rain would soak their skin. Stones would bruise their bodies. Shipwrecks, lashings, martyrdom. But there was a scene in the repertoire of memories that caused them never to look back: the betrayed coming back to find his betrayers, not to scourge them, but to send them. Not to criticize them for forgetting, but to commission them to remember. *Remember* that he who was dead is alive and they who were guilty have been forgiven.

---

Think about the first time you ever saw him. Think about your first encounter with the Christ. Robe yourself in that moment. Resurrect the relief. Recall the purity. Summon forth the passion. Can you remember?

I can. 1965. A red-headed ten-year-old with a tornado of freckles sits in a Bible class on a Wednesday night. What I remember of the class are scenes—school desks with initials carved in them. A blackboard. A dozen or so kids, some listening, some not. A teacher wearing a suit coat too tight to button around his robust belly.

He is talking about Jesus. He is explaining the cross. I know I had heard it before, but that night I heard it for sure. "You can't save yourself; you need a savior." I can't explain why it connected that night as opposed to another, but it did. He simply articulated what I was beginning to understand—I was lost—and he explained what I needed—a redeemer. From that night on, my heart belonged to Jesus.

Many would argue that a ten-year-old is too young for such a decision. And they may be right. All I know is that I never made a more earnest decision in my life. I didn't know much about God, but what I knew was enough. I knew I wanted to go to heaven. And I knew I couldn't do it alone.

No one had to tell me to be happy. No one had to tell me to tell others. They couldn't keep me quiet. I told all my friends at school. I put a bumper sticker on my bicycle. And though I'd never read 2 Corinthians 4:13, I knew what it meant. "I believed; therefore I have spoken." Pardon truly received is pardon powerfully proclaimed.

There is a direct correlation between the accuracy of our memory and the effectiveness of our mission. If we are not teaching people how to be saved, it is perhaps because we have forgotten the tragedy of being lost! If we're not teaching the message of forgiveness, it may be because we don't remember what it was like to be guilty. And if we're not preaching the cross, it could be that we've subconsciously decided that—God forbid—somehow we don't need it.

In what was perhaps the last letter Paul ever wrote, he begged Timothy not to forget. In a letter written within earshot of the sharpening of the blade that would sever his head, he urged Timothy to remember. "Remember Jesus Christ...."[6] You can almost picture the old warrior smiling as he wrote the words. "Remember Jesus Christ, raised from the dead, descended from David. This is my gospel...."

When times get hard, remember Jesus. When people don't listen, remember Jesus. When tears come, remember Jesus. When disappointment is your bed partner, remember Jesus. When fear pitches his tent in your front yard. When death looms, when anger singes, when shame weighs heavily. Remember Jesus.

Remember holiness in tandem with humanity. Remember the sick who were healed with callused hands. Remember the dead called from the grave with a Galilean accent. Remember the eyes of God that wept human tears. And, most of all, remember this descendant of David who beat the hell out of death.

Can you still remember? Are you still in love with him? Remember, Paul begged, remember Jesus. Before you remember anything, remember him. If you forget anything, don't forget him.

Oh, but how quickly we forget. So much happens through the years. So many changes within. So many alterations without. And, somewhere, back there, we leave him. We don't turn away from him…we just don't take him with us. Assignments come. Promotions come. Budgets are made. Kids are born, and the Christ…the Christ is forgotten.

Has it been a while since you stared at the heavens in speechless amazement? Has it been a while since you realized God's divinity and your carnality?

If it has, then you need to know something. He is still there. He hasn't left. Under all those papers and books and reports and years. In the midst of all those voices and faces and memories and pictures, he is still there.

Do yourself a favor. Stand before him again. Or, better, allow him to stand before you. Go into your upper room and wait. Wait until he comes. And when he appears, don't leave. Run your fingers over his feet. Place your hand in the pierced side. And look into those eyes. Those same eyes that melted the gates of hell and sent the demons scurrying and Satan running. Look at them as they look at you. You'll never be the same.

A man is never the same after he simultaneously sees his utter despair and Christ's unbending grace. To see the despair without the grace is suicidal. To see the grace without the despair is upper-room futility. But to see them both is conversion.

1. John 20:19 2. Matthew 28:17 3. Luke 24:52 4. Luke 24:53 5. Acts 2:36
6. 2 Timothy 2:8

ANCHOR POINT 2

# MY FAILURES ARE NOT FATAL

CHAPTER 8

# Fatal Errors

The handwriting was shaky. The stationery was lined, loose-leaf paper. The ink was black and the tone desperate. The note was dated February 6, 1974 and was addressed to the U.S. government.

"I am sending ten dollars for blankets I stole while in World War II. My mind could not rest. Sorry I'm late." It was signed, "an ex-GI." Then there was this postscript, "I want to be ready to meet God."

This recruit was not alone in his guilt. His letter is one of literally tons of letters that have been sent to the U.S. government since it began collecting and storing the letters in 1811. Since that time $3,500,000 has been deposited in what is called the Conscience Fund.

An average of $45,000 per year is received. The biggest year was 1950 in which $350,000 was collected.

One man writing from Brazil sent fifty dollars to cover the cost of two pair of cavalry boots, two pair of trousers, one case of KC rations and thirty pounds of frozen meat he stole from the army between 1943 and 1946.

In some instances the amounts are small; only the remorse is big. One Colorado woman sent in two eight-cent stamps to make up for having used one stamp twice (which for some reason had not been canceled). A former IRS employee mailed in one dollar for four ballpoint pens she had never returned to the office.

A Salem, Ohio, man submitted one dollar with the following note, "When a boy, I put a few pennies on the railroad track and the train flattened them. I also used a dime or a quarter in a silver-coating experiment in high school. I understand there is a law against defacing our money. I have not seen it but I desire to be a law-abiding citizen."

Anxiety over a thirty-year-old mistake? Regret over mashed pennies? A guilty conscience because of ballpoint pens? If the struggle to have a clean conscience wasn't so common, the letters would be funny. But the struggle is common.

What do you do with your failures? Our mistakes come to us as pebbles, small stones that serve as souvenirs of our stumbles. We carry them in our hands, and soon our hands are full. We put them in our pockets, and soon our pockets bulge. We place them in a bag and put it over our shoulder; the burlap scratches and chaps. And soon the bag of yesterday's failures is so heavy we drag it.

Here are some failures that have been dragged into my office.

*Unfaithfulness.* He wanted to try again. She said, "No way." He wanted a second chance. She said, "You blew your chance." He admitted he made a mistake by seeing another woman. He sees now that the mistake was fatal to his marriage.

*Homosexuality.* His wrists bore the scars of a suicide attempt. His arms had tracks from countless needles. His eyes reflected the spirit of one hellbent on self-destruction. His words were those of a prisoner grimly resigned to the judge's sentence. "I'm gay. My dad says I'm a queer. I guess he's right."

*Division.* A church leadership demanded submission. A membership demanded a louder voice. It was a bomb waiting to explode. The eruption resulted in a half-empty building of walking wounded.

*Immorality.* She came to church with a pregnant womb and a repentant spirit. "I can't have a child," she pleaded. "We'll find a home for it," she was assured. She agreed. Then she changed her mind. Her boyfriend funded the abortion. "Can God ever forgive me?" she asked.

Nothing drags more stubbornly than a sack of failures.

Could you do it all over again, you'd do it differently. You'd be a different person. You'd be more patient. You'd control your tongue. You'd finish what you started. You'd turn the other cheek instead of slapping his. You'd get married first. You wouldn't marry at all. You'd be honest. You'd resist the temptation. You'd run with a different crowd.

But you can't. And as many times as you tell yourself, "What's done is done," what you did can't be undone.

That's part of what Paul meant when he said, "The wages of sin is death."[1] He didn't say, "The wages of sin is a bad mood." Or, "The wages of sin is a hard day." Nor, "The wages of sin is depression." Read it again. "The wages of sin is death." Sin is fatal.

*Can* anything be done with it?

Your therapist tells you to talk about it. So you do. You pull the bag into his office and pour the rocks out on his floor and analyze each one. And it's helpful. It feels good to talk and he's nice. But when the hour is up, you still have to carry the bag out with you.

Your friends tell you not to feel bad. "Everyone slumps a bit in this world," they say. "Not very comforting," you say.

Feel-great-about-life rallies tell you to ignore the thing and be happy! Which works—until you wipe the fog off your mirror and take an honest look. Then you see, it's still there.

Legalists tell you to work the weight off. A candle for every rock. A prayer for every pebble. Sounds logical, but what if I run out of time? Or what if I didn't count correctly? You panic.

What *do* you do with the stones from life's stumbles?

My oldest daughter, Jenna, is four years old. Some time ago she came to me with a confession. "Daddy, I took a crayon and drew on the wall." (Kids amaze me with their honesty.)

I sat down and lifted her up into my lap and tried to be wise. "Is that a good thing to do?" I asked her.

"No."

"What does Daddy do when you write on the wall?"

"You spank me."

"What do you think Daddy should do this time?"

"Love."

Don't we all want that? Don't we all long for a father who, even though our mistakes are written all over the wall, will love us anyway? Don't we want a father who cares for us in spite of our failures?

We *do* have that type of a father. A father who is at his best when we are at our worst. A father whose grace is strongest when our devotion is weakest. If your bag is big and bulky, then you're in for some thrilling news: Your failures are not fatal.

1. Romans 6:23

CHAPTER 9

# Cristo Redentor

Ninety feet tall. One thousand three hundred twenty tons of reinforced Brazilian tile. Positioned on a mountain a mile and one-half above sea level. It's the famous *Christ the Redeemer* statue that overlooks the city of Rio de Janeiro, Brazil.

No tourist comes to Rio without snaking up Corcovado Mountain to see this looming monument. The head alone is nine feet tall. The span from fingertip to fingertip—sixty-three feet.

While living in Rio, I saw the statue dozens of times. But no time was as impressive as the first.

I was a college student spending a summer in Brazil. Except for scampers across the Mexican border, this was my first trip outside the continental U.S. I had known this monument only through *National Geographic* magazine. I was to learn that no magazine can truly capture the splendor of *Cristo Redentor.*

Below me was Rio. Seven million people swarming on the lush green mountains that crash into the bright blue Atlantic. Behind me was the *Christ the Redeemer* statue. As I looked at the towering edifice through my telephoto lens, two ironies caught my attention.

I couldn't help but notice the blind eyes. Now, I know what you are thinking—all statues have blind eyes. You are right, they do. But it's as if the sculptor of this statue intended that the eyes be blind. There are no pupils to suggest vision. There are no circles to suggest sight. There are only Little Orphan Annie openings.

I lowered my camera to my waist. *What kind of redeemer is this? Blind? Eyes fixated on the horizon, refusing to see the mass of people at its feet?*

I saw the second irony as I again raised my camera. I followed the features downward, past the strong nose, past the prominent chin, past the neck. My focus came to rest on the cloak of the statue. On the outside of the cloak there is a heart. A Valentine's heart. A simple heart.

A stone heart.

The unintended symbolism staggered me. *What kind of redeemer is this? Heart made of stone? Held together not with passion and love, but by concrete and mortar. What kind of redeemer is this? Blind eyes and stony heart?*

I've since learned the answer to my own question: What kind of redeemer is this? Exactly the kind of redeemer most people have.

Oh, most people would not admit to having a blind redeemer with a stone heart. But take a close look.

For some, Jesus is a good luck charm. The "Rabbit's Foot Redeemer." Pocket sized. Handy. Easily packaged. Easily understood. Easily diagramed. You can put his picture on your wall or you can stick it in your wallet as insurance. You can frame him. Dangle him from your rearview mirror or glue him to your dashboard.

His specialty? Getting you out of a jam. Need a parking place? Rub the redeemer. Need help on a quiz? Pull out the rabbit's foot. No need to have a relationship with him. No need to love him. Just keep him in your pocket next to your four-leaf clover.

For many he's an "Aladdin's Lamp Redeemer." New jobs. Pink Cadillacs. New and improved spouses. Your wish is his command. And what's more, he conveniently reenters the lamp when you don't want him around.

For others, Jesus is a "Monty Hall Redeemer." "All right, Jesus, let's make a deal. For fifty-two Sundays a year, I'll put on a costume—coat and tie, hat and hose—and I'll endure any sermon you throw at me. In exchange, you give me the grace behind pearly gate number three."

The Rabbit's Foot Redeemer. The Aladdin's Lamp Redeemer. The Monty Hall Redeemer. Few demands, no challenges. No need for sacrifice. No need for commitment.

---

Sightless and heartless redeemers. Redeemers without power. That's not the Redeemer of the New Testament.

Compare the blind Christ I saw in Rio to the compassionate one seen by a frightened woman early one morning in Jerusalem.[1]

It's dawn. The early morning sun stretches a golden blanket across the streets of the city. Diamonds of dew cling to blades of grass. A cat stretches as it awakens. The noises are scattered.

A rooster crows his early morning recital.

A dog barks to welcome the day.

A peddler shuffles down the street, his wares on his back.

And a young carpenter speaks in the courtyard.

Jesus sits surrounded by a horseshoe of listeners. Some nod their heads in agreement and open their hearts in obedience. They have accepted the teacher as their teacher and are learning to accept him as their Lord.

Others are curious, wanting to believe yet wary of this one whose claims so stretch the boundaries of belief.

Whether cautious or convinced, they listen keenly. They arose early. There was something about his words that was more comforting than sleep.

We don't know his topic that morning. Prayer, perhaps. Or maybe kindness or anxiety. But whatever it was, it was soon interrupted when people burst into the courtyard.

Determined, they erupt out of a narrow street and stomp toward Jesus. The listeners scramble to get out of the way. The mob is made up of religious leaders, the elders and deacons of their day. Respected and important men. And struggling to keep her balance on the crest of this angry wave is a scantily clad woman.

Only moments before she had been in bed with a man who was not her husband. Was this how she made her living? Maybe. Maybe not. Maybe her husband was gone, her heart was lonely, the stranger's touch was warm, and before she knew it, she had done it. We don't know.

But we do know that a door was jerked open and she was yanked from a bed. She barely had time to cover her body before she was dragged into the street by two men the age of her father. What thoughts raced through her mind as she scrambled to keep her feet?

Curious neighbors stuck heads through open windows. Sleepy dogs yelped at the ruckus.

And now, with holy strides, the mob storms toward the teacher. They throw the woman in his direction. She nearly falls.

"We found this woman in bed with a man!" cries the leader. "The law says to stone her. What do you say?"

Cocky with borrowed courage, they smirk as they watch the mouse go for the cheese.

The woman searches the faces, hungry for a compassionate glance. She finds none. Instead, she sees accusation. Squinty eyes. Tight lips. Gritted teeth. Stares that sentence without seeing.

Cold, stony hearts that condemn without feeling.

She looks down and sees the rocks in their hands—the rocks of righteousness intended to stone the lust out of her. The men squeeze them so tightly that their fingertips are white. They squeeze them as if the rocks were the throat of this preacher they hate.

In her despair she looks at the Teacher. His eyes don't glare. "Don't worry," they whisper, "it's okay." And for the first time that morning she sees kindness.

When Jesus saw her, what did he see? Did he see her as a father sees his grown daughter as she walks down the wedding aisle? The father's mind races back through time watching his girl grow up again—from diapers to dolls. From classrooms to boyfriends. From the prom date to the wedding day. The father sees it all as he looks at his daughter.

As Jesus looked at this daughter, did his mind race back? Did he relive the act of forming this child in heaven? Did he see her as he had originally made her?

"Knitted together" is how the psalmist described the process of God making man.[2] Not manufactured or mass-produced, but knitted. Each thread of personality tenderly intertwined. Each string of temperament deliberately selected.

God as creator. Pensive. Excited. Inventive.

> An artist, brush on pallet, seeking the perfect shade.
>
> A composer, fingers on keyboard, listening for the exact chord.
>
> A poet, pen poised on paper, awaiting the precise word.
>
> The Creator, the master weaver, threading together the soul.

Each one different. No two alike. None identical.

On earth, Jesus was an artist in a gallery of his own paintings.

He was a composer listening as the orchestra interpreted his music. He was a poet hearing his own poetry. Yet his works of art had been defaced. Creation after battered creation.

He had created people for splendor. They had settled for mediocrity. He had formed them with love. They had scarred each other with hate.

> When he saw businessmen using God-given intelligence to feed Satan-given greed…
>
> When he saw tongues he had designed to encourage used as daggers to cut…
>
> When he saw hands that had been given for holding used as weapons for hurting…
>
> When he saw eyes into which he'd sprinkled joy now burning with hatred…

I wonder, did it weary him to see hearts that were stained, even discarded?

Jesus saw such a heart as he looked at this woman. Her feet were bare and muddy. Her arms hid her chest, and her hands clutched each other under her chin. And her heart, her heart was ragged, torn as much by her own guilt as by the mob's anger.

So, with the tenderness only a father can have, he set out to untie the knots and repair the holes.

He begins by diverting the crowd's attention. He draws on the ground. Everybody looks down. The woman feels relief as the eyes of the men look away from her.

The accusers are persistent. "Tell us, teacher! What do you want us to do with her?"

He could have asked why they didn't bring the man. The Law indicted him as well. He could have asked why they were suddenly blowing the dust off an old command that had sat on the shelves for centuries. But he didn't.

He just raised his head and offered an invitation, "I guess if you've never made a mistake, then you have a right to stone this woman." He looked back down and began to draw on the earth again.

Someone cleared his throat as if to speak, but no one spoke. Feet shuffled. Eyes dropped. Then thud…thud…thud…rocks fell to the ground.

And they walked away. Beginning with the grayest beard and ending with the blackest, they turned and left. They came as one, but they left one by one.

Jesus told the woman to look up. "Is there no one to condemn you?" He smiled as she raised her head. She saw no one, only rocks—each one a miniature tombstone to mark the burial place of a man's arrogance.

"Is there no one to condemn you?" he had asked. *There is still one who can,* she thinks. And she turns to look at him.

*What does he want? What will he do?*

Maybe she expected him to scold her. Perhaps she expected him to walk away from her. I'm not sure, but I do know this: What she got, she never expected. She got a promise and a commission.

The promise: "Then neither do I condemn you."

The commission: "Go and sin no more."

The woman turns and walks into anonymity. She's never seen or heard from again. But we can be confident of one thing: On that morning in Jerusalem, she saw Jesus and Jesus saw her. And could we somehow transport her to Rio de Janeiro and let her stand at the base of the *Cristo Redentor*, I know what her response would be.

"That's not the Jesus I saw," she would say. And she would be right. For the Jesus she saw didn't have a hard heart. And the Jesus that saw her didn't have blind eyes.

However, if we could somehow transport her to Calvary and let her stand at the base of the cross…you know what she would say. "That's him," she would whisper. "That's him."

She would recognize his hands. The only hands that had held no stones that day were his. And on this day they still hold no stones. She would recognize his voice. It's raspier and weaker, but the words are the same, "Father, forgive them…." And she would recognize his eyes. How could she ever forget those eyes? Clear and tear filled. Eyes that saw her not as she was, but as she was intended to be.

1. John 8:1-11 2. Psalm 139:13

CHAPTER 10

# THE GOLDEN GOBLET

Flames leap from the hill. Pillows of smoke float upward. Orange tongues crack and pop.

From the midst of the blaze comes a yell—the protest of a prisoner as the dungeon door is locked; the roar of a lion as he feels the heat of the burning jungle.

The cry of a lost son as he looks for his father.

"My God, my God, why have you forsaken me?"

The words ricochet from star to star, crashing into the chamber of the King. Couriers from a bloody battlefield, they stumble into the King's presence. Bruised and broken, they plea for help, for relief.

The soldiers of the King prepare to attack. They mount their steeds and position their shields. They draw their swords.

But the King is silent. It is the hour for which he has planned. He knows his course of action. He has awaited those words since the beginning—since the first poison was smuggled into the kingdom.

It came camouflaged. It came in a golden cup with a long stem. It was in the flavor of fruit. It came not in the hands of a king, but the hands of a prince—the prince of the shadows.

Until this moment there had been no reason to hide in the Garden. The King walked with his children and the children knew their King. There were no secrets. There were no shadows.

Then the prince of shadows entered the Garden. He had to hide himself. He was too ugly, too repulsive. Craters marred his face. So he came in darkness. He came encircled in ebony. He was completely hidden; only his voice could be heard.

"Taste it," he whispered, holding the goblet before her. "It's sweet with wisdom."

The daughter heard the voice and turned. She was intrigued. Her eyes had never seen a shadow. There was something tantalizing about his hiddenness.

The King watched. His army knew the prince of shadows would be no contest for their mighty legion. Eagerly they awaited the command to attack.

But no command was given.

"The choice is hers," the King instructed. "If she turns to us for help, that is your command to deliver her. If she doesn't turn, if she doesn't look to me—don't. The choice is hers."

The daughter stared at the goblet. Rubies embedded in gold filigree invited her touch. Wine wooed her to taste. She reached out and took the cup and drank the poison. Her eyes never looked up.

The venom rushed through her, distorting her vision, scarring her skin, and twisting her heart. She ducked into the shadow of the prince.

Suddenly she was lonely. She missed the intimacy she was made to know. Yet rather than return to the King, she chose to lure another away from him. She replenished the goblet and offered it to the son.

Once again the army snapped into position. Once again they listened for the command of the King. His words were the same. "If he looks to me, then rush to him. If he doesn't, then don't go. The choice is his."

The daughter placed the goblet into the hands of the son. "It's all right," she assured. "It's sweet." The son looked at the delight that danced in her eyes. Behind her stood a silhouetted figure.

"Who is he?" the son asked.

"Drink it," she insisted. Her voice was husky with desire.

The goblet was cold against Adam's lips. The liquid burned his innocence. "More?" he requested as he ran his finger through the dregs on the bottom and put it to his mouth.

The soldiers looked to their King for instructions. His eyes were moist.

"Bring me your sword!" The general dismounted and stepped

quickly toward the throne. He extended the unsheathed blade before the King.

The King didn't take it; he merely touched it. As the tip of his finger encountered the top of the sword, the iron grew orange with heat. It grew brighter and brighter until it blazed.

The general held the fiery sword and awaited the King's command. It came in the form of an edict.

"Their choice will be honored. Where there is poison, there will be death. Where there are goblets, there will be fire. Let it be done."

The general galloped to the Garden and took his post at the gate. The flaming sword proclaimed that the kingdom of light would never again be darkened by the passing of shadows. The King hated the shadows. He hated them because in the shadows the children could not see their King. The King hated the goblets. He hated them because they made the children forget the Father.

But outside the Garden the circle of the shadow grew larger and more empty goblets littered the ground. More faces were disfigured. More eyes saw distortedly. More souls were twisted. Purity was forgotten and all sight of the King was lost. No one remembered that once there was a kingdom without shadows.

In their hands were the goblets of selfishness.

On their lips was the litany of the liar. "Taste it; it's sweet."

And, true to the words of the King, where there was poison, there was death. Where there were goblets, there was fire. Until the day the King sent his Prince.

The same fire that ignited the sword now lit a candle and placed it amidst the shadows.

His arrival, like that of the goblet bearer, did not go unnoticed.

"A star!" was how his coming was announced. "A bright light in a dark sky." A diamond glittering in the dirt.

"Burn brightly, my Son," whispered the King.

Many times the Prince of Light was offered the goblet. Many times it came in the hands of those who'd abandoned the King. "Just a taste, my friend?" With anguish Jesus would look into the eyes of those who tried to tempt him. What is this poison that would make a prisoner try to kill the one who came to release him?

The goblet still bore the seductive flavor of promised power and pleasure. But to the Son of Light its odor was vile. The very sight of the goblet so angered the Prince that he knocked it out of the hand of the tempter, leaving the two alone, locked in an intense glare.

"I will taste the poison," swore the King's Son. "For this I have come. But the hour will be mine to choose."

Finally that hour came. The Son went for one last visit with his Father. He met Him in another garden. A garden of gnarled trees and stony soil.

"Does it have to be this way?"

"It does."

"Is there no one else who can do it?"

The King swallowed. "None but you."

"Do I have to drink from the cup?"

"Yes, my Child. The same cup."

He looked at the Prince of Light. "The darkness will be great." He passed his hand over the spotless face of his Son. "The pain will be awful." Then he paused and looked at his darkened dominion. When he looked up, his eyes were moist. "But there is no other way."

The Son looked into the stars as he heard the answer. "Then, let it be done."

Slowly the words that would kill the Son began to come from the lips of the Father.

"Hour of death, moment of sacrifice, it is your moment. Rehearsed a million times on false altars with false lambs, the moment of truth has come.

"Soldiers, you think you lead him? Ropes, you think you bind him? Men, you think you sentence him? He heeds not your commands. He winces not at your lashes. It is my voice he obeys. It is my condemnation he dreads. And it is your souls he saves.

"Oh, my Son, my Child. Look up into the heavens and see my face before I turn it. Hear my voice before I silence it. Would that I could save you and them. But they don't see and they don't hear.

"The living must die so that the dying can live. The time has come to kill the Lamb.

"Here is the cup, my Son. The cup of sorrows. The cup of sin.

"Slam, mallet! Be true to your task. Let your ring be heard throughout the heavens.

"Lift him, soldiers. Lift him high to his throne of mercy. Lift him up to his perch of death. Lift him above the people that curse his name.

"Now plunge the tree into the earth. Plunge it deep into the heart of humanity. Deep into the strata of time past. Deep into the seeds of time future.

"Is there no angel to save my Isaac? Is there no hand to redeem the Redeemer?

"Here is the cup, my Son. Drink it alone."

God must have wept as he performed his task. Every lie, every lure, every act done in shadows was in that cup. Slowly, hideously they were absorbed into the body of the Son. The final act of incarnation.

The Spotless Lamb was blemished. Flames began to lick his feet.

The King obeys his own edict. "Where there is poison, there will be death. Where there are goblets, there will be fire."

The King turns away from his Prince. The undiluted wrath of a sin-hating Father falls upon his sin-filled Son. The fire envelops him. The shadow hides him. The Son looks for his Father, but his Father cannot be seen.

"My God, my God…why?"

---

The throne room is dark and cavernous. The eyes of the King are closed. He is resting.

In his dream he is again in the Garden. The cool of the evening floats across the river as the three walk. They speak of the Garden—of how it is, of how it will be.

"Father...," the Son begins. The King replays the word again. Father. Father. The word was a flower, petal-delicate, yet so easily crushed. Oh, how he longed for his children to call him Father again.

A noise snaps him from his dream. He opens his eyes and sees a transcendent figure gleaming in the doorway. "It is finished, Father. I have come home."

CHAPTER 11

# Come Home

England. Nineteenth century. Christmas. In a small town there is the tradition of a village party where all the children receive gifts. It is a festive occasion: the bright smiles of the youngsters, a tall tree at the square, colorful packages. There is a young retarded man in the town who, because of his handicap, is the victim of many cruel jokes. The trick played on him this Christmas Day is the cruelest of all.

As the mountain of gifts becomes smaller and smaller, his face grows longer and longer. He is too old for a gift, but he doesn't know that. His childlike heart is heavy as he watches everyone receive presents except himself. Then some of the boys come to him with a gift. His is the last one under the tree. His eyes dance as he looks at the brightly wrapped package. His excitement soars as he tears away the ribbons. His fingers race to rip away the paper. But as he opens the box, his heart sinks.

It's empty.

The packaging was attractive. The ribbons were colorful. The outside was enough to get him into the inside; but when he got to the inside, the box was empty![1]

Ever been there?

Many people have—

A young mother weeps silently into her pillow. All her life she had dreamed of marriage. "If only I could have a home. If only I could have a husband and a house."

So now she's married. The honeymoon has long since ended. The tunnel she dug out of one prison only led her to another. Her Land of Oz has become a land of dirty diapers, car pools, and bills.

She shares a bed with a husband she doesn't love. She listens to the still sleep of a child she doesn't know how to raise. And she feels the sand of her youth slide through her fingers.

A middle-aged businessman sits in his plush office staring blankly out the window. A red German sports car awaits him in the parking lot. There is a gold ring on his finger and a gold card in his wallet. His name is in brass on a walnut door and a walnut desk. His suit is tailored. His shoes are hand sewn, his name well known.

He should be happy. He possesses the package he set out to get when he stood at the bottom of the ladder looking up. But now that he has what he wants, he doesn't want it. Now that he is at the top of the ladder, he sees that it is leaning against the wrong building.

He left his bride in the dust of his ambition. The kids that called him daddy don't call him daddy anymore; they have a new one. And though he has everything that success offers, he'd trade it in a heartbeat to have a home to go home to tonight.

"I've counted the holes in the ceiling tiles a hundred times." The voice shook in spite of an attempt to sound stable. "They say I'll be in this cast for six weeks. They also say I'm lucky to be alive."

His voice was barely audible through the oxygen mask. The skin on his forehead and nose was scraped.

"They keep asking me what I remember. I don't even remember getting into the car, much less driving it. I'd never tried crack before. I guess I tried too much. I'll think before I try it again. In fact, it looks like I'm going to have plenty of time for thinking."

No games. No noise. No flashing lights. Your dreams have come true, but instead of letting you sleep, they are keeping you awake. What do you do at a time like this? Where do you go when the parade stops? Your failures suck the sandy foundation of your future out from under you. Now what do you do?

---

You can blame the world. The prodigal son could have done that. In fact, he probably did.[2]

The boy stared at his reflection in the muddy puddle. He questioned whether the face was really his. It didn't look like him.

The flame in the eyes had been extinguished. The smirk had been humbled. The devil-may-care attitude had been replaced with soberness.

He tumbled headlong and landed face first.

It wasn't enough to be friendless. It wasn't enough to be broke. It wasn't enough to pawn his ring, his coat, even his shoes. The long hours walking the streets didn't break him. You would think that the nights with only a bunkhouse pillow or the days lugging a bucket of pig slop would force a change of heart.

But they didn't. Pride is made of stone. Hard knocks may chip it, but it takes reality's sledgehammer to break it.

His was beginning to crack.

His first few days of destitution were likely steamy with resentment. He was mad at everyone. Everyone was to blame. His friends shouldn't have bailed out on him. And his brother should come and bail him out. His boss should feed him better, and his dad never should have let him go in the first place.

He named a pig after each one of them.

Failure invites finger pointing and buck passing. A person may be out of money, out of a job, and out of friends, but he is never out of people to blame.

Sometimes it's the family:

"If my parents had taken their job more seriously..."

"If my husband wasn't so selfish..."

"If my kids had any respect for me..."

"If I had been potty trained earlier..."

Sometimes it's the system:

"No one can make a good grade in this school!"

"If I had been given an equal shot, I would have been promoted."

"This whole place is rigged."

"There is no way a person can move up in this world."

Even the church has a few bucks passed its way.

"Oh, I'd attend church, but did you know I went to church once back in '58 and no one came to visit me?"

"That group of folks? A bunch of hypocrites."

"I plan on going back to church. Just as soon as I find one that is teaching the proper doctrine, housing all the homeless, feeding all the sick and giving green stamps for attendance awards, then I'll go back."

Soon you are right and everyone else is wrong. You are the victim and the world is your enemy.

---

A second option is to continue playing the games, only this time with a little more abandon.

My wife has a cousin named Rob. Rob is a great guy. His good heart and friendly smile endear him to everyone. He is the kind of fellow you call upon when you can't call on anyone else.

So when the Girl Scouts needed someone to dress up like the Cookie Monster at a fund-raiser, who did they call? You got it. Rob.

There were a few problems. First, no one anticipated the day of the campaign would be so hot. Second, Rob didn't know that the costume would be so big. Third, who would have thought that Rob's glasses would fog up so badly he couldn't see? As he was sitting on the stage waiting his turn to speak, the heat inside the mask covered his glasses with fog. He couldn't wipe them off—his paws were too big to fit in the eyehole.

He started to worry. Any minute he would be called upon to give a talk, and he couldn't even see where the podium was!

He whispered for help. The costume was too thick, and his cries went unheard.

He began to wave his hands. What he heard in response were the squeals of delight from the kids. They thought he was waving at them!

As I heard this story I chuckled…and then I sighed. It was too familiar. Cries for help muffled behind costumed faces? Fear hidden behind a painted smile? Signals of desperation thought to be signs of joy?

Tell me that doesn't describe our world.

Ever since Eve hemmed the fig leaves to fit Adam, we have been disguising our truths.

And we've gotten better with each generation.

Michelangelo's creativity is nothing compared to a bald man's use of a few strands of hair. Houdini would stand in awe at our capacity to squeeze lumberjack waistlines into ballerina-sized pants.

We are masters of the masquerade. Cars are driven to make a statement. Jeans are purchased to portray an image. Accents are acquired to hide a heritage. Names are dropped. Weights are lifted. Yarns are spun. Toys are purchased. Achievements are professed.

And the pain is ignored. And, with time, the real self is forgotten.

The Indians used to say that within every heart there is a knife. This knife turns like the minute hand on a clock. Every time the heart lies, the knife rotates an increment. As it turns, it cuts into the heart. As it turns, it carves a circle. The more it turns, the wider the circle becomes. After the knife has rotated one full circle, a path has been carved. The result? No more hurt, no more heart.

One option the boy in the pigpen had was to walk back into the masquerade party and pretend everything was fine. He could have carved his integrity until the pain disappeared. He could have done what millions do. He could have spent a lifetime in the pigpen pretending it was a palace. But he didn't.

Something told him that this was the moment of—and for—truth.

He looked into the water. The face he saw wasn't pretty—muddy and swollen. He looked away. "Don't think about it. You're no worse off than anybody else. Things will get better tomorrow."

The lies anticipated a receptive ear. They'd always found one before. "Not this time," he muttered. And he stared at his reflection.

"How far I have fallen." His first words of truth.

He looked into his own eyes. He thought of his father. "They always said I had your eyes." He could see the look of hurt on his father's face when he told him he was leaving.

"How I must have hurt you."

A crack zigzagged across the boy's heart.

A tear splashed into the pool. Another soon followed. Then another. Then the dam broke. He buried his face in his dirty hands as the tears did what tears do so well; they flushed out his soul.

His face was still wet as he sat near the pool. For the first time in a long time he thought of home. The memories warmed him. Memories of dinner-table laughter. Memories of a warm bed. Memories of evenings on the porch with his father as they listened to the hypnotic ring of the crickets.

"Father." He said the word aloud as he looked at himself. "They used to say I looked like you. Now you wouldn't even recognize me. Boy, I blew it, didn't I?"

He stood up and began to walk.

The road home was longer than he remembered. When he last traveled it, he turned heads because of his style. If he turned heads this time, it was because of his stink. His clothes were torn, his hair matted, and his feet black. But that didn't bother him, because for the first time in a calendar of heartaches, he had a clean conscience.

He was going home. He was going home a changed man. Not demanding that he get what he deserved, but willing to take whatever he could get. "Give me" had been replaced with "help me," and his defiance had been replaced with repentance.

He came asking for everything with nothing to give in return. He had no money. He had no excuses.

And he had no idea how much his father had missed him.

He had no idea the number of times his father had paused between chores to look out the front gate for his son. The boy had no idea the number of times his father had awakened from restless sleep, gone into the son's room, and sat on the boy's bed. And the son would have never believed the hours the father had sat on the porch next to the empty rocking chair, looking, longing to see that familiar figure, that stride, that face.

As the boy came around the bend that led up to his house, he rehearsed his speech one more time.

"Father, I have sinned against heaven and against you."

He approached the gate and placed his hand on the latch. He began to lift it, then he paused. His plan to go home suddenly seemed silly. "What's the use?" he heard himself asking himself. "What chance do I have?" He ducked, turned around, and began to walk away.

Then he heard the footsteps. He heard the slap, slap, slap of sandals. Someone was running. He didn't turn to look. *It's probably a servant coming to chase me away or my big brother wanting to know what I'm doing back home.* He began to leave.

But the voice he heard was not the voice of a servant nor the voice of his brother; it was the voice of his father.

"Son!"

"Father?"

He turned to open the gate, but the father already had. The son looked at his father standing at the entrance. Tears glistened on his cheeks as arms stretched from east to west inviting the son to come home.

"Father, I have sinned." The words were muffled as the boy buried his face in his father's shoulder.

The two wept. For a forever they stood at the gate intertwined as one. Words were unnecessary. Repentance had been made, forgiveness had been given.

The boy was home.

---

If there is a scene in this story that deserves to be framed, it's the one of the father's outstretched hands. His tears are moving. His smile is stirring. But his hands call us home. Imagine those hands. Strong fingers. Palms wrinkled with lifelines. Stretching open like a wide gate, leaving entrance as the only option.

When Jesus told this parable of the loving father, I wonder, did he use his hands? When he got to this point in the story, did he open his arms to illustrate the point?

Did he perceive the thoughts of those in the audience who were thinking, "I could never go home. Not after my life"? Did he see a housewife look at the ground and a businessman shake his head as if to say, "I can't start over. I've made too big a mess"? And did he open his arms even wider as if to say, "Yes. Yes, you can. You can come home"?

Whether he did that day or not, I don't know. But I know that he did later. He later stretched his hands as open as he could. He forced his arms so wide apart that it hurt. And to prove that those arms would never fold and those hands would never close, he had them nailed open.

They still are.

1. This story is popularly attributed to Harry Emerson Fosdick. 2. Luke 15:11-27

CHAPTER 12

# THE FISH AND THE FALLS

## A LEGEND OF GRACE

### THE JOURNEY

Once upon a distant time, when time was not and rivers had no names, there was a fish.

Born in the cascading bubbles of a rocky mountain stream, this freckled fish learned early the passion of play. He was at home in the water. He raced back and forth in the harbor made by a fallen log. He dared, on occasion, to cross the rapids by darting from rock to rock.

Each morning he witnessed the sun lift the shadowy curtain of night. It was his daily invitation to dance in the clean waters. Then, as the sun climbed higher, its warmth would lull him to slowness, giving him time to stare through the waters at the tall trees that waved and the furred visitors whose tongues would drink and then disappear.

But if the day was his time to play, the night was his time to think. This young trout, not content to know so little, kept his eyes open while others closed theirs. *What is the source of this stream? Where does it go? Why is it here? Why am I here?* He pondered the questions that others never asked. And he listened at length for the answers.

Then one night he heard the roar.

The night was so bright that the moon saw herself in the stream. The fish, awake with his thoughts, recognized for the first time a noise he'd always heard.

A roar. It rumbled under the river. It vibrated the water. Suddenly the fish knew why the water was always moving.

*Who is the maker of this sound? Who is the giver of this noise?*

He had to know.

He swam all night without stopping, nourished by his need to know. The roar grew louder. Its thunder both frightened and compelled him.

He swam until the stars turned pale and the gray pebbles regained their colors. When he could swim no more, weariness overcame curiosity, and he stopped. He slept.

## THE ENCOUNTER

The sun was warm on the trout's back. In his sleep, he dreamt he was playing again. Dashing between the rocks daring the water to catch him. He dreamt he was at home.

Then he awoke, remembering his pilgrimage.

He heard the roar. It sounded near. He opened his eyes and there it was. A wall of white foam. Water tumbling, then falling, then flying, then crashing.

It was like nothing he'd ever seen.

*I will climb it and see it.*

He swam to where the water crashed into the river. He attempted to swim upwards. He would ascend the falls by brute force. But the onrush of the water was too strong. Undaunted, he swam until he could swim no more, then he slept.

The next day he attempted to jump to the top. He plunged downward, deep below the churning foam. He swam deep. He swam until the water was still and dark and the roar was distant. Then he turned upward.

His fins fought from one side to the other, pushing and propelling the trout until he was swimming faster than he'd ever swum. He swam straight for the surface. Higher and higher, faster and faster. He raced through the calm waters toward the surface. He broke through the top of the water and soared high into the air. He soared so high he was sure he would land on the top of the waterfall. But he didn't. He barely rose above the foam. Then he fell.

*I'll try again.* Down he swam. Up he pushed. Out he flew. And down he tumbled.

He tried again. And again. And again. Ever trying to reach the top of the wall. Ever failing at his quest.

Finally night fell and the moon stood vigil over the weary young trout.

He awoke with renewed strength and a new plan. He found a safe pool off to the side of the base of the waterfall. Through the still waters he looked up. He would swim against the gentle trickle of the water as it poured over the rocks. Pleased with his wisdom, he set out. Doggedly he pushed his body to do what it wasn't made to do.

For an entire passing of the sun through the sky he struggled. He pushed on—climbing, falling; climbing, falling; climbing, falling. At one point, when his muscles begged for relief, he actually reached a ledge from which he could look out over the water below. Swollen with his achievements he leaned too far out and tumbled headfirst into the calm pool from which he began.

Wearied from his failure, he slept.

He dreamt of the roar. He dreamt of the glory of leaving the mountain stream and dwelling in the waterfall. But when he awoke, he was still at the bottom.

When he awoke, the moon was still high. It discouraged him to realize that his dream was not reality. He wondered if it was worth it. He wondered if those who never sought to know were happier.

He considered returning. The current would carry him home.

*I've lived with the roar all my life and never heard it. I could simply not hear it again.*

But how do you not hear the yearning of your heart? How do

you turn away from discovery? How can you be satisfied with existence once you've lived with purpose?

The fish wanted nothing more than to ascend the water. But he was out of choices. He didn't know what to do. He screamed at the waterfall. "Why are you so harsh? Why are you so resistant? Why won't you help me? Don't you see I can't do it on my own? I need you!"

Just then the roar of the water began to subside. The foaming slowed. The fish looked around. The water was growing still!

Then, he felt the current again. He felt the familiar push of the rushing water. Only this time the push was from behind. The water gained momentum, slowly at first, then faster and faster until the fish found himself being carried to the tall stone wall over which had flowed the water. The wall was bare and big.

For a moment he feared he would be slammed into it. But just as he reached the rocks, a wave formed beneath him. The trout was lifted upwards. Up he went out of the water on the tip of a rising tongue. The wave elevated him up the wall.

By now the forest was silent. The animals stood still as if they witnessed majesty. The wind ceased its stirring. The moon tilted ever so slightly in an effort not to miss the miracle.

All of nature watched as the fish rode the wave of grace. All of nature rejoiced when he reached the top. The stars raced through the blackness. The moon tilted backwards and rocked in sweet satisfaction. Bears danced. Birds hugged. The wind whistled. And the leaves applauded.

The fish was where he had longed to be. He was in the presence of the roar. What he couldn't do, the river had done. He knew immediately he would spend forever relishing the mystery.

CHAPTER 13

# The Eleventh Hour Gift

Nicodemus came in the middle of the night. The centurion came in the middle of the day. The leper and the sinful woman appeared in the middle of crowds. Zacchaeus appeared in the middle of a tree. Matthew had a party for him.

The educated. The powerful. The rejected. The sick. The lonely. The wealthy. Who would have ever assembled such a crew? All they had in common were their empty hope chests, long left vacant by charlatans and profiteers. Though they had nothing to offer, they asked for everything: a new birth, a second chance, a fresh start, a clean conscience. And without exception their requests were honored.

And now, one more beggar comes with a request. Only minutes from the death of them both, he stands before the King. He will ask for crumbs. And he, like the others, will receive a whole loaf.

Skull's hill—windswept and stony. The thief—gaunt and pale.

Hinges squeak as the door of death closes on his life.

His situation is pitiful. He's taking the last step down the spiral staircase of failure. One crime after another. One rejection after another. Lower and lower he descended until he reached the bottom—a crossbeam and three spikes.

He can't hide who he is. His only clothing is the cloak of his disgrace. No fancy jargon. No impressive résumé. No Sunday school awards. Just a naked history of failure.

He sees Jesus.

Earlier he had mocked the man. When the crowd first chorused its criticism, he'd sung his part.[1] But now he doesn't mock Jesus. He studies him. He begins to wonder who this man might be.

*How strange. He doesn't resist the nails; he almost invites them.*

He hears the jests and the insults and sees the man remain quiet. He sees the fresh blood on Jesus' cheeks, the crown of thorns scraping Jesus' scalp, and he hears the hoarse whisper, "Father, forgive them."

*Why do they want him dead?*

Slowly the thief's curiosity offsets the pain in his body. He momentarily forgets the nails rubbing against the raw bones of his wrists and the cramps in his calves.

He begins to feel a peculiar warmth in his heart: he begins to care; he begins to care about this peaceful martyr.

*There's no anger in his eyes, only tears.*

He looks at the huddle of soldiers throwing dice in the dirt, gambling for a ragged robe. He sees the sign above Jesus' head. It's painted with sarcasm: King of the Jews.

*They mock him as a king. If he were crazy, they would ignore him. If he had no followers, they'd turn him away. If he were nothing to fear, they wouldn't kill him. You only kill a king if he has a kingdom.*

*Could it be...*

His cracked lips open to speak.

Then, all of a sudden, his thoughts are exploded by the accusations of the criminal on the other cross. He, too, has been studying Jesus, but studying through the blurred lens of cynicism.

"So you're the Messiah, are you? Prove it by saving yourself—and us, too, while you're at it!"[2]

It's an inexplicable dilemma—how two people can hear the same words and see the same Savior, and one see hope and the other see nothing but himself.

It was all the first criminal could take. Perhaps the crook who hurled the barb expected the other crook to take the cue and hurl a few of his own. But he didn't. No second verse was sung. What the bitter-tongued criminal did hear were words of defense.

"Don't you fear God?"

Only minutes before these same lips had cursed Jesus. Now they are defending him. Every head on the hill lifts to look at this one who spoke on behalf of the Christ. Every angel weeps and every demon gapes.

Who could have imagined this thief thinking of anyone but himself? He'd always been the bully, the purse-snatching brat. Who could remember the last time he'd come to someone's aid? But as the last grains of sand trickle through his hourglass, he performs man's noblest act. He speaks on God's behalf.

Where are those we would expect to defend Jesus?

A much more spiritual Peter has abandoned him.

A much more educated Pilate has washed his hands of him.

A much more loyal mob of countrymen has demanded his death.

A much more faithful band of disciples has scattered.

When it seems that everyone has turned away, a crook places himself between Jesus and the accusers and speaks on his behalf.

"Don't you even fear God when you are dying? We deserve to die for our evil deeds, but this man hasn't done one thing wrong."[3]

The soldiers look up. The priests cease chattering. Mary wipes her tears and raises her eyes. No one had even noticed the fellow, but now everyone looks at him.

Perhaps even Jesus looks at him. Perhaps he turns to see the one who had spoken when all others had remained silent. Perhaps he fights to focus his eyes on the one who offered this final gesture of love he'd receive while alive. I wonder, did he smile as this sheep straggled into the fold?

For that, in effect, is exactly what the criminal is doing. He is stumbling to safety just as the gate is closing. Lodged in the thief's statement are the two facts that anyone needs to recognize in order to come to Jesus. Look at the phrase again. Do you see them?

"We are getting what we deserve. This man has done nothing wrong."[4]

We are guilty and he is innocent.

We are filthy and he is pure.

We are wrong and he is right.

He is not on that cross for his sins. He is there for ours.

And once the crook understands this, his request seems only natural. As he looks into the eyes of his last hope, he made the same request any Christian has made.

"Remember me when you come into your kingdom."[5]

No stained-glass homilies. No excuses. Just a desperate plea for help.

At this point Jesus performs the greatest miracle of the cross. Greater than the earthquake. Greater than the tearing of the temple curtain. Greater than the darkness. Greater than the resurrected saints appearing on the streets.

He performs the miracle of forgiveness. A sin-soaked criminal is received by a blood-stained Savior.

"Today you will be with me in Paradise. This is a solemn promise."[6]

Wow. Only seconds before the thief was a beggar nervously squeezing his hat at the castle door, wondering if the King might spare a few crumbs. Suddenly he's holding the whole pantry.

Such is the definition of grace.

1. Matthew 27:44 2. Luke 23:39, Living Bible 3. Luke 23:40, Living Bible 4. Luke 23:41 5. Luke 23:42 6. Luke 23:43, Living Bible

ANCHOR POINT 3

# MY DEATH IS NOT FINAL

CHAPTER 14

# GOD VS. DEATH

*"I will tell you something that has been secret: that we are not all going to die, but we shall all be changed."*[1]

I was only going to be in Washington, D.C. for one day, and that day was full. Still, I had to see it. I had read about it, heard about it, seen news reports and pictures of it, but I had to see it for myself.

"You'll only have about ten minutes," my host explained.

"Ten minutes is all I need," I told him.

So he pulled the car over and let me out.

A gray sky was shedding a coat of drizzle. I pulled my overcoat tighter around my neck. The barren trees and dead grass cast an appropriate backdrop for my mission. I walked a few hundred yards, descended a sloping sidewalk, and there it was. The Washington Monument to my left, the Lincoln Memorial to my back, and before me stretched the Vietnam Veterans Memorial.

The wailing wall of a generation. Black marble tablets carved with names that read like the roster of a high school football team more than a list of dead soldiers—Walter Faith, Richard Sala, Michael Andrews, Roy Burris, Emmet Stanton.

Each name a young life. Behind each name was a bereaved widow...an anguished mother...a fatherless child.

I looked down at my feet. There lay a dozen roses, soggy and frosty from the weather. It was the day after Valentine's Day. A girlfriend or wife had come to say, "I still remember. I haven't forgotten."

Next to me stood a trio. By the emotion on their faces, it was obvious they hadn't come out of curiosity. They had come out of grief. The one in the center caught my attention. He wore a green army coat. He was big. He was black. He was bearded. Angry tears steamed down his face. Twenty years of emotion still trying to find an exit.

A couple walked behind me. They were looking for a name. In their hands was a program that told them on what tablet to look. "Did you find it?" I heard the woman ask. "Every name has a number."

*True,* I thought. *Every name does have a number and sooner or later every number is called.*

It was then that I stopped looking at the names and stared at the monument. I relaxed my focus from the lettering and looked at the tablet. What I saw was sobering. I saw myself. I saw my own reflection. My face looked at me from the shiny marble. It reminded me that I, too, have been dying as long as I have been living. I, too, will someday have my name carved in a granite stone. Someday I, too, will face death.

Death. The bully on the block of life. He catches you in the alley. He taunts you in the playground. He badgers you on the way home: "You, too, will die someday."

You see him as he escorts the procession of hearse-led cars. He's in the waiting room as you walk out of the double doors of the intensive care unit. He's near as you stare at the pictures of the bloated bellies of the starving in Zimbabwe. And he'll be watching your expression as you slow your car past the crunched metal and the blanketed bodies on the highway.

"Your time is coming," he jabs.

Oh, we try to prove him wrong. We jog. We diet. We pump iron. We play golf. We try to escape it, knowing all along that we will only, at best, postpone it.

"Everyone has a number," he reminds.

And every number will be called.

He'll make your stomach tighten. He'll leave you wide eyed and flat footed. He'll fence you in with fear. He'll steal the joy of your youth and the peace of your final years. And if he achieves what he sets out to do, he'll make you so afraid of dying that you never learn to live.

That is why you should never face him alone. The bully is too big for you to fight by yourself. That's why you need a big brother.

Read these words and take heart. "Since the children have flesh and blood (that's you and me), he too shared in their humanity (that's Jesus, our big brother) so that by his death he might destroy him who holds the power of death—that is, the devil—and free those who all their lives were held in slavery by their fear of death. For surely it is not angels he helps, but Abraham's descendants (that's us)."[2]

Jesus unmasked death and exposed him for who he really is—a ninety-eight-pound weakling dressed up in a Charles Atlas suit. Jesus had no patience for this impostor. He couldn't sit still while death pulled the veil over life.

In fact, if you ever want to know how to conduct yourself at a funeral, don't look to Jesus for an example. He interrupted each one he ever attended.

A lifeguard can't sit still while someone is drowning. A teacher can't resist helping when a student is confused. And Jesus couldn't watch a funeral and do nothing.

In this last section we are going to watch Jesus when he comes face to face with death. We are going to see his eyes mist as he sees his brothers and sisters bruised and beaten by the bully of death. We are going to see his fists clench as he encounters his enemy. We are going to…well, turn the page and you'll see for yourself.

You'll see why the Christian can face the bully nose to nose and claim the promise that echoed in the empty tomb, "My death is not final."

1. 1 Corinthians 15:51, Jerusalem Bible 2. Hebrews 2:14-16 (parentheses mine)

CHAPTER 15

# FANTASY OR REALITY?

Two crowds. One entering the city and one leaving. They couldn't be more diverse. The group arriving buzzes with laughter and conversation. They follow Jesus. The group leaving the city is solemn—a herd of sadness hypnotized by the requiem of death. Above them rides the reason for their grief—a cold body on a wicker stretcher.

The woman at the back of the procession is the mother. She has walked this trail before. It seems like just yesterday she buried the body of her husband. Her son walked with her then. Now she walks alone, quarantined in her sadness. She is the victim of this funeral.

She is the one with no arm around her shoulder. She is the one who will sleep in the empty house tonight. She is the one who will make dinner for one and conversation with none. She is the one most violated. The thief stole her most treasured diamond—companionship.

The followers of Jesus stop and step aside as the procession shadows by. The blanket of mourning muffles the laughter of the disciples. No one speaks. What could they say? They feel the same despair felt by the bystanders at any funeral. "Someday that will be me."

No one intervenes. What could they do? Their only choice is to stand and stare as the mourners shuffle past.

Jesus, however, knows what to say and what to do. When he sees the mother, his heart begins to break...and his lips begin to tighten. He glares at the angel of death that hovers over the body of the boy. "Not this time, Satan. This boy is mine."

At that moment the mother walks in front of him. Jesus speaks to her. "Don't cry." She stops and looks into this stranger's face. If she wasn't shocked by his presumption, you can bet some of the witnesses were.

Don't cry? Don't cry? What kind of request is that?

A request only God can make.

Jesus steps toward the bier and touches it. The pallbearers stop marching. The mourners cease moaning. As Jesus stares at the boy, the crowd is silent.

The demon had been perched spiderlike over the body. He was enjoying the parade. He was the warden. The people were the prisoners. He was marching the condemned to execution. They were watching from behind invisible bars, imprisoned by their impermanence. He had relished the fear in the faces. He had giggled at their despair.

Then he hears the voice. That voice…he knows the owner. His back arches and he hisses instinctively.

He turns. He doesn't see what others see. He doesn't see the face of a Nazarene. He doesn't hear the voice of a man. He sees the wrath of God. He hears the command of a King.

"Get out of here."

He doesn't have to be told twice.

Jesus turns his attention to the dead boy. "Young man," his voice is calm, "come back to life again."

The living stand motionless as the dead come to life. Wooden fingers move. Gray-pale cheeks blush. The dead man sits up.

Luke's description of what happens next is captivating.

"Jesus gave him back to his mother."[1]

How would you feel at a moment like this? What would you do? A stranger tells you not to weep as you look at your dead son. One who refuses to mourn in the midst of sorrow calls the devil's bluff, then shocks you with a call into the cavern of death. Suddenly what had been taken is returned. What had been stolen is retrieved. What you had given up, you are given back.

Jesus must have smiled as the two embraced. Stunned, the crowd breaks into cheers and applause. They hug each other and slap Jesus on the back. Someone proclaims the undeniable, "God has come to help his people."[2]

Jesus gave the woman much more than her son. He gave her a secret—a whisper that was overheard by us. "That," he says pointing at the cot, "that is fantasy. This," he grins, putting an arm around the boy, "this is reality."

1. Luke 7:15 2. Luke 7:16

CHAPTER 16

# The Sparkle from Eternity

Wallace was an important man. He was the kind of man you would find leading a prayer at the football games or serving as president of the Lion's Club. He wore a title and a collar and had soft hands with no calluses.

He had a nice office just off the sanctuary. His secretary was a bit stale but he wasn't. He had a warm smile that melted your apprehension as you walked through his office door. He sat in a leather swivel chair and had diplomas on the wall. And he had a way of listening that made you willing to tell secrets you'd never told anyone.

He was a good man. His marriage wasn't all it could be, but it was better than most. His church was full. His name was respected. He was a fifteen-handicap golfer, and the church bought him a membership at the country club to commemorate his twentieth year with the congregation. People recognized him in public and flocked to hear him on Easter and Christmas. His retirement account was growing, and he was less than a decade from hanging up the frock and settling down to an autumn of soft wine and good books.

If he committed a sin, no one knew it. If he had a fear, no one heard it—which may have been his gravest sin.

Wallace loved people. This morning, though, he doesn't want people. He wants to be alone. He rings his secretary and advises her that he is not taking any more calls for the rest of the day. She doesn't think it unusual. He's been on the phone all morning. She thinks he needs time to study. She is partly correct. He has been on the phone all morning and he does need time. Not time to study, however. Time to weep.

Wallace looks at the eight-by-ten photo that sits on the mahogany credenza behind his desk. Through watery eyes he gazes at his twelve-year-old daughter. Braces. Pigtails. Freckles. She is a reflection of his wife—blue eyes, brown hair, pug nose. The only thing she got from her father was his heart. She owns that. And he has no intention of requesting that she return it.

She isn't his only child, but she is his last. And she is his only daughter. He'd built a fence of protection around his little girl. Maybe that is why the last few days had hurt so badly. The fence had crumbled.

It began six days ago. She came home early from school feverish and irritable. His wife put her to bed, thinking it was the flu.

During the night the fever rose. The next morning they rushed her to the hospital.

The doctors were puzzled. They couldn't pinpoint the problem. They could only agree on one thing—she was sick and getting sicker.

Wallace had never known such helplessness. He didn't know how to handle his pain. He was so accustomed to being strong, he didn't know how to be weak. He assured all who called that his daughter was fine. He assured all who inquired that God was a great God. He assured everyone but himself.

Inside, his emotions were a mighty river. And his dam was beginning to crack. It was the call from the doctor this morning that broke it. "She is in a coma."

Wallace hangs up the phone and tells his secretary to hold the calls. He reaches over and takes the picture and holds it in his hands. Suddenly the words swirl in his head like a merry-go-round. "It's not fair, it's not fair."

He leans over, holds the picture to his face and weeps.

Nothing is right about it. Nothing. "Why a twelve-year-old girl? Why her, for mercy sakes?" His face hardens as he looks out his window toward the gray sky.

"Why don't you take me?" he screams.

He sits up. He walks over to the coffee table by the couch and picks up the box of tissues he keeps handy for counselees. As he's blowing his nose, he looks out the window into the courtyard of the church. An old man sits reading a paper. Another enters and sits beside him and throws bread crumbs on the cobbles. There's a rustle of wings as a covey of pigeons flutters off the roof and snatches up the food.

*Don't you know my daughter is dying? How can you act as if nothing is wrong?*

He's thinking about his daughter. In the springtime she used to come by every day on the way home from school. She would wait in the courtyard for him to walk her home. He would hear her chasing pigeons below and know it was time to go. He'd stop what he was doing, stand at this same window, and watch her. He'd watch her walk a tightrope on the curb around the garden. He'd watch her pick a wildflower out of the grass. He'd watch her spin around and around until she became so dizzy that she'd fall on her back and watch the clouds spin in the sky.

"Oh, Princess," he'd say. "My little girl." Then he'd stack his books and headaches on his desk and go down to meet her.

But it is not springtime and his daughter is not in the courtyard. It is winter, his little girl is nearly dead, and two old men are sitting on a bench.

"Dear, dear Princess."

Suddenly a third man enters the courtyard. He tells something to the other two. Then the three hurry out. *Must be a fight,* Wallace thinks to himself. Then he remembers. *The teacher. He is here.*

He'd almost forgotten. Jesus was arriving today. As Wallace was leaving the house this morning, his neighbor had asked him if he was going to see the controversial teacher.

Inwardly he'd scoffed at the idea. "No, too busy today," he'd answered with a wave, knowing that even on a slow day he wouldn't take time to go see an itinerant preacher. Especially this one.

The journals from headquarters had branded this guy a maverick. Some even said he was insane. But the crowds hung around him like he was God's gift to humanity.

*I'm going.* Wallace replayed the neighbor's response in his head.

"Yeah," Wallace had said to himself, "you also subscribe to *National Enquirer.*"

"They say he can heal…," he recalled his neighbor saying.

Wallace stood up straight. Then he relaxed. "Don't be foolish."

"Faith healers are an insult to our profession," he had declared while lecturing at the seminary last fall. "Parasites of the people, charlatans of the church, prophets for profit." He'd seen these guys on television, stuffed into double-breasted suits, wearing mannequin smiles and powdered faces. He shakes his head and walks back to his desk. He picks up the photograph.

He stares at the face of the child who is about to be taken from him. "They say he can heal…."

Wallace began to weigh the options. "If I go and am recognized, it will mean my job. But if she dies and he could have done something…" A man reaches a point where his desperation is a notch above his dignity. He shrugs his shoulders. "What choice do I have?"

---

*The events of that afternoon redirected Wallace's life. He told the story whenever he had a chance.*

I circled the bus terminal three times before I found a place to park. The cold wind bit my ears as I fumbled through my pockets looking for parking meter change. I buttoned my overcoat up to the knot of my tie, turned into the wind, and walked.

I passed a pawn shop window still flocked with Season's Greetings. Someone came out of a bar as I walked by. A dozen or so teens in skintight pants leaned against a brick wall. One flipped a cigarette butt at my feet. Three men in leather jackets and jeans warmed hands over a fire in a ten-gallon drum. One of them chuckled as I walked by. "Looky there, a poodle in the pound." I didn't turn around. If he was talking about me, I didn't want to know.

I felt awkward. It had been years since I'd been on this side of town. I glanced over at my reflection in a drugstore window. Wool overcoat. Wing tip shoes. Gray suit. Red tie. No wonder I was turning heads. Their question was written in their eyes. "What brings Mr. White-collar across the tracks?" The bus station was packed. I barely squeezed through the door.

Once I got in I couldn't have gotten out. Heads bobbed and ducked like corks on a lake. Everyone was trying to get across the room to the side where the de-boarded passengers entered the terminal. I managed to squeeze through ahead of them. They were just curious; I was desperate.

As I reached the window, I saw him. He stood near the bus.

He had only been able to advance a couple of strides against the wall of people.

He looked too normal. He wore a corduroy jacket, the kind with patches on the elbows. His slacks weren't new, but they were nice. No tie. His hairline receded a bit before it became a flow of brown curls. I couldn't hear his voice, but I could see his face. His eyebrows were bushy. He had a gleam in his eyes and a grin on his lips—as if he were watching you unwrap the birthday present he just gave you.

He was so different from what I had anticipated I had to ask a lady next to me if that was him.

"That's him," she smiled. "That's Jesus."

He bent over and disappeared for a minute and surfaced holding a toddler. He smiled. With hands around the little boy's chest, he pushed him high into the air and held him there. The hands were rugged and slender. Someone had told me that Jesus grew up in Mississippi—the son of a mechanic in Tupelo. He brought the little boy down and began walking toward the door.

I knew if he entered the bus station, I'd never get him out. I put my hands flat against the window pane and began edging along the window. People complained but I moved anyway.

When I got to the doorway, so did Jesus. Our eyes met. I froze. I guess I hadn't considered what I would say to him. Maybe I thought he would recognize me. Maybe I thought he'd ask me if there was anything he could do. "Oh, my daughter is sick and I thought you might say a prayer...."

That's not how it came out. The words logjammed in my throat. I felt my eyes water, my chin quiver, and my knees hit the uneven pavement. "It's my daughter, my little girl.... She's very sick. Could you please touch her so she won't die?"

I regretted the words as soon as I said them. If he's a man, then I've asked the impossible. If he's more than a man, what right do I have to make such a request?

I didn't dare look up. I was ashamed. If the crowd was going anywhere, they were going to have to move around me. I didn't have the courage to raise my face.

I guess he knew I didn't. He did it for me.

I felt his fingers under my chin. He lifted my head. He didn't have to raise it far. He had knelt down in front of me. I looked into his eyes. The gaze of this young preacher embraced this old pastor like the arms of an old friend. I knew, then, that I knew this man. From somewhere I'd seen that look. I knew those eyes.

"Take me to her." His hand moved under my arm. He helped me stand. "Where is your car?"

"A car? This way!" I grabbed his hand and began to fight a path through the crowd. It wasn't easy. With my free hand I moved people like I was parting stalks of corn in a cornfield. Faces tumbled in on us. Young mothers wanting a blessing for their children. Old faces with caved-in mouths wanting release from pain.

Suddenly I lost his hand. It slipped out. I stopped and turned and saw him standing and looking. His abrupt stop surprised the crowd. They hushed. I noticed his face was pale. He spoke as if speaking to himself.

"Someone touched me."

"What?" one of his own men inquired.

"Someone touched me."

I thought he was telling a joke. He turned, slowly studying each face. For the life of me, I couldn't tell if he was angry or delighted. He was looking for someone he didn't know but knew he'd know when he saw her.

"I touched you." The voice was beside me. Jesus pivoted.

"It was me. I'm sorry." The curtain of the crowd parted, leaving a girl on center stage. She was thin, almost frail. I could have wrapped my hand around her upper arm and touched my finger to my thumb. Her skin was dark, and her hair was in a hundred braids with beads on each end. She was coatless. She hugged her arms to herself—hands squeezing bony elbows as much out of fear as out of cold.

"Don't be afraid," Jesus assured. "What is wrong?"

"I have AIDS."

Someone behind me gasped. Several took a step back.

Jesus stepped towards her. "Tell me about it."

She looked at him, looked around at the throng of people, swallowed, and began. "I am out of money. The doctors say it is just a matter of time. I didn't have anywhere else to go. But now..."

She lowered her eyes and began to smile. She smiled as if someone had just whispered some good news in her ear.

I looked back at Jesus. My lands, if he wasn't smiling too! The two stood there and stared at each other, smiling like they were the only two kids in class who knew the answer to the teacher's question.

It was then I saw the look again. The same gaze met her that only moments before met me as I looked up from the pavement. Those same eyes that I knew I'd seen I saw again. Where? Where had I seen those eyes?

I turned and looked at the girl. For a moment she looked at me. I wanted to say something to her. I think she felt the same urge. We were so different, but suddenly we had everything in common: What a strange couple we were. She with her needle-tracked arms and midnight lovers; I with my clean fingernails and sermon outlines. I had spent my life telling people not to be like her. She'd spent her life avoiding hypocrites like me. But now we were thrust together against the enemy of death, desperately hoping that this country preacher could tie a knot in the end of our frazzled ropes so we could hang on.

Jesus spoke. "It was your faith that did it. Now go and enjoy life."

She resisted all effort to hide her joy. She smiled, looked back at Jesus, and jumped up and kissed him on the cheek.

The crowd laughed, Jesus blushed, and she disappeared.

I hadn't noticed, but while Jesus was speaking, some other men had worked their way into the crowd. They were standing behind me. When I heard them speak, I immediately recognized their voices. They were from my congregation.

One put his hand on my shoulder. "There's no need to bother this teacher anymore; your daughter is dead."

The words came at me like darts, but Jesus intercepted them: "Don't be afraid; just trust me."

The next few moments were a blur of activity. We raced through the crowd, jumped in the car of the man who brought the news, and sped to the hospital.

The waiting room was chaotic. Church members, neighbors, and friends were already gathering. Several wept openly. My wife, seated in one of the chairs, was pale and speechless. Her eyes were red. Her hand trembled as she brushed away a tear.

As I entered, people came to comfort me. Jesus stepped in front of them. They stopped and stared at this stranger.

"Why are you crying?" he asked. "She isn't dead; she's only asleep."

They were stunned. They were insulted. "Of all the insensitive things to say," someone shouted. "Who are you anyway?"

"Get that joker out of here!"

But leaving was the last thing Jesus had on his agenda. He turned and within a few seconds was standing in front of my daughter's hospital room. He signaled for a few of us to follow. We did.

The six of us stood at my daughter's bedside. Her face was ashen. Her lips dry and still. I touched her hand. It was cold. Before I could say anything, Jesus' hand was on mine. With the exception of one instant he never took his eyes off my daughter. But during that instant he looked at me. He looked at me with that same look, that same slight smile. He was giving another gift and couldn't wait to see the response when it was opened.

"Princess," the words were said softly, almost in a whisper, "get up!"

Her head turned slightly as if hearing a voice. Jesus stood back. Her upper body leaned forward until she was upright in bed. Her eyes opened. She turned and put her bare feet on the floor and stood.

No one moved as my wife and I watched our girl walk toward us. We held her for an eternity—half believing it couldn't be true and half not wanting to know if it wasn't. But it was.

"Better get her something to eat," Jesus teased with a smile. "She's probably famished." Then he turned to leave.

I reached out and touched his shoulder. My willingness was in my eyes. "Let me return the favor. I'll introduce you to the right people. I'll get you speaking engagements at the right places."

"Let's keep this between us, okay?" and he and three speechless friends left the room.

For weeks after that day I was puzzled. Oh, of course I was exuberant. But my joy was peppered with mystery. Everywhere I went I saw his face. His look followed me. Even as I write this, I can see it.

Head cocked just a bit. Tender twinkle of anticipation under bushy brows. That look that whispered, "Come here. I've got a secret."

And now I know where I'd seen it before. In fact I've seen it again—several times.

I saw it in the eyes of the cancer patient I visited yesterday. Bald from chemotherapy. Shadowed eyes from the disease. Her skin was soft and her hand bony. She recognized me when she awoke. She didn't even say hello. She just lofted her eyebrows, sparkled that sparkle, and said, "I'm ready, Wallace. I'm ready to go."

I saw it last week as I spoke at a funeral. The widower, a wrinkled-faced man with white hair and bifocals. He didn't weep like the others. In fact, at one point I think I saw him smile. I shook his hand afterwards. "Don't worry about me," he exclaimed. Then he motioned for me to lean down so he could say something in my ear. "I know where she is."

But it was this morning that I saw it the clearest. I'd wanted to ask her for days, but the right moment never came. This morning it did. At the breakfast table, just the two of us, she with her cereal, I with my paper, I turned to my daughter and asked her. "Princess?"

"Uh huh?"

"What was it like?"

"What?"

"While you were gone. What was it like?"

She didn't say anything. She just turned her head slightly and looked out the window. When she turned around again, the sparkle was there. She opened her mouth and then closed it, then opened it again. "It's a secret, Dad. A secret too good for words."

Peace where there should be pain. Confidence in the midst of crisis. Hope defying despair. That's what that look says. It is a look that knows the answer to the question asked by every mortal, "Does death have the last word?" I can see Jesus wink as he gives the answer. "Not on your life."

(Based on Mark 5:22-43; Matthew 9:18-26; and Luke 8:41-56)

CHAPTER 17

# "LAZARUS, COME OUT!"

When the famous agnostic Robert Ingersoll died, the printed funeral program left this solemn instruction, "There will be no singing."

Few feel like singing in the face of death. Running, perhaps. Crying, probably. But singing? Not at death. Death steals our reason to sing. Death takes the songs from our lips and leaves in their place stilled tongues and tear-flooded cheeks.

*There was no singing at the funeral Jesus attended either. Mourning. Weeping. Wailing. But no singing.*

*The house was more like a prison than a residence. People shuffled about aimlessly, their faces pasty white and their eyes full moons of fear. On their lips was no music, no laughter—only the foreboding news that reminded them of their own fate: Another prisoner had been marched from death row to the gallows. Lazarus was dead. They were in prison awaiting their turn.*

Shokoi Yokoi spent twenty-eight years in a prison. Not a prison of walls, but a prison of fear. When the tide began to turn in World War II, Shokoi was a Japanese soldier on the island of Guam. Fearing that defeat meant certain capture by American forces, he ran into the jungle and hid in a cave. He later learned the war was over by reading one of the thousands of leaflets that were dropped into the jungle by American planes. Still, he feared being taken as prisoner, so he remained in his cave.

For over a quarter of a century he came out only at night. He existed on frogs, rats, roaches, and mangoes. It was only when some hunters discovered him that he was convinced it was safe to leave the jungle.

"Shocking," we say. "How could a man be so blind?"

"Tragic," we sigh. "What a waste of life."

"A pity," we lament, "that a human would be so imprisoned by fear that he would cease to live."

A life wasted pacing up and down in a self-made cell of fear. It is shocking. It is tragic. It is a pity. And it is also very common.

The fear of death has filled a thousand prisons. You can't see the walls. You can't see the warden. You can't see the locks. But you can see the prisoners. You can see them as they sit on their bunks and bemoan their fate. They want to live, but they can't because they are doomed to do what they most want to avoid—they will die.

And, oh how restrictive is the ball and chain of death. You try to run away from it—you can't. You try to run with it—it is too heavy. You try to ignore it, and it yanks you into reality.

Just yesterday I visited a home that was wearing the black wreath of death. The youngest of three daughters, a recently married twenty-two-year-old, had been killed in a collision between an eighteen-wheeler and a bus. The eyes that met me at the door were those of a prisoner. The family was held hostage by the answerless questions. Taken captive by sadness, they couldn't take a dozen steps without walking into a brick wall of disbelief.

It was enough to make you cry. It is enough to make God cry.

*Jesus' throat tightened as he walked among the inmates. He gazed at the chalky faces through watery eyes. How long would they listen to Satan's lie? How long would they be in bondage? What would he have to do to convince them? Hadn't he proven it at Nain? Was the raising of Jairus's daughter not proof enough? How long would these people lock themselves into this man-made prison of fear? He had shown them the key to unlock their door. Why didn't they use it ?*

*"Show me the tomb."*

*They led him to the burial place of Lazarus. It was a cave with a stone laid across the entrance. Over the stone was spun the spider web of finality. "No more!" the stone boasted. "No more shall these hands move. No longer shall this tongue speak. No more!"*

*Jesus wept. He wept not for the dead but for the living. He wept not for the one in the cave of death but for those in the cave of fear. He wept for those who, though alive, were dead. He wept for those who, though free, were prisoners, held captive by their fear of death.*

*"Move the stone." The command was soft but firm.*

*"But, Jesus, it will...it will stink."*

*"Move the stone so you will see God."*

Stones have never stood in God's way. They didn't in Bethany two thousand years ago. And they didn't in Europe a hundred years ago.

She was a Hanoverian countess. If she was known for anything, she was known for her disbelief in God and her conviction that no one could call life from a tomb.

Before her death, she left specific instructions that her tomb was to be sealed with a slab of granite; she asked that blocks of stone be placed around her tomb and that the corners of the blocks be fastened together and to the granite slab by heavy iron clamps.

This inscription was placed on the granite rock:

*This burial place,*
*purchased to all eternity,*
*must never be opened.*

All that any man could do to seal the tomb was done. The countess had insured that her tomb would serve as a mockery to the belief in the resurrection. A small birch tree, however, had other plans. Its root found its way between the slabs and grew deep into the ground. Over the years it forced its way until the iron clamps popped loose and the granite lid was raised. The stone cover is now resting against the trunk of the birch, the boastful epitaph permanently silenced by the work of a determined tree...or a powerful God.

*"Lazarus, come out!"*

*It took only one call. Lazarus heard his name. His eyes opened beneath the wrap. The cloth-covered hands raised. Knees lifted, feet touched the ground, and the dead man came out.*

*"Take the grave clothes off of him and let him go."*[1]

There is a story told in Brazil about a missionary who discovered a tribe of Indians in a remote part of the jungle. They lived near a large river. The tribe was friendly and in need of medical attention. A contagious disease was ravaging the population and people were dying daily. An infirmary was located in another part of the jungle and the missionary determined that the only hope for the tribe was to go to the hospital for treatment and inoculations. In order to reach the hospital, however, the Indians would have to cross the river—a feat they were unwilling to perform.

The river, they believed, was inhabited by evil spirits. To enter the water meant certain death. The missionary set about the difficult task of overcoming the superstition of the tribe.

He explained how he had crossed the river and arrived unharmed. No luck. He led the people to the bank and placed his hand in the water. The people still wouldn't believe him. He walked out into the river and splashed water on his face. The people watched closely, yet were still hesitant. Finally he turned and dove into the water. He swam beneath the surface until he emerged on the other side.

Having proven that the power of the river was a farce, the missionary punched a triumphant fist into the air. He had entered the water and escaped. The Indians broke into cheers and followed him across.

Jesus saw people enslaved by their fear of a cheap power. He explained that the river of death was nothing to fear. The people wouldn't believe him. He touched a boy and called him back to life. The followers were still unconvinced. He whispered life into the dead body of a girl. The people were still cynical. He let a dead man spend four days in a grave and then called him out. Is that enough? Apparently not. For it was necessary for him to enter the river, to submerge himself in the water of death before people would believe that death had been conquered.

But after he did, after he came out on the other side of death's river, it was time to sing…it was time to celebrate.

1. John 11:1-44

CHAPTER 18

# The Celebration

A party was the last thing Mary Magdalene expected as she approached the tomb on that Sunday morning. The last few days had brought nothing to celebrate. The Jews could celebrate—Jesus was out of the way. The soldiers could celebrate—their work was done. But Mary couldn't celebrate. To her the last few days had brought nothing but tragedy.

Mary had been there. She had heard the leaders clamor for Jesus' blood. She had witnessed the Roman whip rip the skin off his back. She had winced as the thorns sliced his brow and wept at the weight of the cross.

In the Louvre there is a painting of the scene of the cross. In the painting the stars are dead and the world is wrapped in darkness. In the shadows there is a kneeling form. It is Mary. She is holding her hands and lips against the bleeding feet of the Christ.

We don't know if Mary did that, but we know she could have. She was there. She was there to hold her arm around the shoulder of Mary the mother of Jesus. She was there to close his eyes. She was there.

So it's not surprising that she wants to be there again.

In the early morning mist she arises from her mat, takes her spices and aloes, and leaves her house, past the Gate of Gennath and up to the hillside. She anticipates a somber task. By now the body will be swollen. His face will be white. Death's odor will be pungent.

A gray sky gives way to gold as she walks up the narrow trail. As she rounds the final bend, she gasps. The rock in front of the grave is pushed back.

"Someone took the body." She runs to awaken Peter and John. They rush to see for themselves. She tries to keep up with them but can't.

Peter comes out of the tomb bewildered and John comes out believing, but Mary just sits in front of it weeping. The two men go home and leave her alone with her grief.

But something tells her she is not alone. Maybe she hears a noise. Maybe she hears a whisper. Or maybe she just hears her own heart tell her to take a look for herself.

Whatever the reason, she does. She stoops down, sticks her head into the hewn entrance, and waits for her eyes to adjust to the dark.

"Why are you crying?" She sees what looks to be a man, but

he's white—radiantly white. He is one of two lights on either end of the vacant slab. Two candles blazing on an altar.

"Why are you crying?" An uncommon question to be asked in a cemetery. In fact, the question is rude. That is, unless the questioner knows something the questionee doesn't.

"They have taken my Lord away, and I don't know where they have put him."

She still calls him "my Lord." As far as she knows his lips were silent. As far as she knows, his corpse had been carted off by graverobbers. But in spite of it all, he is still her Lord.

Such devotion moves Jesus. It moves him closer to her. So close she hears him breathing. She turns and there he stands. She thinks he is the gardener.

Now, Jesus could have revealed himself at this point. He could have called for an angel to present him or a band to announce his presence. But he didn't.

"Why are you crying? Who is it you are looking for?"[1]

He doesn't leave her wondering long, just long enough to remind us that he loves to surprise us. He waits for us to despair of human strength and then intervenes with heavenly. God waits for us to give up and then—surprise!

Has it been a while since you let God surprise you? It's easy to reach the point where we have God figured out.

We know exactly what God does. We break the code. We chart his tendencies. God is a computer. If we push all the right buttons and insert the right data, God is exactly who we thought he was.

No variations. No alterations. God is a jukebox. Insert a tithe. Punch in the right numbers and—bam—the divine music we want fills the room.

I look across my desk and see a box of tissues. Ten minutes ago that box sat in the lap of a young woman—midthirties, mother of three. She told me of the telephone call she received from her husband this morning. He wants a divorce. She had to leave work and weep. She wanted a word of hope.

I reminded her that God is at his best when our life is at its worst. God has been known to plan a celebration in a cemetery. I told her, "Get ready, you may be in for a surprise."

Have you got God figured out? Have you got God captured on a flowchart and frozen on a flannelboard? If so, then listen. Listen to God's surprises.

Hear the rocks meant for the body of the adulterous woman drop to the ground.

Listen as Jesus invites a death-row convict to ride with him to the kingdom in the front seat of the limo.

Listen as the Messiah whispers to the Samaritan woman, "I who speak to you am he."

Listen to the widow from Nain eating dinner with her son who is supposed to be dead.

And listen to the surprise as Mary's name is spoken by a man she loved—a man she had buried.

"Miriam."[2]

God appearing at the strangest of places. Doing the strangest of things. Stretching smiles where there had hung only frowns. Placing twinkles where there were only tears. Hanging a bright star in a dark sky. Arching rainbows in the midst of thunderclouds. Calling names in a cemetery.

"Miriam," he said softly, "surprise!"

Mary was shocked. It's not often you hear your name spoken by an eternal tongue. But when she did, she recognized it. And when she did, she responded correctly. She worshiped him.

The scene has all the elements of a surprise party—secrecy, wide eyes, amazement, gratitude. But this celebration is timid in comparison with the one that is being planned for the future. It will be similar to Mary's, but a lot bigger. Many more graves will open. Many more names will be called. Many more knees will bow. And many more seekers will celebrate.

It's going to be some party. I plan to make sure my name is on the guest list. How about you?

> "No eye has seen,
> no ear has heard,
> no mind has conceived
> what God has prepared for those who love him."[3]

1. John 20:1-18 2. "Miriam" is the Aramaic form of "Mary." 3. 1 Corinthians 2:9

CHAPTER 19

# THE FINAL GLANCE

"Max, your dad's awake." I had been watching a movie on television. One of those thrillers that takes you from the here and now and transports you to the somewhere and sometime. My mother's statement seemed to come from another world. The real world.

I turned toward my father. He was looking at me.

His head was all he could turn. Lou Gehrig's disease had leeched his movement, taking from him everything but his faith...and his eyes.

It was his eyes that called me to walk over to his bedside. I had been home for almost two weeks, on special leave from Brazil, due to his worsening condition. He had slept most of the last few days, awakening only when my mother would bathe him or clean his sheets.

Next to his bed was a respirator—a metronome of mortality

that pushed air into his lungs through a hole in his throat. The bones in his hand protruded like spokes in an umbrella. His fingers, once firm and strong, were curled and lifeless. I sat on the edge of his bed and ran my hands over his barreled rib cage. I put my hand on his forehead. It was hot…hot and damp. I stroked his hair.

"What is it, Dad?"

He wanted to say something. His eyes yearned. His eyes refused to release me. If I looked away for a moment, they followed me and were still looking when I looked back.

"What is it?"

I'd seen that expression before. I was seven years old, eight at the most. Standing on the edge of a diving board for the first time, wondering if I would survive the plunge. The board dipped under my seventy pounds. I looked behind me at the kids who were pestering me to hurry up and jump. I wondered what they would do if I asked them to move over so I could get down. Tar and feather me, I supposed.

So caught between ridicule and a jump into certain death, I did the only thing I knew to do—I shivered.

Then I heard him, "It's all right, son. Come on in." I looked down. My father had dived in. He was treading water awaiting my jump. Even as I write, I can see his expression—tanned face, wet hair, broad smile, and bright eyes. His eyes were assuring and earnest. Had he not said a word, they would have conveyed the message. But he did speak. "Jump. It's all right."

So I jumped.

Twenty-three years later the tan was gone, the hair thin, and the face drawn. But the eyes hadn't changed. They were bold. And their message hadn't changed. I knew what he was saying. Somehow he knew I was afraid. Somehow he perceived I was shivering as I looked into the deep. And somehow, he, the dying, had the strength to comfort me, the living.

I placed my cheek in the hollow of his. My tears dripped on his hot face. I said softly what his throat wanted to, but couldn't. "It's all right," I whispered. "It's going to be all right."

When I raised my head, his eyes were closed. I would never see them open again.

He left me with a final look. One last statement of the eyes. One farewell message from the captain before the boat would turn out to sea. One concluding assurance from a father to a son, "It's all right."

---

Perhaps it was a similar look that stirred the soul of the soldier during those six hours one Friday.

He was uneasy. He had been since noon.

It wasn't the deaths that troubled him. The centurion was no stranger to finality. Over the years he'd grown callous to the screams of the crucified. He'd mastered the art of numbing his heart. But this crucifixion plagued him.

The day began as had a hundred others—dreadfully. It was bad enough to be in Judea, but it was hell to spend hot afternoons on a rocky hill supervising the death of pickpockets and rabble-rousers. Half the crowd taunted, half cried. The soldiers griped. The priests bossed. It was a thankless job in a strange land. He was ready for the day to be over before it began.

He was curious at the attention given to the flatfooted peasant. He smiled as he read the sign that would go on the cross. The condemned looked like anything but a king. His face was lumpy and bruised. His back arched slightly and his eyes faced downward. "Some harmless hick," mused the centurion. "What could he have done?"

Then Jesus raised his head. He wasn't angry. He wasn't uneasy. His eyes were strangely calm as they stared from behind the bloody mask. He looked at those who knew him—moving deliberately from face to face as if he had a word for each.

For just a moment he looked at the centurion—for a second the Roman looked into the purest eyes he'd ever seen. He didn't know what the look meant. But the look made him swallow and his stomach feel empty. As he watched the soldier grab the Nazarene and yank him to the ground, something told him this was not going to be a normal day.

As the hours wore on, the centurion found himself looking more and more at the one on the center cross. He didn't know what to do with the Nazarene's silence. He didn't know what to do with his kindness.

But most of all, he was perplexed by the darkness. He didn't know what to do with the black sky in midafternoon. No one could explain it.... No one even tried. One minute the sun, the next the darkness. One minute the heat, the next a chilly breeze. Even the priests were silenced.

For a long while the centurion sat on a rock and stared at the three silhouetted figures. Their heads were limp, occasionally rolling from side to side. The jeering was silent...eerily silent. Those who had wept, now waited.

Suddenly the center head ceased to bob. It yanked itself erect. Its eyes opened in a flash of white. A roar sliced the silence. "It is finished."[1] It wasn't a yell. It wasn't a scream. It was a roar...a lion's roar. From what world that roar came the centurion didn't know, but he knew it wasn't this one.

The centurion stood up from the rock and took a few paces toward the Nazarene. As he got closer, he could tell that Jesus was staring into the sky. There was something in his eyes that the soldier had to see. But after only a few steps, he fell. He stood and fell again. The ground was shaking, gently at first and now violently. He tried once more to walk and was able to take a few steps and then fall...at the foot of the cross.

He looked up into the face of this one near death. The King looked down at the crusty old centurion. Jesus' hands were fastened; they couldn't reach out. His feet were nailed to timber; they couldn't walk toward him. His head was heavy with pain; he could scarcely move it. But his eyes...they were afire.

They were unquenchable. They were the eyes of God.

Perhaps that is what made the centurion say what he said. He saw the eyes of God. He saw the same eyes that had been seen by a near-naked adulteress in Jerusalem, a friendless divorcée in Samaria, and a four-day-dead Lazarus in a cemetery. The same eyes that didn't close upon seeing man's futility, didn't turn away at man's failure, and didn't wince upon witnessing man's death.

"It's all right," God's eyes said. "I've seen the storms and it's still all right."

The centurion's convictions began to flow together like rivers. "This was no carpenter," he spoke under his breath. "This was no peasant. This was no normal man."

He stood and looked around at the rocks that had fallen and the sky that had blackened. He turned and stared at the soldiers as they stared at Jesus with frozen faces. He turned and watched as the eyes of Jesus lifted and looked toward home. He listened as the parched lips parted and the swollen tongue spoke for the last time.

"Father, into your hands I entrust my spirit."[2]

Had the centurion not said it, the soldiers would have. Had the centurion not said it, the rocks would have—as would have the angels, the stars, even the demons. But he did say it. It fell to a nameless foreigner to state what they all knew.

"Surely this man was the Son of God."[3]

Six hours on one Friday. Six hours that jut up on the plain of human history like Mount Everest in a desert. Six hours that have been deciphered, dissected, and debated for two thousand years.

What do these six hours signify? They claim to be the door in time through which eternity entered man's darkest caverns. They mark the moments that the Navigator descended into the deepest waters to leave anchor points for his followers.

What does that Friday mean?

For the life blackened with failure, that Friday means forgiveness.

For the heart scarred with futility, that Friday means purpose.

And for the soul looking into this side of the tunnel of death, that Friday means deliverance.

Six hours. One Friday.

What do *you* do with those six hours on that Friday?

1. John 19:30 2. Luke 23:46 3. Matthew 27:54

# Study Guide

# ANCHORING DEEP

**A Message from Max**

Do you know many people who have intentionally turned their backs on God and stomped away in anger? Neither do I. Do you know many people who gradually lost their faith over an extended period of time? So do I.

Few abandon the faith out of anger at God or disbelief in the Scriptures. If you vacate your church pew, you probably won't do so overnight. It will be a subtle, casual abandonment. Read these words from Hebrews and see how one writer describes the process: "We must pay more careful attention, therefore, to what we have heard, so that we do not drift away" (Hebrews 2:1).

What is the danger that faces any person attempting to stay spiritually afloat? Drifting. Getting off course. Aimlessly floating. A directionless meander that leaves you in uncharted and unfamiliar waters.

If you lose your faith, you will probably do so gradually. In tiny increments you will get spiritually sloppy. You will let a few days slip by without consulting your compass. Your sails will go untrimmed. Your rigging will go unprepared. And worst of all, you will forget to anchor your boat. And, before you know it, you'll be bouncing from wave to wave in stormy seas.

And unless you anchor deep, you could go down.

How do you anchor deep? Look at the verse again.

"We must pay more careful attention, therefore, to *what we have heard. . . .*"

Stability in the storm comes not from seeking a new message but from understanding an old one. The most reliable anchor points are not recent discoveries, but are time-tested truths that have held their ground against the winds of change. Truths like:

My life is not futile.
My failures are not fatal.
My death is not final.

Attach your soul to these boulders and no wave is big enough to wash you under.

My prayer is that *Six Hours One Friday* has been a tool to help you anchor to these rocks.

The following study guide will help you even more. It is ideal for personal devotional time, small group study, or classroom exploration. The guide invites you to reexamine each chapter of the book on three levels.

**Level One: Mind Anchors.** This first part gleans crucial quotes from the chapter and invites you to reexamine them by answering some probing questions.

**Level Two: Soul Anchors.** This section uses parallel Scriptures to reinforce and clarify the thrust of the chapter.

**Level Three: Life Anchors.** Here is where you take the message home. Want to keep from drifting? Spend some time meditating over the exercises in this section.

I am deeply indebted to Steve Halliday and Liz Heaney for their work on this study guide.

One final word. Don't be content to depend on someone else's anchor points. Don't settle for a faith inherited from your family or borrowed from your friends. Their help is important and their teaching is vital, but you never know when you'll have to face a hurricane alone. So be sure that *your* heart is safely secured. Take the advice of the sailor, "Anchor deep, say a prayer, and hold on!"

CHAPTER 1

HURRICANE WARNINGS

## Mind Anchors

I. *Anchor points. Firm rocks sunk deeply in a solid foundation. Not casual opinions or negotiable hypotheses, but ironclad undeniables that will keep you afloat. How strong are yours?*

1. Why are anchor points necessary in developing a strong life of faith? What happens if you don't have them?
2. What anchor points can you identify in your own life? How strong are they?

II. *Three anchor points were planted firmly in bedrock two thousand years ago by a carpenter who claimed to be the Christ. And it was all done in the course of a single day. A single Friday. All done during six hours, one Friday.*

1. What does it mean that these anchor points were "planted firmly in bedrock"? What gives them such strength?
2. What set apart these six hours from any other six hours in history? Why is it remarkable that Jesus' work was accomplished in such a short time?

III. *There is one stone to which you should tie. It's large. It's round. And it's heavy. It blocked the door of a grave. It wasn't big enough, though. The tomb it sealed was the tomb of a transient. He only went in to prove he could come out.*

1. In what sense was Jesus a "transient"? What Scripture verses can you think of that would say this in another way?
2. Why was it necessary for Jesus to *"prove* he could come out" of the tomb? Why leave evidence?

IV. *To the casual observer the six hours are mundane.... But to the handful of awestruck witnesses the most maddening of miracles is occurring. God is on a cross. The creator of the universe is being executed.... And there is no one to save him, for he is sacrificing himself.*

1. How is the crucifixion of Jesus a "miracle"? What thoughts do you imagine went through Jesus' mind during his ordeal?
2. Why is it significant that Jesus sacrificed himself? How does your answer make you feel?

**Soul Anchors**

Read Hebrews 12:2-13.

1. According to verses 2-3, what should Christians do to avoid growing weary or losing heart in the face of personal hurricanes? In what practical ways can this advice help you?
2. How do we sometimes "make light of" hardships or "lose heart" because of them? What use does God sometimes make of these hardships, according to verse 6?

3. What is an ultimate purpose of God in allowing "hurricanes" into our lives, according to verse 10?
4. How do we feel about these hardships, according to verse 11? Does it help to know that God understands how we feel about this? Why?
5. According to verse 11, what kind of people reap the benefits of such difficult experiences?
6. What connection is there between verse 12 and verses 2-3? What anchor points are mentioned in this passage?

**Life Anchors**

1. On a clean sheet of paper write down five of your personal anchor points. Put this list in a safe, accessible place and reread it when hurricanes blow into your life.
2. Think of the last time you went through a personal hurricane. How did you react? Did you rely on any anchor points? If not, why not? If so, which ones?
3. What do you think were Jesus' anchor points when he walked on this earth? Which ones do you think he relied upon while he spent those six hours on the cross?
4. Take five minutes to thank God for providing firm anchor points for your faith. If you haven't been relying on these anchor points as you should, confess it and ask the Lord to help you the next time a hurricane blows your way.

CHAPTER 2

GOD'S FORMULA FOR FATIGUE

## Mind Anchors

I. *You are tired. You are weary. Weary of being slapped by the waves of broken dreams. Weary of being stepped on and run over in the endless marathon to the top. Weary of trusting in someone only to have that trust returned in an envelope with no return address.*

1. Have you ever felt this way? If so, explain. If not, think of someone you know who has felt this way. What caused such feelings?

II. Is it worth it? When I get what I want, will it be worth the price I paid? *Perhaps those were the thoughts of a San Antonio lawyer I read about recently. Apparently his success wasn't enough. One day, he came home, took a gun out of his vault, climbed into a sleeping bag, and took his life. His note to his bride read, "It's not that I don't love you, it's just that I'm tired and I want to rest."*

1. In what ways can weariness distort one's thinking?
2. Do you think this lawyer achieved what he was after? Why?

III. *Jesus was the only man to walk God's earth who claimed to have an answer for man's burdens. "Come to me," he invited them. My prayer is that you, too, will find rest. And that you will sleep like a baby.*

1. Many groups today claim to have an answer for man's problems. How is Jesus' answer different from theirs?
2. Describe this answer that Jesus claimed to have for man's burdens. How do you evaluate his answer?
3. Does this wish for "sleeping like a baby" mean that believers are shielded from situations that rob them of sleep? Explain.

**Soul Anchors**

Read Matthew 11:28-29.

1. What kind of people does Jesus invite to come to him? What does he promise them?
2. The phrase "take my yoke upon you" is unfamiliar to many of us today. Read what William Hendriksen had to say about it and then answer the questions that follow:

   In Jewish literature a "yoke" represents the sum total of obligations which, according to *the teaching* of the rabbis, a person must take upon himself.... Because of their misinterpretation, alteration, and augmentation of God's holy law, the yoke which Israel's teachers placed upon the shoulders of the people was that of a totally unwarranted legalism. It was the system of *teaching* that stressed salvation by means of strict obedience to a host of rules and regulations. Now here in 11:29 Jesus places his own teaching over against that to which the people had become accustomed. When he says, "Take my yoke upon you and

> learn from me,"...he means, "Accept my teaching, namely, that a person is saved by means of simple trust in me...." Symbolically speaking, Jesus here assures the oppressed persons whom he addresses, both then and now, that *his* yoke, that is, the one he urges them to wear, is kindly, and his burden, that is, that which he requires of us, is light. What he is really saying, therefore, is that simple trust in him and obedience to his commands out of gratitude for the salvation already imparted by him is delightful. It brings peace and joy. The person who lives this kind of life is no longer a slave. He has become free.[1]

What "yokes" are you carrying today? How does Jesus suggest you can shed them?

Read Hebrews 4:1-11.

3. How does a person enjoy the rest of God?
4. How did some people in the past fail to enjoy this rest?
5. What is the link between the rest mentioned in Matthew 11:28-29 and that in Hebrews 4:1-11?

**Life Anchors**

1. Do you believe you normally enjoy the rest Jesus provides? Why or why not? What things keep you from enjoying it?
2. If it's your desire to enjoy Jesus' offer of rest, but you're not sure what to do, begin with these three things:
    a. Reread chapter two, "God's Formula for Fatigue."
    b. Read once more Matthew 11:28-29 and Hebrews 4:1-11.

   c. Sit down with a piece of paper and a pencil and write out specific steps you find in these two sources which describe how to enjoy God's rest.

3. Keep a personal journal for one week, each day recording any events which keep you from enjoying the rest of Jesus. At the end of the week, do two things:

   a. Pray about each of those events, asking God for his help in enjoying his rest. Be sure to thank him for those times when you did enjoy his rest.

   b. Analyze the events, looking for clues which might indicate how you got off track.

1. William Hendricksen, *The Gospel of Matthew* (Grand Rapids, Mich.: Baker Book House, 1973), 504-05.

# CHAPTER 3

# TWO TOMBSTONES

## Mind Anchors

I. *"Sleeps, but rests not. Loved, but was loved not. Tried to please, but pleased not. Died as she lived—alone."*

1. What for you is the most chilling phrase in this epitaph? Why?
2. If you were to write an epitaph for yourself that expresses your current lot in life, what would it say?

II. *How many people will die in the loneliness in which they are living? The homeless in Atlanta. The happy-hour hopper in L.A. A bag lady in Miami. The preacher in Nashville. Any person who doubts whether the world needs him. Any person who is convinced that no one really cares.*

1. How do you identify people living in loneliness? What characterizes them outwardly?
2. What lonely people do you know?
3. Have you ever fit any of the descriptions in this passage? Which one(s)?

III. *The woman asked the question that revealed the gaping hole in her soul. "Where is God? My people say he is on the mountain. Your people say he is in Jerusalem. I don't know where he is."*

1. Have you ever met someone who was asking these kinds of questions? What did you tell him or her?
2. Have you ever asked these questions yourself? If so, what prompted the questions?

IV. *Barbara's difficult home life had left her afraid and insecure. While the other children talked, she sat. While the others sang, she was silent. While the others giggled, she was quiet. Always present. Always listening. Always speechless.*

*Until the day Joy gave a class on heaven. Joy talked about seeing God. She talked about tearless eyes and deathless lives. Barbara listened with hunger. Then she raised her hand. "Mrs. Joy?"*

*"Yes, Barbara?"*

*"Is heaven for girls like me?"*

1. Describe the emotional impact this story has on you. Why is Barbara's question so poignant?
2. What do you think caused Barbara to ask such a question?
3. If you had been Joy, how would you have answered Barbara's question?

**Soul Anchors**

Read John 4:4-42.

1. Jews of Jesus' day avoided passing through Samaria at all costs, even taking long detours to bypass the area. Yet John 4:4 says Jesus "had" to go though Samaria. Why do you think he "had" to do so?

2. How did Jesus use his own needs as tools for evangelism (vv. 6-15)? What can we learn from this?
3. What is the "living water" Jesus talks about in verse 10? What does it do?
4. What kind of people does God seek to worship him (vv. 23-24)? Could this Samaritan woman qualify? Do you?
5. How did Jesus use his own needs as tools for teaching (vv. 31-38)? What can we learn from this?
6. How did the woman's report about Jesus affect the people of her town (vv. 39-42)? Taking into account her background (vv. 17-18), why is this remarkable?
7. Identify the single greatest lesson you have learned from this story.

**Life Anchors**

1. Sit down with a close friend or your spouse and write out what gives your life purpose and meaning. Be specific. The next time you are overwhelmed by the rising tides of futility, take out that list and read it.
2. Do you know any Grace Llewellen Smiths? What can you do to help make them feel more significant? Why not do it today?

CHAPTER 4

LIVING PROOF

## Mind Anchors

I. *One step into the classroom and the cat of curiosity pounced on Jenna. And I walked away. I gave my daughter up. Not much. And not as much as I will have to in the future. But I gave her up as much as I could today.*

1. In what other ways will Jenna (or your boy or girl) have to be given up in the future?
2. Does it help to know that all this "giving up" doesn't have to be done at once? Why?

II. *I gave up my child fully aware that were she to need me I would be at her side in a heartbeat. You, God, said good-bye to your son fully aware that when he would need you the most, when his cry of despair would roar through the heavens, you would sit in silence. The angels, though positioned, would hear no command from you. Your son, though in anguish, would feel no comfort from your hands.*

1. Why did God give up his son so completely?
2. Imagine, if you can, what it might have been like in heaven's throne room while Christ suffered on the cross. What is the mood of the angels surrounding God? Somber? Sad? Happy? Angry? Confused?

III. *Before the day was over, I sat in silence a second time. This time not beside my daughter, but before my Father. This time not sad over what I had to give, but grateful for what I'd already received—living proof that God does care.*

1. What is the "living proof" to which this passage refers?
2. How do you respond to this "living proof"?

**Soul Anchors**

Read Romans 8:32-39.

1. For what purpose did God give up his son (v. 32)?
2. Finish the following phrase, based on the second half of verse 32: "Because God was willing to give up his only son for us, we should never think that he__________ ______________________________________________ ______________________________________________."
3. What does it mean that Christ even now "intercedes" for us (v. 34)? How does this make you feel?
4. In a passage of Scripture aimed at helping believers understand their safe position with God, what is Paul's point in quoting a text that says, "For your sake we face death all day long; we are considered as sheep to be slaughtered"?
5. What things, according to Paul, can separate a believer from the love of Christ (vv. 35-39)?

**Life Anchors**

1. Think about past hurricanes in your life. What gives you

"living proof" that God loves you? Make a list of these specifics.

2. Do you help others experience your love for them? Who are the significant people in your life? Think of one thing you can give them as "living proof" of your love for them, and do it.
3. If you have not been able to experience God's love for you, ask God to open your heart so that you would recognize his hand in your life. Then go to a Christian friend whom you regard as spiritually mature and ask what he or she would do in your shoes.

## CHAPTER 5
## FLAMING TORCHES AND LIVING PROMISES

### Mind Anchors

I. *Had any visits from Doubt lately ? If you find yourself going to church in order to be saved and not because you are saved, then you've been listening to him. If you find yourself doubting if God could forgive you* again *for* that, *you've been sold some snake oil. If you are more cynical about Christians than sincere about Christ, then guess who came to dinner.*

1. Explain the phrase "If you find yourself going to church in order to be saved and not because you are saved, then you've been listening to him." How is this statement a reflection of doubt?
2. To which lies of Doubt are you most susceptible?

II. *The invisible God had drawn near to Abraham to make his immovable promise: "To your descendants I give this land." And though God's people often forgot their God, God didn't forget them. He kept his word. The land became theirs. God didn't give up. He never gives up.*

1. In what situations are you most likely to forget God?
2. How does it make you feel to know that God "never gives up"? At what times in your life has this knowledge been especially comforting?

III. *So, the next time that obnoxious neighbor Doubt walks in, escort him out. Out to the hill. Out to Calvary. Out to the cross where, with holy blood, the hand that carried the flame wrote the promise, "God would give up his only son before he'd give up on you."*

1. Why is Calvary a good place to put doubt to rest?

**Soul Anchors**

Read 2 Timothy 2:8-13.

1. One good way to combat doubt is to remember what things are essential. What does Paul ask Timothy to "remember" in verse 8? How is this essential?
2. Verse 11 promises that we will live with Christ if we "died with him." What does it mean to "die with him"? How do you do that?
3. How is "enduring" connected with "reigning" in verse 12? How does this idea relate to verse 10?
4. What warning is included in verse 12? How does doubt sometimes enter in here? How does Paul's warning here compare to Jesus' own words in Luke 12:8-9?
5. What great hope is found in verse 13? Upon what is this hope built?
6. What does it mean to you that God is absolutely faithful?

**Life Anchors**

1. This chapter has listed many times when God did not

give up on his people. Think about your own life. Can you recall times when you were unfaithful but God was faithful to you? Write these down and tell a friend about them.

2. Is doubt ever a good thing? Have there been times in your life when you looked your doubts in the face and they strengthened your faith? Talk about these times with a friend or write about them. How can this encourage you the next time doubt comes your way?
3. For more insight into doubt and God's faithfulness, read *Disappointment with God* by Philip Yancey.

CHAPTER 6

ANGELIC MESSAGES

## Mind Anchors

I. *What if God had responded to my grumblings? What if he'd heeded my complaints? He could have. He could have answered my carelessly mumbled prayers. And had he chosen to do so, a prototype of the result had just appeared at my door.*

1. What prayers have you mumbled which you're glad God hasn't answered? Why do you think grumbling comes so easy to us?
2. What "angels" have crossed your path recently?

II. *God sent the boy with a message. And the point the boy made was razor sharp: "You cry over spilled champagne. Your complaints are not over the lack of necessities but the abundance of benefits. You bellyache over the frills, not the basics; over benefits, not essentials. The source of your problems is your blessings."*

1. Do you believe God would make these same statements to you? Why or why not?
2. Try to name your personal "Top Ten Blessings."

III. *Gajowniczek survived the Holocaust. He made his way back to his hometown. Every year, however, he goes back to Auschwitz. Every August 14 he goes back to say thank you to the man who died in his place. In his backyard there is a plaque. On the plaque is a tribute he carved with his own hands. A tribute to Maximilian Kolbe—the man who died so Gajowniczek could live.*

1. What makes Gajowniczek trek back to Auschwitz every August 14? If you were in his place, would you continue the trips? Why?
2. The statement about Kolbe—"he died so that I could live"—is also a good way to think about Jesus' relationship to redeemed sinners. Explain how this is so.

**Soul Anchors**

Read John 11:45-52.

1. In the verses just prior to this passage, John tells how Jesus had raised Lazarus from the dead. What happened because of this miracle (v. 45)? How did this make Lazarus an "angel" to others?
2. In what two ways did people respond to this "angel" (vv. 45-46; Luke 12:9-11)? In what ways can we respond to the "angels" God sends us?
3. What did *Caiaphas* mean by his speech in verses 49-50?
4. What did *God* mean by that same speech (vv. 51-52)?
5. How are these two interpretations of the same speech typical of the way God often works (see also Acts 4:24-28)?
6. For what purpose did Jesus die, according to verses 51-52? For whom did he die? Are you included in this list? If so, how?

**Life Anchors**

1. Who are the people for whom you are most grateful? Do they know how you feel? If not, tell them of your appreciation and why they mean so much to you. Ask God to help you encourage them in both the timing and the selection of your words.
2. Take a couple of hours this week to go with a friend and visit a homeless shelter or mission. Talk to the people there, finding out who they are and what has happened to them. Also talk with those who work there. What needs do their clients have? How does the community respond to the have-nots in your city? What might you do to help meet some of these needs?

# CHAPTER 7
# REMEMBER

## Mind Anchors

I. *The church of Jesus Christ began with a group of frightened men in a second-floor room in Jerusalem.*

1. What frightened these men?
2. Why do you think modern-day disciples are frightened?

II. *The one betrayed sought his betrayers. What did he say to them? Not, "What a bunch of flops!" Not, "I told you so." No "Where-were-you-when-I-needed-you?" speeches. But simply one phrase, "Peace be with you." The very thing they didn't have was the very thing he offered: peace.*

1. How important is it that Jesus "sought his betrayers"? What likely would have happened if he hadn't done so?
2. What was the purpose behind Jesus' speech? Why did these men need it?

III. *What unlocked the doors of the apostles' hearts? Simple. They saw Jesus. They encountered the Christ. Their sins collided with their Savior, and their Savior won! What lit the boiler of the apostles was a red-hot conviction that the very one who should have sent them to hell went to hell for them and came back to tell about it.*

1. Explain the phrase "Their sins collided with their Savior, and their Savior won!"

2. What should it matter to us how Jesus interacted with a group of men two thousand years ago?

IV. *Think about the first time you ever saw him. Think about your first encounter with the Christ. Robe yourself in that moment. Resurrect the relief. Recall the purity. Summon forth the passion. Can you remember?*

1. Describe the first time you "saw Christ."
2. How long ago did you first "see Christ"? If you could climb in a time machine and revisit that moment, would you? Why?

V. *There is a direct correlation between the accuracy of our memory and the effectiveness of our mission. If we are not teaching people how to be saved, it is perhaps because we have forgotten the tragedy of being lost! If we're not teaching the message of forgiveness, it may be because we don't remember what it was like to be guilty. And if we're not preaching the cross, it could be that we've subconsciously decided that—God forbid—somehow we don't need it.*

1. Try to recall what it was like to be "lost." Describe it. Did you feel guilt? In what way(s)?
2. Do you think you need the cross? Why?

VI. *A man is never the same after he simultaneously sees his utter despair and Christ's unbending grace. To see the despair without the grace is suicidal. To see the grace without the despair is upper-room futility. But to see them both is conversion.*

1. Why are both "despair" and "grace" necessary for conversion?

**Soul Anchors**

Read Acts 23:6-15.

1. For what reason was Paul in custody at this time (v. 6)? Would there have been an uproar had he kept silent about Jesus? Explain.
2. What incident gave Paul great strength and courage in the midst of his hardships (v. 11)? How would this have helped?
3. Did the Lord's promise of help shield Paul from trouble (vv. 12-15)? What did the promise secure for Paul?
4. What is it about seeing Jesus that gives boldness and strength?
5. Can you "see Jesus" without having an actual vision of him? If so, how?

**Life Anchors**

1. Take about half an hour and meditate on the cross. You could do this in several ways—
   a. Remember who you are and who Jesus is and what he did for you. What is it about Jesus that particularly amazes you?
   b. Use a familiar hymnbook and focus on hymns about the cross. Try reading them aloud or singing them.

c. Ask God to fill you with awe that he—the God of the universe—would die for you. Read Psalm 22 and use it to guide your thoughts.

2. Find a partner and take turns asking the following questions. Write down your answers, but don't evaluate what was said until all questions are answered. Say what you really think, not what you believe you should think.

    a. What does Jesus think about your relationship with him? How would he describe it?

    b. How does he view you?

    c. How do you view him?

    d. Do you believe he would offer you peace as he did the disciples, or do you think he would reprimand you? Why?

    Once the questions have been answered, go over them together and summarize what your answers reveal.

3. What hardships are you facing right now? Write these down and beside each note how Jesus can help you weather this storm.

CHAPTER 8

FATAL ERRORS

## Mind Anchors

I. *Could you do it all over again, you'd do it differently. You'd be a different person. You'd be more patient. You'd control your tongue. You'd finish what you started. You'd turn the other cheek instead of slapping his. You'd get married first. You wouldn't marry at all. You'd be honest. You'd resist the temptation. You'd run with a different crowd.*

*But you can't. And as many times as you tell yourself "What's done is done," what you did can't be undone.*

1. What major decisions or actions in your own life would you change if you could?
2. What dangers are there in rehearsing past personal errors? What benefits?

II. *Don't we all long for a father who, even though our mistakes are written all over the wall, will love us anyway? Don't we want a father who cares for us in spite of our failures?*

1. How would you answer these questions? Why would you answer like this?

III. *What kind of heavenly father do we have? A father who is at his best when we are at our worst. A father whose grace is strongest when our devotion is weakest.*

1. What specific comfort do you receive from the thought in this passage? What does this statement mean for you?
2. Name three instances where you experienced the truth of this passage.

**Soul Anchors**

Compare Acts 13:13 and 15:36-41 to 2 Timothy 4:11.

1. Describe the failure of John Mark. How serious, in Paul's mind, was this failure?
2. What happened in Acts 15:36-41 as a direct result of this failure?
3. The text doesn't mention how John Mark felt about this controversy. If you were in his shoes, what might you have felt?
4. How does 2 Timothy 4:11 show that Mark's failure was not fatal? What had changed over time?
5. What lessons can you learn from the experience of John Mark?

**Life Anchors**

1. If you find it difficult to believe that God accepts your failures, begin with these two things:
   a. Reread "Fatal Errors," slowly and meditatively, asking God to let the truths of the chapter sink into your soul.
   b. Go back to the story of John Mark in Acts 13:13 and 15:36-41, then write out the lesson you learn from

John Mark and how you can apply this lesson to your life.

2. If you have trouble experiencing God's grace, it will take time for you to feel free of your guilt. Over the next week, take time to identify those things which keep you from accepting failure as a normal part of life. Here are some things to think through and write down:
   a. Do you have specific memories of times when you have failed and then been punished?
   b. How have the significant people in your life affected your view of failure?
   c. Can you remember times when you have failed and the results were used for good in your life?
3. Analyze how you responded to the questions above and then pray that God will renew your mind and help you see yourself as he sees you.

# CHAPTER 9

# CRISTO REDENTOR

## Mind Anchors

I. What kind of redeemer is this? *I thought.* Blind eyes and stony heart? *I've since learned the answer to my own question: exactly the kind of redeemer most people have.*

1. Do you agree with this observation? Explain your answer.
2. What kind of redeemer do you think your next-door neighbor has? Your closest co-worker? You?

II. *In her despair the woman looks at the Teacher. His eyes don't glare. "Don't worry," they whisper. "It's okay." And for the first time that morning she sees kindness.*

1. Imagine you are this woman. What would you have *expected* to see in Jesus' eyes? What is running through your mind?
2. Does this passage mean that Jesus winks at sin? What does it mean?

III. *On earth, Jesus was an artist in a gallery of his own paintings. He was a composer listening as the orchestra interpreted his music. He was a poet hearing his own poetry. Yet his works of art had been defaced, creation after battered creation. He had created people for splendor. They had settled for mediocrity. He had formed them with love. They had scarred each other with hate.*

1. How are these images of "artist," "composer," and "poet" meant to remind us of Jesus? To what aspects of his personality or work do they refer?
2. Give five specific, personally observed examples that illustrate the point of this passage.

IV. *"Is there no one to condemn you?" Jesus asked.* There is still one who can, *she thinks. And she turns to look at him.* What does he want? What will he do?

1. Why does the woman think, "There is still one who can"?
2. What do you think Jesus wants of you?

V. *She would recognize his eyes. How could she ever forget those eyes? Clear and tear filled. Eyes that saw her not as she was, but as she was intended to be.*

1. What did Jesus intend this woman to be? What does he intend you to be?
2. Does this passage give you hope? Why?

**Soul Anchors**

Read Luke 7:36-50.

1. What things does the woman in this story have in common with the woman described in John 8?
2. What do you see in the eyes of this Pharisee when he looks at the woman (see verse 39)?
3. Compare the way Jesus dealt with the woman in this

passage to the way he interacted with the woman of John 8. What things did he do similarly? What did he do differently?

4. What is the point of the story Jesus tells in verses 41-43? With which character in the story do you most identify? Why?
5. How would you answer the question raised in verse 49?
6. Do you think Jesus could repeat his words found in verse 50 to you? Why or why not?

**Life Anchors**

1. Ask your closest friend to tell you honestly what your behavior reveals about the kind of redeemer you have. Find out why he or she says this and make any changes you see are necessary.
2. Reread the story in Luke 7:41-43. Write down the sins for which you have been forgiven—be sure to mention only those for which you have *experienced* God's forgiveness.
3. If you do not feel as if God has forgiven you for much, pray that he will make you sensitive to the sin in your life. If you feel that your sins are so terrible that a holy God could not forgive you, read this chapter again, putting yourself in the place of the woman.

CHAPTER 10

THE GOLDEN GOBLET

## Mind Anchors

I. *"The choice is hers," the King instructed. "If she turns to us for help, that is your command to deliver her. If she doesn't turn, if she doesn't look to me—don't go. The choice is hers."*

1. With help so near, why do you think the woman chose as she did?
2. Why do you think God refused to send help unless the woman asked for it?

II. *"Their choice will be honored. Where there is poison, there will be death. Where there are goblets, there will be fire. Let it be done."*

1. In your own words, describe the spiritual principle outlined in this passage.

III. *"I will taste the poison," swore the King's Son. "For this I have come. But the hour will be mine to choose."*

1. What did the son mean by, "I will taste the poison"? How was his "tasting" different from all those who had tasted before?
2. What was important about the son choosing the hour of his "tasting"? What is significant about the timing?

IV. *"Here is the cup, my Son. Drink it alone."*

*God must have wept as he performed his task. Every lie, every lure, every act done in shadows was in that cup. Slowly, hideously they were absorbed into the body of the Son. The final act of incarnation. The Spotless Lamb was blemished. Flames began to lick his feet.... The King turns away from his Prince. The undiluted wrath of a sin-hating Father falls upon his sin-filled Son. The fire envelops him. The shadow hides him. The Son looks for his Father, but his Father cannot be seen.*

*"My God, my God...why?"*

1. What one word would you pick to describe how the son must have felt at the moment he drank the cup?
2. Do you think an answer to the son's agonized question would have eased his pain? Explain your answer.

V. *A noise snaps the King from his dream. He opens his eyes and sees a transcendent figure gleaming in the doorway. "It is finished, Father. I have come home."*

1. What emotional impact do these lines have upon you?
2. What part of this story is most memorable for you? Why?

**Soul Anchors**

Read 2 Corinthians 5:21.

1. Who "had no sin"? What does this mean?
2. How did this one "become sin" for us? What was the purpose?

Read Galatians 3:13-14.

3. How did Christ "redeem us from the curse of the law"? When did this happen?
4. What was the purpose for Christ's becoming a curse for us?
5. How do we receive "the promise of the Spirit"?

Read Romans 8:3-4.

6. Why was the law "powerless" to bring us to God?
7. How did God overcome this powerlessness?
8. If sinful men are unable to meet the requirements of the law, how can they be saved (v. 4)?

**Life Anchors**

1. "The Golden Goblet" paints a picture of the spiritual warfare that raged in Eden, but that warfare continues all around us. Are you currently engaged in a spiritual struggle? What is it? Describe it to a friend and ask for prayer that you will embrace God's help to win the battle. Ask to be held accountable.
2. Pray that God will make you more sensitive to spiritual warfare and the power of prayer to defeat Satan.
3. For more insight into spiritual warfare, read *Counterattack* by Jay Carty or *This Present Darkness* by Frank Peretti.

CHAPTER 11

COME HOME

## Mind Anchors

I. *Pride is made of stone. Hard knocks may chip it, but it takes reality's sledgehammer to break it.*

1. In what sense is pride "made of stone"?
2. Why is it hard for the proud to accept the gospel?

II. *His first few days of destitution were likely steamy with resentment. He was mad at everyone. Everyone was to blame. His friends shouldn't have bailed out on him. And his brother should come and bail him out. His boss should feed him better, and his dad never should have let him go in the first place. He named a pig after each one of them.*

1. Is it easy for you to blame others for your own mistakes? Explain.
2. What gave the young man satisfaction in naming a pig after each one of the people mentioned? Do you ever act like this? How?

III. *It is so familiar: Cries for help muffled behind costumed faces. Fear hidden behind a painted smile. Signals of desperation thought to be signs of joy. Tell me that doesn't describe our world.*

1. In what ways does this describe your world?

2. In what ways does this describe you?

IV. *He was going home a changed man. Not demanding that he get what he deserved, but willing to take whatever he could get. "Give me" had been replaced with "help me," and his defiance had been replaced with repentance.*

1. What factors helped cause this man's transformation?
2. Try to think of someone you know who has gone through a similar transformation. Describe him or her before/after.

V. *Jesus stretched his hands as open as he could. He forced his arms so wide apart that it hurt. And to prove that those arms would never fold and those hands would never close, he had them nailed open. They still are.*

1. What does the last phrase mean?
2. What significance does this passage have for you?

**Soul Anchors**

Read Luke 15:11-32.

1. What drove this young man to reconsider his way of living (vv. 14-16)? How is this story often replayed in the modern world?
2. Compare what the young man says in verse 18 to what King David said in Psalm 51:4. What sentiment is the same in both?
3. How does the father in verse 20 picture our heavenly

father? Do you think it is a good picture? Why?

4. Compare verses 18-19 with verse 21. Note which part of the son's prepared speech gets left off. Why do you think the son was unable to finish the whole speech?
5. Was the young man worthy of the treatment he received in verses 22-24? How is this scene a picture of grace?
6. Have you ever felt like the older brother in verses 25-30? Explain.
7. How is the father's description of his son in verse 32 a good description of every Christian?

**Life Anchors**

1. For the next week or so, carefully monitor what you do when you catch yourself making a mistake. Do you own up to your faults? Are you critical of yourself, or do you tend to blame others? What sort of things do you say to yourself? Write down your observations and use them to guide your prayer schedule.
2. Ask someone you trust to name which of the three characters in Luke 15:1-32 you most resemble. Have your friend describe what he or she sees in you that prompts that response. With this input, consider whether you need to make some changes in your behavior and attitude. Choose three things you can do to help make those changes.
3. Take some time this week to think about how you believe

God views your failures. Here are some questions to ask yourself:

a. Do I have any failures from which I have never recovered?

b. If I were to die and go to heaven today, what would Jesus say to me about my life?

c. Can I see positive outcomes from my failures?

4. For more insight into how you can change, read *Inside Out* by Larry Crabb.

CHAPTER 12

THE FISH AND THE FALLS

## Mind Anchors

I. *The fish swam to where the water crashed into the river. He attempted to swim upwards. He would ascend the falls by brute force. But the onrush of the water was too strong. Undaunted, he swam until he could swim no more, then he slept.*

1. How does this passage picture man's attempt to reach God by unaided human strength? What is the outcome?

II. *But how do you not hear the yearning of your heart? How do you turn away from discovery? How can you be satisfied with existence once you've lived with purpose?*

1. How would you answer these questions?
2. What purpose is there in your life?

III. *All of nature watched as the fish rode the wave of grace. All of nature rejoiced when he reached the top. The stars raced through the blackness. The moon tilted backwards and rocked in sweet satisfaction. Bears danced. Birds hugged. The wind whistled. And the leaves applauded. The fish was where he had longed to be. He was in the presence of the roar.*

*What he couldn't do the river had done. He knew immediately he would spend forever relishing the mystery.*

1. How is the scene depicted here like Jesus' own statement in Luke 15:10?
2. How is the wave like God's grace? In what way is the fish like you? Where would the fish be without the wave? Where would you be without God's grace?

**Soul Anchors**

Read Romans 5:6-11.

1. What word does Paul use to describe our inability to save ourselves (v. 6)? Why is this tough to swallow?
2. For whom did Christ die (v. 6)? Who could be characterized like this?
3. How does Paul try to get us to see the enormity of God's sacrifice for us in verses 7-8?
4. By what are Christians "justified" (v. 9)? How does this relate to the cross?
5. From what will all Christians be saved (v. 9)? What makes this possible?
6. How does Paul teach that people can go from being God's "enemies" in verse 10 to "rejoicing in God" in verse 11? What does it mean to "rejoice in God"?

**Life Anchors**

1. Do you know anyone who is struggling to understand the concept of God's grace? Do you know someone who has trouble believing that God's acceptance and approval have

nothing to do with our efforts? Who is that person? What can you do to be a picture of grace to him or her?

2. Think through the gospel message as clearly as you can, making sure you identify all the major parts (see especially 1 Corinthians 15:1-11; Ephesians 2:8-9). Then "borrow" a child (not your own) from a close friend or neighbor and see if you can successfully communicate this message to him or her. Do a "debriefing" session afterwards to evaluate how you did.

CHAPTER 13

THE ELEVENTH HOUR GIFT

## Mind Anchors

I. *And now, one more beggar comes with a request. Only minutes from the death of them both, he stands before the King. He will ask for crumbs. And he, like the others, will receive a whole loaf.*

1. What are the "crumbs" this man asked for? What was the "whole loaf" he received?
2. Why did the beggar receive such a great gift? How is this a picture of grace?

II. *It's an inexplicable dilemma—how two people can hear the same words and see the same Savior, and one see hope and the other see nothing but himself.*

1. Describe a contemporary example of what this passage teaches.

III. *Lodged in the thief's statement are the two facts that anyone needs to recognize in order to come to Jesus. Look at the phrase again. Do you see them?*

*"We are getting what we deserve. This man has done nothing wrong."*

1. Name the two facts that must be recognized in order for someone to come to Jesus.

2. What makes these two facts indispensable for coming to Jesus?

**Soul Anchors**

Read Colossians 1:21-23.

1. Before the Colossians became Christians, what was their relationship to God (v. 22)? What areas of their lives were affected?
2. Who made the first move toward reconciliation? What was his purpose in doing so (v. 22)?
3. How did God accomplish this reconciliation? What was his purpose in doing so (v. 22)?
4. How does one gain this new relationship to God (v. 23)?
5. Paul says the gospel holds great "hope." What hope in the gospel is there for you?
6. What does Paul mean when he says that he has become a servant of the gospel? How can we follow his example?

**Life Anchors**

1. Who are the people God has placed in your life? Consider neighbors, friends, co-workers, relatives, and service people. What message of God's grace do they hear from you? Why not decide today to make a conscious effort to tell one of these people the hope of the gospel? Plan out how and when you will do this.
2. Think about someone in your life who has treated you

poorly or unfairly. Now suppose this person has come to you to ask your forgiveness. What will you do? In order to answer honestly, ask yourself these questions:

a. Am I a forgiving person—or do I hold grudges?
b. Can I remember specific incidents when a person asked for my forgiveness? What was my response?
c. Have I ever been refused forgiveness? If so, how might this affect my ability to forgive someone else?

CHAPTER 14

GOD VS. DEATH

**Mind Anchors**

I. *At that moment I stopped looking at the names and stared at the monument. I relaxed my focus from the lettering and looked at the tablet. What I saw was sobering. I saw myself. I saw my own reflection. My face looked at me from the shiny marble. It reminded me that I, too, have been dying as long as I have been living. I, too, will someday have my name carved in a granite stone. Someday I, too, will face death.*

1. What circumstances or events prompt you to ponder your own death?
2. What feelings do thoughts of your own death create in you? Why?

II. *Jesus unmasked death and exposed him for who he really is—a ninety-eight-pound weakling dressed up in a Charles Atlas suit. Jesus had no patience for this impostor. He couldn't sit still while death pulled the veil over life.*

1. In what way is death an "impostor"? How is it "a ninety-eight-pound weakling dressed up in a Charles Atlas suit"?
2. Why couldn't Jesus "sit still while death pulled the veil over life"?

III. *If you ever want to know how to conduct yourself at a funeral, don't look to Jesus for an example. He interrupted each one he ever attended.*

1. Why might this statement make you smile?
2. What point was Jesus making by interrupting all these funerals? How was this important?

**Soul Anchors**

Read Hebrews 2:14-16.

1. What two reasons are given in verses 14-15 for Christ's becoming human and dying on the cross?
2. How is it ironic that Christ's death was God's means of destroying the devil?
3. How does death hold people in slavery? Does it hold you? Why or why not?
4. Who is included in "Abraham's descendants" (see also Romans 4:16-17; Galatians 3:26-29)?
5. What advantage do redeemed men and women have over angels (v. 16)?

**Life Anchors**

1. One of the most exciting results of the gospel is that the Christian does not have to fear death. Death *is* an impostor. Take some time this week to delight in this truth. Look up 1 Corinthians 15:51-57. Meditate on these verses, asking God to let the wonder of his power over death encourage you.

2. If, after reading this chapter, you realize you have some fears about your own dying, try some of these ideas to help fortify your faith:
   a. Talk to someone about your fears. Ask for help in sorting out the rational from the irrational. Make a list of those fears which you need to overcome.
   b. Find out the name of someone who has faced death and has experienced God's peace. Ask the person how he or she feels and why. What can you learn from the person that would help you?

CHAPTER 15

# FANTASY OR REALITY?

## Mind Anchors

I. *The followers of Jesus stop and step aside as the funeral procession shadows by. The blanket of mourning muffles the laughter of the disciples. No one speaks. What could they say? They feel the same despair felt by the bystanders at any funeral. "Someday that will be me." No one intervenes. What could they do? Their only choice is to stand and stare as the mourners shuffle past.*

1. Think of the last funeral you attended. What parts of this description fit what you saw there?
2. Does it bother you to ponder your own mortality? Why?

II. *How would you feel at a moment like this? What would you do? A stranger tells you not to weep as you look at your dead son. One who refuses to mourn in the midst of sorrow calls the devil's bluff, then shocks you with a call into the cavern of death. Suddenly what had been taken is returned. What had been stolen is retrieved. What you had given up, you are given back.*

1. Answer the questions in the first two sentences of the passage.
2. How do you picture Jesus' demeanor in this incident? How do you picture that of the disciples?

III. *Jesus gave the woman much more than her son. He gave her a secret—a whisper that was overheard by us. "That," he says pointing at the cot, "that is fantasy. This," he grins, putting an arm around the boy, "this is reality."*

1. In your own words, describe the secret Jesus whispered to the woman.

**Soul Anchors**

Read Luke 7:11-17.

1. How did the Lord react when he saw this distraught mother (v. 13)? How is this typical of him?
2. Did the Lord require the mother to exercise faith before he performed the miracle?
3. The text doesn't tell us, but what do you imagine the young man might have said after Jesus raised him from the dead (v. 15)?
4. How did the people respond to Jesus' miracle?
5. Did the people fully understand who Jesus was? How can you tell?
6. Why is it that believers today do not seem as intent on "spreading the news" about Jesus as were the people back then (v. 17)?

**Life Anchors**

1. Do you know someone who is dying or who has recently lost a person he or she cared about? What can you do to

encourage him or her? Here are some suggestions—

a. Read him the last section of this book.
b. Spend time with her and listen to any of her fears.
c. Pray with him about those fears.
d. Commit yourself to pray for her and to keep in contact so she doesn't feel abandoned.

2. Make a list of some practical things you could do to help someone who was dying. Some things to include are—

   a. Help with meals and transportation.
   b. Help with correspondence and communication.
   c. Volunteer to take care of the children.
   d. Offer to help make sure his or her financial affairs are in order, or identify someone who can.

   Keep this list in a place of easy access so that when the time comes you are ready to help.

3. If you have never lost a loved one, you may feel uncomfortable around those who are grieving. A classic on the subject is *The Last Thing We Talk About* by Joe Bayley.

CHAPTER 16

THE SPARKLE FROM ETERNITY

**Mind Anchors**

I. *Wallace had never known such helplessness. He didn't know how to handle his pain. He was so accustomed to being strong, he didn't know how to be weak. He assured all who called that his daughter was fine. He assured all who inquired that God was a great God. He assured everyone but himself.*

1. Why do you think it is hard for "strong" people to show weakness? How is this sometimes a handicap?
2. Do you ever feel that God is not as great as you say he is? Explain.

II. *Wallace began to weigh his options. Should he go to see the Teacher? "If I go and am recognized, it will mean my job. But if she dies and he could have done something..." A man reaches a point where his desperation is a notch above his dignity. He shrugs his shoulders. "What choice do I have?"*

1. Have you ever reached a point of desperation similar to Wallace's? What happened?
2. What is it about trying circumstances that often bring people to Jesus?

III. *This Jesus looked too normal. He wore a corduroy jacket, the kind with patches on the elbows. His slacks weren't new, but they were nice. No tie. His hairline receded a bit before it became a flow of brown curls. I couldn't hear his voice, but I could see his face. His eyebrows were bushy. He had a gleam in his eyes and a grin on his lips—as if he were watching you unwrap the birthday present he just gave you.*

1. If Jesus were to appear on earth today, do you think this description might fit him? Why or why not?
2. How do you normally picture Jesus?

IV. *Wallace regretted the words as soon as he said them.* If he's a man, then I've asked the impossible. If he's more than a man, what right do I have to make such a request?

1. Where do you agree or disagree with Wallace's reasoning?
2. What would the granting of Wallace's request imply about the identity of Jesus?

V. *Peace where there should be pain. Confidence in the midst of crisis. Hope defying despair. That's what that look says. It is a look that knows the answer to the question asked by every mortal: "Does death have the last word?" I can see Jesus wink as he gives the answer. "Not on your life."*

1. Are you confident that Jesus has mastered death? Why or why not?
2. How does your answer to the previous question affect the way you live?

**Soul Anchors**

Read Mark 5:21-43.

1. Why were large crowds always following Jesus? Had you been alive at the time, do you believe you would have been among them? Why?
2. What was important to Jesus about identifying the woman who had been healed of her affliction? Why not just overlook it?
3. What does Jesus' declaration to the woman (v. 34) have in common with his instruction to Jairus (v. 36)?
4. What reasons can you name to explain why Jesus required Jairus to show faith, but not the distraught mother of Luke 7:11-17? What might this suggest about the way God works in the world?
5. Note how Jesus gave orders for the little girl to be fed after he raised her from the dead (v. 43). What does this tell you about Jesus?

**Life Anchors**

1. Did you notice how Jesus responded to Jairus's request for help? Even though he was busy, Jesus didn't hesitate: "Jesus went with him" (Mark 5:24).

   How receptive are you to cries for help? Do your friends see you as a caring and compassionate person—someone they can call on if they are in need? Whom do you feel free to call on? Ask those people if they feel the same toward you, and why.

2. Look more closely at those people you cited as being willing to help. What qualities or characteristics do they have that make them approachable? Write these down and evaluate your own strengths in these areas. If you see that you need to change, you can begin the process by—
    a. Praying that God will help you grow in those areas in which you are weak.
    b. Choosing one or two characteristics you can begin to cultivate today. Decide how you can do that.
    c. Asking someone to give you feedback on any changes he or she sees in you.
3. Why wait until someone asks you for help? What could you do today that would help or encourage someone? Go do it.

CHAPTER 17

"LAZARUS, COME OUT!"

## Mind Anchors

I. *A life wasted pacing up and down in a self-made cell of fear. It is shocking. It is tragic. It is a pity. And it is also very common.*

1. Give several examples of what this passage describes.
2. Have you ever wasted part of your life "pacing up and down in a self-made cell of fear"? How did you escape?

II. *Jesus wept. He wept not for the dead but for the living. He wept not for the one in the cave of death but for those in the cave of fear. He wept for those who, though alive, were dead. He wept for those who, though free, were prisoners, held captive by their fear of death.*

1. How can someone be "alive" yet "dead"?
2. What does Jesus' weeping tell you about his character or personality? How does this affect your perception of him?

III. *Jesus saw people enslaved by their fear of a cheap power. He explained that the river of death was nothing to fear. The people wouldn't believe him. He touched a boy and called him back to life. The followers were still unconvinced. He whispered life into the dead body of a girl. The people were still cynical. He let a dead man spend four days in a grave and then called him out. Is that enough? Apparently not. For it was necessary for him to enter the river, to submerge himself in the water of death before people would believe that death had been conquered.*

1. How was Jesus' resurrection different from the boy's, the girl's, or Lazarus's?
2. Do you believe that Jesus has conquered death? Why or why not?

**Soul Anchors**

Read John 11:1-44.

1. How could Jesus say in verse 4, "This sickness will not *end* in death," when he knew very well that Lazarus would die?
2. How was Jesus glorified through this incident, as he predicted in verse 4?
3. In what way are verses 25-26 the heart of the gospel? How do you respond to Jesus' question here?
4. What was Jesus doing that caused the Jews to say of his relationship to Lazarus, "See how he loved him!" (v. 36)? How do his actions color your picture of him?
5. Compare Martha's words in verse 27 to those in verse 39. Does her faith remind you of your own at times? If so, how?
6. What is the strongest impression you get of Jesus from reading these three stories of his resurrecting the dead?

**Life Anchors**

1. Make an appointment to visit a funeral home. Ask the funeral director questions about how he arranges funeral

details, how he deals with those in grief, the differences between "religious" and "secular" services, his personal view of death, etc. When you return home, write a page or two describing how your visit affected your views of death and Christianity.

2. The next time you see a movie or television show which includes scenes of death, ask yourself how the show's producers depict death. Do they see it as final? Triumphant? Glorious? Frightening? Then sit down with a family member or friend and try to imagine how you, as a director with a Christian viewpoint, would have staged those same scenes. What would you do differently? The same?

CHAPTER 18

THE CELEBRATION

## Mind Anchors

I. *"Why are you crying?" An uncommon question to be asked in a cemetery. In fact, the question is rude. That is, unless the questioner knows something the questionee doesn't.*

1. What did the questioner know that the questionee didn't?
2. Of what significance is this knowledge?

II. *Jesus doesn't leave her wondering long, just long enough to remind us that he loves to surprise us. He waits for us to despair of human strength and then intervenes with heavenly. God waits for us to give up and then—surprise!*

1. Why do you think Jesus "waits for us to despair of human strength"?
2. Have you experienced any of God's surprises? Describe them.

III. *"Miriam," Jesus said softly, "surprise!"*

*Mary was shocked. It's not often you hear your name spoken by an eternal tongue. But when she did, she recognized it. And when she did, she responded correctly. She worshiped him.*

1. Why was worship Mary's correct response? What does it mean to worship?

2. What is the correct response to Jesus today? How are you responding to him?

**Soul Anchors**

Read John 20:1-18.

1. What was Mary's concern when she saw the stone rolled away from Jesus' tomb?
2. What was remarkable about the items Peter and John found in the tomb (vv. 5-7)? What made John "believe" (v. 8)?
3. Three times Mary expresses her belief that someone has carried away the dead body of Jesus (vv. 2, 13, 15). What makes her change her belief (v. 16)?
4. What task did Jesus give Mary to do? What did she do?
5. Are you glad that God is a God of surprises? Explain your answer.

**Life Anchors**

1. Since God invites us to share in his work, and since he is a God of surprises, plan and give a surprise party or event for a friend who wouldn't expect it.
2. Keep a personal journal for two weeks in which you record any surprises God springs on you during that time. At the end of the two weeks, take your journal and go someplace quiet where you can thank him for these special works in your life. Pray also that you might respond well to any surprises that aren't so welcome.

3. Celebrate the resurrection with your family or friends. Some ideas include:
    a. Have communion and a time of worship.
    b. Present a gift to someone who cannot return the favor.
    c. Attend a theatrical performance or rent a movie that highlights Jesus' victory over death.
    d. Identify an unbelieving friend and ask that person to read and give his or her reaction to one of the chapters in this section of the book.
    e. Discuss as a group how your lives would be different if the resurrection had never happened.

CHAPTER 19

THE FINAL GLANCE

## Mind Anchors

I. *My dad left me with a final look. One last statement of the eyes. One farewell message from the captain before the boat would turn out to sea. One concluding assurance from a father to a son, "It's all right."*

1. The phrase "it's all right" pops up frequently in this book, even in this story of a dying father. What's the point?
2. For whom does the phrase "it's all right" fit? For whom does it not fit?

II. *For a long while the centurion sat on a rock and stared at the three silhouetted figures. Their heads were limp, occasionally rolling from side to side. The jeering was silent, eerily silent.... Suddenly the center head ceased to bob. It yanked itself erect. Its eyes opened in a flash of white. A roar sliced the silence. "It is finished." It wasn't a yell. It wasn't a scream. It was a roar, a lion's roar. From what world that roar came the centurion didn't know, but he knew it wasn't this one.*

1. What was "finished" in this story? Why was it said so forcefully?
2. Many Christians find great hope and comfort in these three words, "It is finished." Why?

III. *Had the centurion not said it, the soldiers would have. Had the centurion not said it, the rocks would have—as would have the angels, the stars, even the demons. But he did say it. It fell to a nameless foreigner to state what they all knew. "Surely this man was the Son of God."*

1. If the centurion fully understood his words, what course of action should he have taken?
2. If it is true that Jesus is the Son of God, what course of action should you take? What is your relationship to him?

**Soul Anchors**

Read Mark 15:33-39.

1. What statement was God making by causing darkness to fall over the land for three solid hours during the height of the afternoon?
2. Read through Psalm 22:1-18. This portion of Scripture was written hundreds of years before Christ was born, yet it contains detailed descriptions of what would happen at the crucifixion. What details presented in Psalm 22 can you match with the gospel account in Mark 15?
3. What prompted the centurion to say of Jesus, "Surely this man was the Son of God!" (v. 39)?
4. Who do you think Jesus is? On what basis do you give your answer?

## Life Anchors

1. Pick a favorite spot where you can be alone and think. Go there and spend some time reflecting on how this book has challenged you to change certain aspects of your life. What specific changes is God asking you to make in:

   your family life?
   your work life?
   your church life?
   your relationship to friends?
   your reading habits?
   your recreational time?
   your spending priorities?
   your giving patterns?
   your use of time?
   your conversation or vocabulary?
   other areas?

2. Write a letter to a close friend, expressing how this book has changed your view of God. Be as personal and specific as possible.

Max Lucado speaks weekly at the Oak Hills Church of Christ in San Antonio, Texas. He can be heard daily on the radio program *UpWords.* For a station listing or a catalog of tape messages, please write:

UpWords
P. O. Box 5860
San Antonio, Texas 78201

# The G·I·F·T for all people

THOUGHTS ON GOD'S GREAT GRACE

MAX LUCADO

Multnomah® Publishers *Sisters, Oregon*

THE GIFT FOR ALL PEOPLE
published by Multnomah Publishers, Inc.


International Standard Book Number: 1-59052-233-8 (3-in-1 ABA)

Compiled and edited by Karen Hill
Cover photograph by Mike Houska
Design by Kirk DouPonce, Teri Sharp, and Mark Mickel

Much of the content of this book is taken from previously published work.
A complete list of references can be found in the back of the book.



Printed in the United States of America



For information:
MULTNOMAH PUBLISHERS, INC.
POST OFFICE BOX 1720
SISTERS, OREGON 97759

Library of Congress Cataloging-in-Publication Data

Lucado, Max.
The gift for all people / Max Lucado.
p. cm.
Includes bibliographical references.
ISBN 1-57673-464-1 (alk. paper)
1. Devotional literature, English. 2. Jesus Christ—Devotional literature. I. Title.
BV4832.2.L77 1999
242—dc21 98-31656
CIP

03 04 05 06 — 13 12 11 10

# CONTENTS

## *The Choice*

# PROLOGUE

✦

"Bright future" said it all. Single, good looking, recent college grad. His family loved him, girls noticed him, career opportunities invited him.

And yet, while Eric appeared confident without, he was tormented within. Tormented by inner voices he could not quiet. Tortured by mental images he could not avoid and by thoughts he could not understand. So, desperate to escape the torment, Eric decided to escape from life. On a gray, rainy February day, Eric walked out the back door of his home. He never returned.

When Eric walked away, someone was watching. His sister Debbie saw her brother leave, his tall frame ambling down the street. She assumed he would return. He didn't. She hoped he would call. He didn't. She thought she could find him. She couldn't. Hours became years. Years of wandering and wondering. As Eric wandered, Debbie wondered. Where could he be? What could have happened? Is he all right? Is he alive?

Where Eric journeyed, only God and Eric know. But we know that he ended up thousands of miles from his home. And somewhere along his path, somehow, Eric began to believe he had been given an assignment. Someone noticed Eric going through a dumpster, looking for food. And that someone suggested Eric sweep up in exchange for the garbage. Eric interpreted this comment as an assignment: he believed he had been given a permanent commission to clean up a roadside in San Antonio, Texas.

To the local residents, Eric's lanky form and bearded face became a familiar feature as he walked up and down his "assigned" section of Interstate 10, gathering trash. Through the years many tried to assist him, but Eric resisted. He was content to survive on what he collected. He created a home out of a hole in a vacant lot. He designed a wardrobe out of split trousers and a torn sweatshirt. Summer sun was deflected by an old hat, winter chill softened by a plastic bag covering his shoulders.

His weathered skin and stooped shoulders made him look twice his forty-four years. But then, sixteen years living on the side of the road would do that to you.

It had been sixteen years since Debbie had seen her brother. And she might never have seen him again, had it not been for two events. The first was the construction of a car lot on top of Eric's hovel. The second was a pain in Eric's abdomen. The car lot took Eric's shelter. The pain took Eric's health.

When EMS found Eric curled in a ball on the roadside, he was already dying of cancer. Another few months and Eric would be gone. And with no known family or relatives, he would die as he'd lived—alone.

Eric's court-appointed temporary guardian couldn't handle this thought. *Surely someone is looking for this man,* reasoned the attorney. So the attorney searched the Internet for anyone missing a brown-haired adult male with Eric's last name.

A reply came from a New Hampshire woman. Could this homeless man in Texas be the brother she'd been seeking for so long? The description seemed to match, but she had to know for sure. So Debbie, her husband, and two children headed for Texas.

By the time Debbie arrived, Eric had been released from the hospital. Debbie found him near his old home, resting against the side of a building. One look was all it took to convince her—the search was over. She saw beyond the sun-dried skin, beneath the unkempt hair and beard. She saw her brother.

Eric, however, didn't recognize his sister. The years had ravaged his mind. Debbie longed to embrace this long-lost sibling, but her instincts told her she must await his cue.

And then something small led the way. Eric noticed an angel pin Debbie was wearing. He was intrigued by it. When Debbie offered the pin to Eric, he said yes. He even allowed her to pin the angel on his shirt. And with that one gesture, she, at long last, touched her brother.

Debbie came to Texas planning to spend a week. But a week passed and she couldn't leave. She rented an apartment, began homeschooling her children and reaching out to her brother. It wasn't easy. He didn't always recognize her. He wouldn't call her by name. One day he cursed her. He refused to sleep in her apartment. He didn't want her food. He didn't want to talk. He just wanted his vacant lot. He wanted his "job."

But Debbie didn't give up on Eric. Weeks became months, and still the sister stayed. She understood that he didn't understand. So she stayed. I came to know her as she began to attend our church. After hearing her story, I asked what you would have asked. Why? Why didn't she give up? "Simple," she told me. "He's my brother."

Her pursuit reminds us of another, doesn't it? Another kind heart who left home in search of the confused. Another compassionate soul who couldn't bear the thought of a brother in pain. So, like Debbie, he left home. Like Debbie, he found his sibling.

And when God found us, we acted like Eric. We didn't recognize the one who came to help us. When he told us we were part of his family, we didn't believe him. When he offered a safe place to stay, we didn't follow him. We ignored him. Some even cursed him and told him to leave.

But he didn't leave. He lingered. And still he lingers. He

understands that we don't understand. He knows that we are torn by many voices and infected by a cancerous sin. He knows we are near death. But he doesn't want us to die alone.

Like Debbie, he wants to give us something before it's too late. He wants to give us a place in his family. And he wants to hold our hand when we die.

So God follows us. He pursues us along every roadside; he follows us down every highway. He follows us all the days of our lives. "Surely goodness and mercy shall follow me all the days of my life. And I will dwell in the house of the Lord forever" (Psalm 23:6).

What a surprising way to describe God. A God who pursues us.

Dare we envision a mobile, active God who chases us, tracks us, following us with goodness and mercy all the days of our lives? He's not hard to find. He's there in Scripture, looking for Adam and Eve. They're hiding in the bushes, partly to cover their bodies, partly to cover their sin. Does God wait for them to come to him? No, the words ring in the garden. "Where are you?" God asks (Genesis 3:9), beginning his quest to redeem the heart of man. A quest to follow his children until his children follow him.

Moses can tell you about it. After forty years in the desert, he looked over his shoulder and saw a bush blazing. God had followed him into the wilderness.

Jonah can tell you about it. He was a fugitive on a boat when he looked over his shoulder and saw clouds brewing. God had followed him onto the ocean.

The disciples of Jesus knew the feeling of being followed by God. They were rain-soaked and shivering when they looked over their shoulders and saw Jesus walking. God had followed them into the storm.

An unnamed Samaritan woman knew the same feeling. Alone in life and alone at the well, she looked over her shoulder and saw a Messiah speaking. God had followed her through her pain.

The apostle John, banished on Patmos, looked over his shoulder and saw the skies begin to open. God had followed him into his exile.

Lazarus had been dead for three days in a sealed tomb when a voice awakened him. He lifted his head and looked over his shoulder to see Jesus. God had followed him into death.

Peter the Apostle had denied his Lord and gone back to fishing when he heard his name and looked over his shoulder and saw Jesus cooking breakfast. God had followed him in spite of his failure.

Sin, wilderness, ocean, storm, pain, exile, death—our God is the God who follows. Have you sensed him following you? He is the one who came to seek and save the lost. Have you sensed him seeking you?

Have you felt his presence through the kindness of a stranger? Through the majesty of a sunset or the mystery of romance? Through the question of a child or the commitment of a spouse? Through a word well spoken or a touch well timed, have you sensed him?

Like Eric, we have left home. But, like Debbie, God has followed us. Like Eric, we are quick to turn away. But, like Debbie, God is slow to anger and determined to stay. We don't accept God's gifts. Yet God still gives them.

God gives us himself. Even when we choose our hovel over his house and our trash over his grace, still he follows. Never forcing us. Never leaving us. Patiently persistent. Faithfully present. He uses all his power to convince us that he is who he is and he can be trusted to lead us home.

By the way, Debbie's faithful persistence moved Eric's heart. Before his life ended, he acknowledged her as his sister. In doing so, he found his way home.

And that's what God wants for you. He simply wants you home with him. And to bring you home, he offers you a gift.

My prayer is that through these pages you'll see his gift like you've never seen it.

If you've already accepted it, you'll thank him again.

And if you've never accepted it, you will. For it's the gift of a lifetime, a gift for all people.

# The Gift of a Savior

✦

*The Word became a human and lived among us.... The Word was in the world and the world was made by him, but the world did not know him.... But to all who did accept him and believe in him he gave the right to become children of God.... Because he was full of grace and truth, from him we all received one gift after another.*

JOHN 1:14, 10, 12, 16

IT WAS ABOUT TO BEGIN—GOD'S PLAN FOR HUMANITY, CRAFTED IN THE HALLS OF HEAVEN AND CARRIED OUT ON THE PLAINS OF EARTH. ONLY HOLINESS COULD HAVE IMAGINED IT. ONLY DIVINITY COULD HAVE ENACTED IT. ONLY RIGHTEOUSNESS COULD HAVE ENDURED IT. AND ONCE THE PLAN BEGAN, THERE WOULD BE NO TURNING BACK. THE CREATOR KNEW IT. THE SON KNEW IT. AND SOON, EARTH ITSELF WOULD WITNESS HEAVEN'S MAJESTY ALIGHTING ON THE PLANET.

# IT BEGAN IN A MANGER

✦

It all happened in a most remarkable moment... A moment like no other. For through that segment of time a spectacular thing occurred.

God became a man. Divinity arrived. Heaven opened herself and placed her most precious one in a human womb.

The omnipotent, in one instant, became flesh and blood. The one who was larger than the universe became a microscopic embryo. And he who sustains the world with a word chose to be dependent upon the nourishment of a young girl.

God had come near.

He came, not as a flash of light or as an unapproachable conqueror, but as one whose first cries were heard by a peasant girl and a sleepy carpenter. Mary and Joseph were anything but royal. Yet heaven entrusted its greatest treasure to these simple parents. It began in a manger, this momentous moment in time. He looked anything but a king. His face, prunish and red. His cry, still the helpless and piercing cry of a dependent baby.

Majesty in the midst of the mundane. Holiness in the filth of sheep manure and sweat. This baby had overseen the universe. These rags keeping him warm were the robes of eternity. His golden throne room had been abandoned in favor of a dirty sheep pen. And worshiping angels had been replaced with kind but bewildered shepherds.

Curious, this royal throne room. No tapestries covering the windows. No velvet garments on the courtiers. No golden scepter or glittering crown. Curious, the sounds in the court. Cows munching, hooves crunching, a mother humming, a babe nursing.

It could have begun anywhere, the story of the king. But, curiously, it began in a manger. Step into the doorway, peek through the window.

He is here!

# A DAY FOR GOOD-BYE

✦

It was time for Jesus to leave. The carpentry shop had been his home, his refuge. He had come to say good-bye, to smell the sawdust and lumber just one more time.

Life was peaceful here. Life was so safe. Here he had spent countless hours of contentment. On this dirt floor he had played as a toddler while his father worked. Here Joseph had taught him how to grip a hammer. And on this workbench he had built his first chair.

It was here that his human hands shaped the wood his divine hands had created. And it was here that his body matured while his spirit waited for the right moment, the right day.

And now that day had arrived.

I wonder if he wanted to stay.

I wonder because I know he had already read the last chapter. He knew that the feet that would step out of the safe shadow of the carpentry shop would not rest until they'd been pierced and placed on a Roman cross.

You see, he didn't have to go. He had a choice. He could have stayed. He could have ignored the call or at least postponed it. And had he chosen to stay, who would have known? Who would have blamed him?

He could have come back as a man in another era when society wasn't so volatile, when religion wasn't so stale, when people would listen better.

He could have come back when crosses were out of style.

But his heart wouldn't let him. If there was hesitation on the part of his humanity, it was overcome by the compassion of his divinity. His divinity heard the voices. His divinity heard the hopeless cries of the poor, the bitter accusations of the abandoned, the dangling despair of those who are trying to save themselves.

And his divinity saw the faces. Some wrinkled. Some weeping. Some hidden behind veils. Some obscured by fear. Some earnest with searching. Some blank with boredom. From the face of Adam to the face of the infant born somewhere in the world as you read these words, he saw them all.

And you can be sure of one thing. Among the voices that found their way into that carpentry shop in Nazareth was your voice. Your silent prayers uttered on tearstained pillows were heard before they were said. Your deepest questions about death and eternity were answered before they were asked. And your direst need, your need for a Savior, was met before you ever sinned.

And not only did he hear you, he saw you. He saw your face aglow the hour you first knew him. He saw your face in shame the hour you first fell. The same face that looked back at you from this morning's mirror, looked at him. And it was enough to kill him.

He left because of you.

He laid his security down with his hammer. He hung tranquillity on the peg with his nail apron. He closed the window shutters on the sunshine of his youth and locked the door on the comfort and ease of anonymity.

Since he could bear your sins more easily than he could bear the thought of your hopelessness, he chose to leave.

It wasn't easy. But it was love.

# GOD IN THE FLESH

✦

God chose to reveal himself through a human body. The tongue that called forth the dead was a human one. The hand that touched the leper had dirt under its nails. The feet upon which the woman wept were callused and dusty. And his tears…oh, don't miss the tears…they came from a heart as broken as yours or mine ever has been.

So, people came to him. My, how they came to him! They came at night; they touched him as he walked down the street; they followed him around the sea; they invited him into their homes and placed their children at his feet. Why? Because he refused to be a statue in a cathedral or a priest in an elevated pulpit. He chose instead to be a touchable, approachable, reachable Jesus.

There is not a hint of one person who was afraid to draw near him. There were those who mocked him. There were those who were envious of him. There were those who misunderstood him. There were those who revered him. But there was not one person who considered him too holy, too divine, or too celestial to touch. There was not one person who was reluctant to approach him for fear of being rejected.

# COMPASSIONATE SAVIOR

✦

*They were like sheep without a shepherd.*
*So he began teaching them many things.*

MARK 6:34

*When Jesus landed and saw a large crowd,*
*he had compassion on them and healed their sick.*

MATTHEW 14:14

It's a good thing those verses weren't written about me. It's a good thing thousands of people weren't depending on Max for their teaching and nourishment. Especially on a day when I'd just heard of the death of a dear friend. Especially on a day when I wanted to be alone with my friends. Especially after I'd gotten into a boat to escape the crowds. Had that been me in Jesus' sandals on that Bethsaida beach, the verses would read something like:

> They were like sheep without a shepherd. So Max told them to quit grazing on his pasture and head back to their pens.

> When Max landed and saw a large crowd, he mumbled something about how hard it was to get a day off and radioed for the helicopter. Then he and the disciples escaped to a private retreat.

It's a good thing I wasn't responsible for those people. I would have been in no mood to teach them, no mood to help them. I would have had no desire even to be with them.

But, as I think about it, Jesus had no desire to be with them either. After all, he did leave them, didn't he? He had every intention of getting away and being alone. So what happened? Why didn't he tell them to get lost? What made him change his mind and spend the day with the people he was trying to avoid?

Answer? "He had *compassion* on them" (Matthew 14:14).

The Greek word for compassion is *splanchnizomai,* which won't mean much to you unless you are in the health professions and studied "splanchnology" in school. If so, you remember that "splanchnology" is a study of the visceral parts. Or, in contemporary jargon, a study of the gut.

When Matthew writes that Jesus had compassion on the people, he is not saying that Jesus felt casual pity for them. No, the term is far more graphic. Matthew is saying that Jesus felt their hurt in his gut:

> He felt the limp of the crippled.
> He felt the hurt of the diseased.
> He felt the loneliness of the leper.
> He felt the embarrassment of the sinful.

And once he felt their hurts, he couldn't help but heal their hurts. He was moved in the stomach by their needs. He was so touched by their needs that he forgot his own needs. He was so moved by the people's hurts that he put his hurts on the back burner. When Jesus arrived at Bethsaida, he was sorrowful, tired, and anxious to be alone with the disciples. No one would have blamed him had he dismissed the crowds a second time. No one would have criticized him had he waved away the people. But he didn't. Later he would. Later he would demand their departure and seek solitude.

But not before he "healed their sick" (Matthew 14:14) and taught them "many things" (Mark 6:34). Self was forgotten and others were served by the compassionate Savior.

# JESUS KNOWS HOW YOU FEEL

✦

Jesus knows how you feel. You're under the gun at work? Jesus knows how you feel. You've got more to do than is humanly possible? So did he. People take more from you than they give? Jesus understands. Your teenagers won't listen? Your students won't try? Jesus knows how you feel.

You are precious to him. So precious that he became like you so that you would come to him.

When you struggle, he listens. When you yearn, he responds. When you question, he hears. He has been there.

Like the little boy in the following story, Jesus sees you with a heart of compassion. He knows that you are special....

A boy went into a pet shop, looking for a puppy. The store owner showed him a litter in a box. The boy looked at the puppies. He picked each one up, examined it, and put it back in the box.

After several minutes, he walked back to the owner and said, "I picked one out. How much will it cost?"

The man gave him the price, and the boy promised to be back in a few days with the money. "Don't take too long," the owner cautioned. "Puppies like these sell quickly."

The boy turned and smiled knowingly. "I'm not worried," he said. "Mine will still be here."

The boy went to work—weeding, washing windows, cleaning yards. He worked hard and saved his money. When he had enough for the puppy, he returned to the store.

He walked up to the counter and laid down a pocketful of wadded bills. The store owner sorted and counted the cash. After verifying the amount, he smiled at the boy and said, "All right, son, you can go get your puppy."

The boy reached into the back of the box, pulled out a skinny dog with a limp leg, and started to leave.

The owner stopped him.

"Don't take that puppy," he objected. "He's crippled. He can't play. He'll never run with you. He can't fetch. Get one of the healthy pups."

"No, thank you, sir," the boy replied. "This is exactly the kind of dog I've been looking for."

As the boy turned to leave, the store owner started to speak but remained silent. Suddenly he understood. For extending from the bottom of the boy's trousers was a brace—a brace for his crippled leg.

Why did the boy want the dog? Because he knew how it felt. And he knew it was very special.

# FAITH BEHELD, FAITH BLESSED

✦

*A few days later, when Jesus came back to Capernaum,*
*the news spread that he was at home. Many people gathered together*
*so that there was no room in the house, not even outside the door.*
*And Jesus was teaching them God's message. Four people came, carrying a*
*paralyzed man. Since they could not get to Jesus because of the crowd,*
*they dug a hole in the roof right above where he was speaking.*
*When they got through, they lowered the mat with the paralyzed man on it.*
*When Jesus saw the faith of these people, he said to the paralyzed man,*
*"Young man, your sins are forgiven."*

MARK 2:1-5

Jesus was moved by this demonstration of faith. Four men had enough hope in him and love for their friend that they took a chance. The stretcher above was a sign from above—somebody believes! Someone was willing to risk embarrassment and injury for just a few moments with the Galilean.

Jesus was moved. So he applauds—if not with his hands, at least with his heart. And not only does he applaud, he blesses. And we witness a divine loveburst.

The friends want him to heal their friend. But Jesus won't settle for a simple healing of the body—he wants to heal the soul. He leapfrogs the physical and deals with the spiritual. To heal the body is temporal; to heal the soul is eternal.

The request of the friends is valid—but timid. The expectations of the crowd are high—but not high enough. They expect Jesus to say, "I heal you." Instead he says, "I forgive you."

They expect him to treat the body, for that is what they see.

He chooses to treat not only the body, but also the spiritual, for that is what he sees.

They want Jesus to give the man a new body so he can walk. Jesus gives grace so the man can live.

Remarkable. Sometimes God is so touched by what he sees that he gives us what we need and not simply that for which we ask.

By the way, Jesus hasn't changed since the day a stretcher was lowered into his presence on the cords of hope.

What happened then still happens today. When we take a step of faith, God sees. The same face that beamed at the paralytic beams at the alcoholic refusing the bottle. The same eyes that danced at the friends dance at the mom and dad who will do whatever it takes to get their child to Jesus. And the same lips that spoke to the man in Capernaum speak to the man in Detroit, to the woman in Belfast, to the child in Moscow...to any person anywhere who dares to come into the presence of God and ask for help.

And though we can't hear it here, the angels can hear him there. All of heaven must pause as another burst of love declares the only words that really matter: "Your sins are forgiven."

# THE GREAT EXCHANGE

✦

A friend of mine was at Disney World some time back. He and his family sought a place to rest in Cinderella's castle. Unfortunately, so did everyone else. The place was packed with kids and parents. Suddenly all the children rushed to one side. Had it been a boat, the castle would have tipped over. Cinderella had entered.

Cinderella. The pristine princess. A gorgeous young girl with each hair in place, flawless skin, and a beaming smile. She stood waist-deep in a garden of kids, each wanting to touch and be touched.

The other side of the castle was now vacant except for a boy maybe seven or eight years old. His age was hard to determine because of the disfigurement of his body. Dwarfed in height, face deformed, he stood watching quietly and wistfully, holding the hand of an older brother.

Don't you know what he wanted? He wanted to be with the children. He longed to be in the middle of the kids reaching for Cinderella, calling her name. But can't you feel his fear, fear of yet another rejection? Fear of being taunted again, mocked again?

Don't you wish Cinderella would go to him? Guess what? She did!

She noticed the little boy. She immediately began walking in his direction. Politely but firmly inching through the crowd of children, she finally broke free. She walked quickly across the floor, knelt at eye level with the stunned little boy, and placed a kiss on his face.

The story reminds me of another royal figure. The names are different, but isn't the story almost the same? Rather than a princess of Disney, these essays are about the Prince of Peace. Rather than a boy in a castle, our story is about you and me. In both cases a gift was given. In both cases love was shared. In both cases the lovely one performed a gesture beyond words.

But Jesus did more than Cinderella. Oh, so much more.

Cinderella gave only a kiss. When she stood to leave, she took her beauty with her. The boy was still deformed. What if Cinderella had done what Jesus did? What if she'd assumed his state? What if she had somehow given him her beauty and taken on his disfigurement?

That's what Jesus did.

"He took our suffering on him and felt our pain for us.... He was wounded for the wrong we did; he was crushed for the evil we did. The punishment, which made us well, was given to him, and we are healed because of his wounds"(Isaiah 53:4–5).

Make no mistake:

Jesus gave more than a kiss—he gave his beauty.

He paid more than a visit—he paid for our mistakes.

He took more than a minute—he took away our sin.

# EYES ON THE SAVIOR

✦

A group of climbers set out to scale a large mountain in Europe. The view boasted a breathtaking peak of snowcapped rocks. On clear days the crested point reigned as king on the horizon. Its white tip jutted into the blue sky inviting admiration and offering inspiration.

On days like that the hikers made the greatest progress. The peak stood above them like a compelling goal. Eyes were called upward. The walk was brisk. The cooperation was unselfish. Though many, they climbed as one, all looking to the same summit.

Yet on some days the peak of the mountain was hidden from view. The cloud covering would eclipse the crisp blueness with a drab, gray ceiling and block the vision of the mountaintop. On those days the climb became arduous. Eyes were downward and thoughts inward. The goal was forgotten. Tempers were short. Weariness was an uninvited companion. Complaints stung like thorns on the trail.

We're like that, aren't we? As long as we can see our dream, as long as our goal is within eyesight, there is no mountain we can't climb or summit we can't scale. But take away our vision, block our view of the trail's end, and the result is as discouraging as the journey.

Think about it. Hide the Nazarene who calls to us from the mountaintop and see what happens.

Listen to the groans of the climbers as they stop and sit by the side of the path. Why continue if there is no relief in sight? Pilgrims with no vision of the promised land become proprietors of their own land. They set up camp. They exchange hiking boots for loafers and trade in their staffs for new recliners.

Instead of looking upward at him, they look inward at themselves and outward at each other. The result? Cabin fever. Quarreling families. Restless leaders. Fence-building. Staked-off territory. No trespassing! signs are hung on hearts and homes. Spats turn into fights as myopic groups turn to glare at each other's weaknesses instead of turning to worship their common Strength.

Mark it down. We are what we see. If we see only ourselves, our tombstones will have the same epitaph Paul used to describe enemies of Christ: "Their god is their own appetite, they glory in their shame, and this world is the limit of their horizon" (Philippians 3:19).

Humans were never meant to dwell in the stale fog of the lowlands with no vision of their Creator.

That's why God came near. To be seen.

And that's why those who saw him were never the same. "We saw his glory," exclaimed one follower.

"We were eyewitnesses of his majesty," whispered a martyr. They saw the peak. They breathed the fresh air of the high country. They caught a glimpse of the pinnacle. And they refused to quit climbing until they reached the top. They wanted to see Jesus.

Seeing Jesus is what Christianity is all about. Christian service, in its purest form, is nothing more than imitating him who we see. To see his majesty and to imitate him, that is the sum of Christianity.

This is why those who see him today are never the same again.

Acquiring a vision of your Maker can be like starting a whole new life. It can be like a new birth. In fact, the One who inspired this book said that new beginnings and good eyesight are inseparable. "Unless a man is born again, he cannot see the kingdom of God."

If Jesus is who he says he is, there is no truth more worthy of your time and no god more worthy of your devotion. Keep climbing. And keep looking up. But make sure your eyes are on the Savior.

# COME AND SEE

✦

*Nathanael said to Philip,*
*"Can anything good come from Nazareth?"*
*Philip answered, "Come and see."*

JOHN 1:46

Nathanael's question still lingers, even two thousand years later. Is the life of the young Nazarene really worth considering?

The answer of Philip still suffices. "Come and see."

Come and see the rock that has withstood the winds of time. Hear his voice.

The truth undaunted,
grace unspotted,
loyalty undeterred.

Come and see the flame that tyrants and despots have not extinguished.

Come and see the passion that oppression has not squelched.

Come and see the hospitals and orphanages rising beside the crumbling ruins of humanism and atheism. Come and see what Christ has done.

Can anything good come out of Nazareth? Come and see.

Come and see the changed lives:
the alcoholic now dry,
the embittered now joyful,
the shamed now forgiven.

Come and see the marriages rebuilt, the orphans embraced, the imprisoned inspired.

Journey into the jungles and hear the drums beating in praise.

Sneak into the corners of communism and find believers worshiping under threat of death.

Walk on death row and witness the prisoner condemned by man yet liberated by God.

Can anything good come out of Nazareth?

Come and see the pierced hand of God touch the most common heart, wipe the tear from the wrinkled face, and forgive the ugliest sin.

Come and see. He avoids no seeker. He ignores no probe. He fears no search. Come and see. Nathanael came. And Nathanael saw. And Nathanael discovered: "Teacher, you are the Son of God; you are the King of Israel."

# Ransom for Sinners

✦

*But God showed his great love*
*for us in this way: Christ died for us*
*while we were still sinners.*
ROMANS 5:8

JESUS, DO YOU GIVE NO THOUGHT TO SAVING YOURSELF? WHAT KEEPS YOU THERE? WHAT HOLDS YOU TO THE CROSS? NAILS DON'T HOLD GODS TO TREES. WHAT MAKES YOU STAY?

# ROAD TO CALVARY

✦

Christ came to earth for one reason: to give his life as a ransom for you, for me, for all of us. He sacrificed himself to give us a second chance. He would have gone to any lengths to do so. And he did. He went to the cross, where man's utter despair collided with God's unbending grace. And in that moment when God's great gift was complete, the compassionate Christ showed the world the cost of his gift.

Trace the path of this Savior, the God who swapped heavenly royalty for earthly poverty. His bed became, at best, a borrowed pallet—and usually the hard earth. He was dependent on handouts for his income. He was sometimes so hungry he would eat raw grain or pick fruit off a tree. He knew what it meant to have no home. He was ridiculed. His neighbors tried to lynch him. Some called him a lunatic. His family tried to confine him to their house. His friends weren't always faithful to him.

He was accused of a crime he never committed. Witnesses were hired to lie. The jury was rigged. A judge swayed by politics handed down the death penalty.

They killed him.

And why? Because of the gift that only he could give.

He who was perfect gave that perfect record to us, and our imperfect record was given to him. Jesus was "not guilty, but he suffered for those who are guilty to bring you to God" (1 Peter 3:18). As a result, God's holiness is honored and his children are forgiven.

# THE FOG OF A BROKEN HEART

✦

*They went to a place called Gethsemane, and Jesus said to his disciples, "Sit here while I pray." He took Peter, James and John along with him, and he began to be deeply distressed and troubled. Horror and dismay came over him, and he said to them, "My heart is ready to break with grief; stop here, and stay awake." Then he went forward a little, threw himself on the ground, and prayed that, if it were possible, this hour might pass him by. "Abba, Father," he said, "all things are possible to thee; take this cup away from me. Yet not what I will, but what you will."*

MARK 14:32–36

Look at those phrases. "*Horror* and *dismay* came over him." "My heart is ready to *break* with grief." "He went a little forward and *threw* himself on the ground."

Does this look like the picture of a saintly Jesus resting in the palm of God? Hardly. Mark used black paint to describe this scene. We see an agonizing, straining, and struggling Jesus. We see a "man of sorrows." We see a man struggling with fear, wrestling with commitments, and yearning for relief.

We see Jesus in the fog of a broken heart.

The writer of Hebrews would later pen, "During the days of Jesus' life on earth, he offered up prayers and petitions with loud cries and tears to the one who could save him from death" (Hebrews 5:7).

My, what a portrait! Jesus is in pain. Jesus is on the stage of fear. Jesus is cloaked, not in sainthood, but in humanity.

The next time the fog finds you, you might do well to remember Jesus in the garden. The next time you think that no one understands, reread the fourteenth chapter of Mark. The next time your self-pity convinces you that no one cares, pay a visit to Gethsemane. And the next time you wonder if God really perceives the pain that prevails on this dusty planet, listen to him pleading among the twisted trees.

Seeing God like this does wonders for our own suffering. God was never more human than at this hour. God was never nearer to us than when he hurt. The Incarnation was never so fulfilled as in the garden.

As a result, time spent in the fog of pain could be God's greatest gift. It could be the hour that we finally see our Maker. If it is true that in suffering God is most like man, maybe in our suffering we can see God like never before.

Watch closely. It could very well be that the hand that extends itself to lead you out of the fog is a pierced one.

# PARTNER IN THE PLAN

✦

*Jesus was given to you, and with the help of those who don't know the law, you put him to death by nailing him to a cross. But this was God's plan which he had made long ago; he knew this would happen. God raised Jesus from the dead and set him free from the pain of death, because death could not hold him.*

ACTS 2:23–24

The cross was no accident.

Jesus' death was not the result of a panicking cosmological engineer. The cross wasn't a tragic surprise. Calvary was not a knee-jerk response to a world plummeting toward destruction. It wasn't a patch-up job or a stop-gap measure. The death of the Son of God was anything but an unexpected peril.

No, it was part of an incredible plan. A calculated choice.

The moment the forbidden fruit touched the lips of Eve, the shadow of a cross appeared on the horizon. And between that moment and the moment the man with the mallet placed the spike against the wrist of God, a master plan was fulfilled.

What does that mean? It means Jesus planned his own sacrifice.

It means Jesus intentionally planted the tree from which his cross would be carved.

It means he willingly placed the iron ore in the heart of the earth from which the nails would be cast.

It means he voluntarily placed his Judas in the womb of a woman.

It means Christ was the one who set in motion the political machinery that would send Pilate to Jerusalem.

And it also means he didn't have to do it—but he did.

It was no accident—would that it had been! Even the cruelest of criminals is spared the agony of having his death sentence read to him before his life even begins.

But Jesus was born crucified. Whenever he became conscious of who he was, he also became conscious of what he had to do. The cross-shaped shadow could always be seen. And the screams of hell's imprisoned could always be heard.

This explains the glint of determination on his face as he turned to go to Jerusalem for the last time. He was on his death march (Luke 9:51).

This explains the resoluteness in the words, "The reason my Father loves me is that I lay down my life—only to take it up again. No one takes it from me, but I lay it down of my own accord" (John 10:17–18).

The cross explains why John the Baptist introduced Jesus to the crowds as the "Lamb of God, who takes away the sin of the world!" (John 1:29).

Maybe it's why he tore the grass out by the roots in Gethsemane. He knew the hell he'd endure for saying, "Thy will be done."

Maybe the cross was why he so loved children. They represented the very thing he would have to give: Life.

The ropes used to tie his hands and the soldiers used to lead him to the cross were unnecessary. They were incidental. Had they not been there, had there been no trial, no Pilate, and no crowd, the very same crucifixion would have occurred. Had Jesus been forced to nail himself to the cross, he would have done it. For it was not the soldiers who killed him, nor the screams of the mob: It was his devotion to us.

So call it what you wish: An act of grace. A plan of redemption. A martyr's sacrifice. But whatever you call it, don't call it an accident. It was anything but that.

# HE SAW YOU

✦

The final prayer of Jesus was about you. His final pain was for you. His final passion was for you. Before he went to the cross, Jesus went to the garden. And when he spoke with his Father, you were in his prayers. As Jesus looked into heaven, you were in his vision. As Jesus dreamed of the day when we will be where he is, he saw you there....

Never had he felt so alone. What had to be done, only he could do. An angel couldn't do it. No angel has the power to break open hell's gates. A man couldn't do it. No man has the purity to destroy sin's claim. No force on earth can face the force of evil and win—except God.

And God couldn't turn his back on you. He couldn't because he saw you, and one look at you was all it took to convince him. Right there in the middle of a world which isn't fair. He saw you cast into a river of life you didn't request. He saw you betrayed by those you love. He saw you with a body which gets sick and a heart which grows weak.

He saw you in your own garden of gnarled trees and sleeping friends. He saw you staring into the pit of your own failures and the mouth of your own grave. He saw you in your Garden of Gethsemane—and he didn't want you to be alone.

He wanted you to know that he has been there, too. He

knows what it's like to be plotted against. He knows what it's like to be confused. He knows what it's like to be torn between two desires. He knows what it's like to smell the stench of Satan. And, perhaps most of all, he knows what it's like to beg God to change his mind and to hear God say so gently, but firmly, "No."

For that is what God said to Jesus. And Jesus accepted the answer. At some moment during that midnight hour an angel of mercy came over the weary body of the man in the garden. Jesus stood, the anguish gone from his eyes. His heart will fight no more.

The battle has been won. The sign of conquest? Jesus at peace in the olive trees.

On the eve of the cross, Jesus made his decision. He would rather go to hell for you than go to heaven without you.

# HEAVEN'S SILENCE

✦

During the darkest night of his life, Jesus experienced unanswered prayer, unfruitful service, and unbelievable betrayal. Jesus had just offered an anguished appeal to God. "My Father, if it is possible, do not give me this cup of suffering. But do what you want, not what I want" (Matthew 26:39). Matthew says that Jesus was "very sad and troubled" (Matthew 26:37). The Master "fell to the ground" (Matthew 26:39) and cried out to God. Luke tells us that Jesus was "full of pain" and that "his sweat was like drops of blood falling to the ground" (Luke 22:44).

Never has earth offered such an urgent request. And never has heaven offered more deafening silence. The prayer of Jesus was unanswered. Jesus and unanswered prayer in the same phrase? Isn't that an oxymoron? Would the son of Henry have no Ford or the child of Bill Gates own no computer? Would God, the one who owns the cattle on a thousand hills, keep something from his own Son? He did that night. And that was just the beginning. Look who showed up next:

Judas arrived with an angry crowd (Matthew 26:47, 51). Not only did Jesus have to face unanswered prayer, he also had to deal with unfruitful service. The very people he came to save had now come to arrest him.

Unbelievable betrayal: *All* pledged loyalty, and yet *all* ran. The disciples have left him. Unfruitful service: The people have rejected him. And, perhaps most hurtful: unanswered prayer. God hasn't heard him. From a human point of view, Jesus' world has collapsed. No answer from heaven, no help from the people, no loyalty from his friends.

Yet somehow, despite all the pain, Jesus was able to see good in the bad, the purpose in the pain, and God's presence in the problem.

He found good in the bad. It would be hard to find someone worse than Judas. The Bible says, "Judas...was a thief. He was the one who kept the money box, and he often stole from it" (John 12:6). Somehow Judas was able to live in the presence of God and experience the miracles of Christ and remain unchanged. In the end he decided he'd rather have money than a friend, so he sold Jesus for thirty pieces of silver. Judas was a scoundrel, a cheat, and a bum. How could anyone see him any other way?

Somehow Jesus did. Only inches from the face of his betrayer, Jesus looked at him and said, "Friend, do what you came to do" (Matthew 26:50). What Jesus saw in Judas as worthy of being called a friend, I can't imagine. But I do know that Jesus doesn't lie, and in that moment he saw something good in a very bad man.

Not only did Jesus find good in the bad, he found purpose in the pain. Of the ninety-eight words Jesus spoke at his arrest, thirty refer to the purpose of God. "It must happen this way to bring about what the Scriptures say" (Matthew 26:54). "All these things have happened so that it will come about as the prophets wrote" (Matthew 26:56).

Jesus chose to see his immediate struggle as a necessary part of a greater plan. He viewed the Gethsemane conflict as an important but singular act in the grand manuscript of God's drama.

Where we see unanswered prayer, Jesus saw answered prayer. Where we see the absence of God, Jesus saw the plan of God. Note especially verse 53: "Surely you know I could ask my Father, and he would give me more than twelve armies of angels."

Jesus saw what mattered. He saw his Father. He saw his Father's presence in the problem.

# AT ANY COST

✦

God on a cross. The ultimate act of creative compassion. The Creator being sacrificed for the creation. God convincing man once and for all that he would give anything, pay any price to save his children. He could have given up. He could have turned his back. He could have walked away from the wretched mess the world became, but he didn't.

God didn't give up.

When people from his own hometown tried to push him over a cliff, he didn't give up.

When his brothers ridiculed him, he didn't give up.

When he was accused of blaspheming God by people who didn't fear God, he didn't give up.

When Peter worshiped him at the supper and cursed him at the fire, he didn't give up.

When people spat in his face, he didn't spit back. When the bystanders slapped him, he didn't slap them. When a whip ripped his sides, he didn't turn and command the awaiting angels to stuff that whip down that soldier's throat.

And when human hands fastened the divine hands to a cross with spikes, it wasn't the soldiers who held the hands of Jesus steady. It was God who held them steady. Those same hands that formed the oceans and built the mountains. Those same hands that designed the dawn and crafted each cloud. Those same hands that blueprinted one incredible plan for you and me.

Take a stroll out to the hill. Out to Calvary. Out to the cross where, with holy blood, the hand that placed you on the planet wrote the promise, "God would give up his only Son before he'd give up on you."

# RIGHT OR RIGHTEOUS?

✦

It wasn't right that people spit into the eyes that had wept for them. It wasn't right that soldiers ripped chunks of flesh out of the back of their God. It wasn't right that spikes pierced the hands that formed the earth. And it wasn't right that the Son of God was forced to hear the silence of God.

It wasn't right, but it happened.

For while Jesus was on the cross, God sat on his hands. He turned his back. He ignored the screams of the innocent.

He sat in silence while the sins of the world were placed upon his Son. And he did nothing while a cry a million times bloodier than John's echoed in the black sky: "My God, my God, why have you forsaken me?"

Was it right? No.

Was it fair? No.

Was it love? Yes.

In a world of injustice, God once and for all tipped the scales in the favor of hope. And he did it by sitting on his hands so that we could know the kingdom of God.

# HEARTBROKEN FOR YOU

✦

It was the most gut-wrenching cry of loneliness in history, and it came not from a prisoner or a widow or a patient. It came from a hill, from a cross, from a Messiah.

"My God, my God!" he screamed. "Why did you abandon me!"

Never have words carried so much hurt. Never has one being been so lonely.

The despair is darker than the sky. The two who have been one are now two. Jesus, who had been with God for eternity, is now alone. The Christ, who was an expression of God, is abandoned. The Trinity is dismantled. The Godhead is disjointed. The unity is dissolved.

It is more than Jesus can take. He withstood the beatings and remained strong at the mock trials. He watched in silence as those he loved ran away. He did not retaliate when the insults were hurled nor did he scream when the nails pierced his wrists.

But when God turned his head, that was more than he could handle.

"My God!" The wail rises from parched lips. The holy heart is broken. The Sinbearer screams as he wanders in the eternal wasteland. Out of the silent sky come the words screamed by all who walk in the desert of loneliness. "Why? Why did you abandon me?"

I can't understand it. I honestly cannot. Why did Jesus do it? Oh, I know, I know. I have heard the official answers. "To gratify the old law." "To fulfill prophecy." And these answers are right. They are. But there is something more here. Something very compassionate. Something yearning. Something personal.

What is it?

Could it be that his heart was broken for all the people who cast despairing eyes toward the dark heavens and cry the same "Why?" Could it be that his heart was broken for the hurting? Could it be his desire to take on their pain propelled him to the cross? If he could have, wouldn't he have run to the cross on behalf of all the pain in the world?

I imagine him, bending close to those who hurt. I imagine him listening. I picture his eyes misting and a pierced hand brushing away a tear. And although he may offer no answer, although he may solve no dilemma, although the question may freeze painfully in midair, he who also was once alone, understands.

# "IT IS FINISHED!"

✦

Are any words in history more splendid? Three words, at once shattering and victorious.

"It is finished."

Stop and listen a moment. Let the words wind through your heart. Imagine the cry from the cross. The sky is dark. The other two victims are moaning. Jeering mouths of the crowd are silent. Perhaps there is thunder. Perhaps there is weeping. Perhaps there is silence. Then Jesus draws in a deep breath, pushes his feet down on that Roman nail, and cries, "It is finished!"

What was finished?

The history-long plan of redeeming man was finished. The message of God to man was finished. The works done by Jesus as a man on earth were finished. The task of selecting and training ambassadors was finished. The job was finished. The song had been sung. The blood had been poured. The sacrifice had been made. The sting of death had been removed. It was over.

A cry of defeat? Hardly. Had his hands not been fastened down I dare say that a triumphant fist would have punched the dark sky. No, this is no cry of despair. It is a cry of completion. A cry of relief. A roar of fulfillment. A shout of victory.

"Father!" (The voice is hoarse.)
The voice that called forth the dead,
the voice that taught the willing,
the voice that screamed at God,
now says, "Father!"
"Father."

It's over.
An angel sighs. A star wipes away a tear.

"Take me home."
Yes, take him home.
Take this prince to his king.
Take this Son to his Father.
Take this pilgrim to his home.
    (He deserves a rest.)
"Take me home."

Come, ten thousand angels! Come and take this
    wounded Troubadour to
        The cradle of his Father's arms!

Farewell, manger's infant.
Bless you, holy ambassador.
Go home, death slayer.
Rest well, sweet soldier.
    The battle is over.

# *Bounteous Grace*

✦

*God showed his love for us in this way:*
*Christ died for us while we were still sinners.*

ROMANS 5:8

*And you never again have to wonder who your father is—you've been adopted by God and are therefore an "heir of God through Christ."*

GALATIANS 4:7

PONDER THE ACHIEVEMENT OF GOD. HE DOESN'T CONDONE OUR SIN, NOR DOES HE COMPROMISE HIS STANDARD. HE DOESN'T IGNORE OUR REBELLION, NOR DOES HE RELAX HIS DEMANDS. RATHER THAN DISMISS OUR SIN, HE ASSUMES OUR SIN AND, INCREDIBLY, SENTENCES HIMSELF. GOD'S HOLINESS IS HONORED. OUR SIN IS PUNISHED...AND WE ARE REDEEMED. GOD DOES WHAT WE CANNOT DO SO WE CAN BE WHAT WE DARE NOT DREAM: PERFECT BEFORE GOD.

# GRACIOUS PROMISES

✦

*Therefore, there is now no condemnation*
*for those who are in Christ Jesus.*
ROMANS 8:1

*[God] justifies those who have faith in Jesus.*
ROMANS 3:26

*For I will forgive their wickedness*
*and will remember their sins no more.*
HEBREWS 8:12

For those in Christ, these promises are not only a source of joy. They are also the foundations of true courage. You are guaranteed that your sins will be filtered through, hidden in, and screened out by the sacrifice of Jesus. When God looks at you, he doesn't see you; he sees the One who surrounds you. That means that failure is not a concern for you. Your victory is secure. How could you not be courageous?

Picture it this way. Imagine that you are an ice-skater in competition. You are in first place with one more round to go. If you perform well, the trophy is yours. You are nervous, anxious, and frightened.

Then, only minutes before your performance, your trainer rushes to you with the thrilling news: "You've already won! The judges tabulated the scores, and the person in second place can't catch you. You are too far ahead."

Answer the big question of eternity, and the little questions of life fall into perspective.

# PARDON AND PEACE

✦

Through Christ's sacrifice, our past is pardoned and our future secure. And, "Since we have been made right with God by our faith, we have peace with God" Romans 5:1.

Peace with God. What a happy consequence of faith! Not just peace between countries, peace between neighbors, or peace at home; salvation brings peace with God.

Once a monk and his apprentice traveled from the abbey to a nearby village. The two parted at the city gates, agreeing to meet the next morning after completing their tasks. According to plan, they met and began the long walk back to the abbey. The monk noticed that the younger man was unusually quiet. He asked him if anything was wrong. "What business is it of yours?" came the terse response.

Now the monk was sure that his brother was troubled, but he said nothing. The distance between the two began to increase. The apprentice walked slowly, as if to separate himself from his teacher. When the abbey came in sight, the monk stopped at the gate and waited for the student. "Tell me, my son. What troubles your soul?"

The boy started to react again, but when he saw the warmth in his master's eyes, his heart began to melt. "I have sinned greatly," he sobbed. "Last night I slept with a woman and abandoned my vows. I am not worthy to enter the abbey at your side."

The teacher put his arm around the student and said, "We will enter the abbey together. And we will enter the cathedral together. And together we will confess your sin. No one but God will know which of the two of us fell."

Doesn't that describe what God has done for us? When we kept our sin silent, we withdrew from him. We saw him as an enemy. We took steps to avoid his presence. But our confession of fault alters our perception. God is no longer a foe, but a friend. We are at peace with him. He did more than the monk did, much more. More than share in our sin, Jesus was "crushed for the evil we did. The punishment which made us well was given to him" (Isaiah 53:5). "He accepted the shame" (Hebrews 12:2). He leads us into the presence of God.

# GRASPING GRACE

✦

"Lord, if it's you," Peter says, "tell me to come to you on the water" (Matthew 14:28).

Peter is not testing Jesus; he is pleading with Jesus. Stepping onto a stormy sea is not a move of logic; it is a move of desperation. Peter grabs the edge of the boat. Throws out a leg…follows with the other. Several steps are taken. It's as if an invisible ridge of rocks runs beneath his feet. At the end of the ridge is the glowing face of a never-say-die friend.

We do the same, don't we? We come to Christ in an hour of deep need. We abandon the boat of good works. We realize, like Moses, that human strength won't save us. So we look to God in desperation. We realize, like Paul, that all the good works in the world are puny when laid before the Perfect One. We realize, like Peter, that spanning the gap between us and Jesus is a feat too great for our feet.

So we beg for help. Hear his voice. And step out in fear, hoping that our little faith will be enough.

Faith is not born at the negotiating table where we barter our gifts in exchange for God's goodness. Faith is not an award given to the most learned. It's not a prize given to the most disciplined. It's not a title bequeathed to the most religious.

Faith is a desperate dive out of the sinking boat of human

effort and a prayer that God will be there to pull us out of the water. The apostle Paul wrote about this kind of faith:

"For it is by grace you have been saved, through faith—and this not from yourselves, it is the gift of God—not by works, so that no one can boast" (Ephesians 2:8–9).

The supreme force in salvation is God's grace. Not our works. Not our talents. Not our feelings. Not our strength.

Grace is God's sudden, calming presence during the stormy seas of our lives. We hear his voice; we take the step.

Why? Because we are great sinners and we need a great Savior.

We, like Peter, are aware of two facts: We are going down and God is standing up. So we scramble out. We leave behind the Titanic of self-righteousness and stand on the solid path of God's grace.

And, surprisingly, we are able to walk on water. Death is disarmed. Failures are forgivable. Life has real purpose. And God is not only within sight, he is within reach.

# GRACE MEANS...

✦

Here's a secret about grace—ten little words that explain all you need to know: "If God is for us, who can be against us?" (Romans 8:31). That's really all you need to know. And while it sounds simple, there's a profound message contained within those ten words.

Let's take a look at four words in this verse that deserve your attention. Read slowly the phrase, "God is for us." Please pause for a minute before you continue. Read it again, aloud. God is for us. Repeat the phrase four times, this time emphasizing each word. (Come on, you're not in that big of a hurry.)

God is for us.

God is for us.

God is for us.

God is for us.

God is for you. Your parents may have forgotten you, your teachers may have neglected you, your siblings may be ashamed of you; but within reach of your prayers is the maker of the oceans. God!

God is for you. Not "may be," not "has been," not "was," not "would be," but "God is!" He is for you. Today. At this hour. At this minute. As you read this sentence. No need to wait in line or come back tomorrow. He is with you. He could not be closer than he is at this second. His loyalty won't increase if you are better nor lessen if you are worse. He is for you.

God is *for* you. Turn to the sidelines; that's God cheering your run. Look past the finish line; that's God applauding your steps. Listen for him in the bleachers, shouting your name. Too tired to continue? He'll carry you. Too discouraged to fight? He's picking you up. God is for you.

God is for you. Had he a calendar, your birthday would be circled. If he drove a car, your name would be on his bumper. If there's a tree in heaven, he's carved your name in the bark. We know he has a tattoo, and we know what it says. "I have written your name on my hand," he declares (Isaiah 49:16).

"Can a mother forget the baby at her breast and have no compassion on the child she has borne?" God asks (Isaiah 49:15). What a bizarre question. Can you mothers imagine feeding your infant and then later asking, "What was that baby's name?" No. I've seen you care for your young. You stroke the hair, you touch the face, you sing the name over and over. Can a mother forget? No way. But "even if she could forget…I will not forget you," God pledges (Isaiah 49:15).

God is for you. Knowing that, who is against you? Can death harm you now? Can disease rob your life? Can your purpose be taken or your value diminished? No. Though hell may set itself against you, no one can defeat you. You are protected. God is for you.

And that's what grace means.

# WITH TOWEL AND BASIN

✦

*It was almost time for the Jewish Passover Feast.*
*Jesus knew that it was time for him to leave this world and go back to the Father. He had always loved those who were his own in the world, and he loved them all the way to the end....*
*So during the meal Jesus stood up...poured water into a bowl and began to wash the followers' feet.*

JOHN 13:1–5

Behold the gift Jesus gives his followers! He knows what these men are about to do. He knows they are about to perform the vilest act of their lives. By morning they will bury their heads in shame and look down at their feet in disgust. And when they do, he wants them to remember how his knees knelt before them and he washed their feet. He wants them to realize those feet are still clean.

Remarkable. He forgave their sin before they even committed it. He offered mercy before they even sought it. Aside from geography and chronology, our story is the same as the disciples'. We weren't in Jerusalem, and we weren't alive that night. But what

Jesus did for them he has done for us. He has cleansed us. He has cleansed our hearts from sin.

Even more, he is still cleansing us! "We are being cleansed from every sin by the blood of Jesus" (1 John 1:7). In other words, we are always being cleansed. The cleansing is not a promise for the future but a reality in the present. Let a speck of dust fall on the soul of a saint, and it is washed away. Let a spot of filth land on the heart of God's child, and the filth is wiped away. Jesus still cleans his disciples' feet. Jesus still washes away stains. Jesus still purifies his people.

Our Savior kneels down and gazes upon the darkest acts of our lives. But rather than recoil in horror, he reaches out in kindness and says, "I can clean that if you want." And from the basin of his grace, he scoops a palm full of mercy and washes our sin.

# ADOPTION OF THE HEART

✦

Family therapist Paul Faulkner tells of the man who set out to adopt a troubled teenage girl. One would question his logic. She was destructive, disobedient, and dishonest.

One day she came home from school and ransacked the house looking for money. By the time he arrived, she was gone and the house was in shambles.

Upon hearing of her actions, a friend urged him not to finalize the adoption. "You haven't completed the paperwork. You haven't signed any documents. Let her go."

His response was simply, "But I've already promised her that she would be my daughter."

God, too, has made a covenant to adopt his people. His covenant is not invalidated by our rebellion. It's one thing to love us when we are strong, obedient, and willing. But when we ransack his house and steal what is his? This is the test of love.

And God passes the test. "For God shows his great love for us in this way: Christ died for us while we were still sinners" (Romans 5:8).

The father didn't look at the wrecked house and say, "Come back when you've learned respect."

God didn't look at our frazzled lives and say, "I'll die for you when you deserve it."

No, despite our sin, in the face of our rebellion, he chose to adopt us. And for God, there's no going back. His grace is a come-as-you-are promise from a one-of-a-kind King. You've been found, called, and adopted; so trust your Father and claim this verse as your own: "God showed his love for us in this way: Christ died for us while we were still sinners" (Romans 5:8). And you never again have to wonder who your father is—you've been adopted by God and are therefore an "heir of God through Christ" (Galatians 4:7).

# THE SOURCE OF MY STRENGTH

✦

During the early days of the Civil War a Union soldier was arrested on charges of desertion. Unable to prove his innocence, he was condemned and sentenced to die a deserter's death. His appeal found its way to the desk of Abraham Lincoln. The president felt mercy for the soldier and signed a pardon. The soldier returned to service, fought the entirety of the war, and was killed in the last battle. Found within his breast pocket was the signed letter of the president.

Close to the heart of the soldier were his leader's words of pardon. He found courage in grace. I wonder how many thousands more have found courage in the emblazoned cross of their heavenly king.

If you need a bit of courage, let me show you a source of strength for your journey. Keep these words close to your heart and be confident that, because of grace:

You are beyond condemnation (Romans 8:1).
You are delivered from the law (Romans 7:6).
You are near God (Ephesians 2:13).
You are delivered from the power of evil (Colossians 1:13).
You are a member of his kingdom (Colossians 1:13).

You are justified (Romans 5:1).
You are perfect (Hebrews 10:14).
You have been adopted (Romans 8:15).
You have access to God at any moment (Ephesians 2:18).
You are a part of his priesthood (1 Peter 2:5).
You will never be abandoned (Hebrews 13:5).
You have an imperishable inheritance (1 Peter 1:4).
You are a partner with Christ in life (Colossians 3:4), privilege (Ephesians 2:6), suffering (2 Timothy 2:12), and service (1 Corinthians 1:9).

And know that in the heart of God, you are a:

member of his body (1 Corinthians 12:13)
branch in the vine (John 15:5)
stone in the building (Ephesians 2:19-22)
bride for the groom (Ephesians 2:25-27)
saint in the new generation (1 Peter 2:9)
dwelling place of the Spirit (1 Corinthians 6:19).

You possess (get this!) every spiritual blessing possible. "In Christ, God has given us every spiritual blessing in the heavenly world" (Ephesians 1:3). This is the gift offered to the lowliest sinner on earth. Who could make such an offer but God? "From him we have all received one gift after another" (John 1:16).

Everything comes from him;
Everything comes through him;
Everything ends up in him.
Always glory! Always praise! Yes. Yes. Yes.
Romans 11:33–36, THE MESSAGE

# The Choice

✦

*And being found in appearance as a man, [Jesus] humbled himself and became obedient to death—even death on a cross! Therefore God exalted him to the highest place and gave him the name that is above every name, that at the name of Jesus every knee should bow, in heaven and on earth and under the earth, and every tongue confess that Jesus Christ is Lord, to the glory of God the Father.*

PHILIPPIANS 2:8–11

ON ONE SIDE STANDS THE CROWD.

JEERING. BAITING. DEMANDING.

ON THE OTHER STANDS A PEASANT.

SWOLLEN LIPS. LUMPY EYE. LOFTY PROMISE.

ONE PROMISES ACCEPTANCE, THE OTHER A CROSS.

ONE OFFERS FLESH AND FLASH, THE OTHER OFFERS FAITH.

THE CROWD CHALLENGES, "FOLLOW US AND FIT IN."

JESUS PROMISES, "FOLLOW ME AND STAND OUT."

THEY PROMISE TO PLEASE. GOD PROMISES TO SAVE.

A BASIN OF WATER? OR THE BLOOD OF THE SAVIOR?

GOD LOOKS AT YOU AND ASKS...

WHICH WILL BE YOUR CHOICE?

# THE GOD WHO INVITES

✦

God is an inviting God. He invited Mary to birth his son, the disciples to fish for men, the adulteress woman to start over, and Thomas to touch his wounds. God is the King who prepares the palace, sets the table, and invites his subjects to come in.

In fact, it seems his favorite word is *come.*

"*Come,* let us talk about these things. Though your sins are like scarlet, they can be as white as snow."

"All you who are thirsty, *come* and drink."

"*Come* to me all, all of you who are tired and have heavy loads, and I will give you rest."

"*Come* to the wedding feast."

"*Come* follow me, and I will make you fish for people."

"Let anyone who is thirsty *come* to me and drink."

God is a God who invites. God is a God who calls. God is a God who opens the door and waves his hand, pointing pilgrims to a full table.

His invitation is not just for a meal, however; it is for life. An invitation to come into his kingdom and take up residence in a tearless, graveless, painless world. Who can come? Whoever wishes. The invitation is at once universal and personal.

To know God is to receive his invitation. Not just to hear it, not just to study it, not just to acknowledge it, but to receive it. It is possible to learn much about God's invitation and never respond to it personally.

Yet his invitation is clear and nonnegotiable. He gives all and we give him all. Simple and absolute. He is clear in what he asks and clear in what he offers. The choice is up to us. Isn't it incredible that God leaves the choice to us? Think about it. There are many things in life we can't choose. We can't, for example, choose the weather. We can't control the economy.

We can't choose whether or not we are born with a big nose or blue eyes or a lot of hair. We can't even choose how people respond to us.

But we can choose where we spend eternity. The big choice, God leaves to us. The critical decision is ours.

That is the only decision which really matters. Whether or not you take the job transfer is not critical. Whether or not you buy a new car is not crucial. What college you choose or what profession you select is important, but not compared to where you spend eternity. That is the decision you will remember. It is the choice of a lifetime.

# LEAVING THE PORCH LIGHT ON

✦

He's waiting for you. God is standing on the porch of heaven, expectantly hoping, searching the horizon for a glimpse of his child. You're the one God is seeking.

God is the waiting Father, the caring Shepherd in search of his lamb. His legs are scratched, his feet are sore, and his eyes are burning. He scales the cliffs and traverses the fields. He explores the caves. He cups his hands to his mouth and calls into the canyon.

And the name he calls is yours.

He is the Housewife in search of the lost coin. No matter that he has nine others; he won't rest until he has found the tenth. He searches the house. He moves furniture. He pulls up rugs. He cleans out the shelves. All other tasks can wait. Only one matters–the coin of great value to him. He owns it. He will not stop until he finds it.

The coin he seeks is you.

God is the Father pacing the porch. His eyes are wide with his quest. His heart is heavy. He seeks his prodigal. He searches the horizon, yearning for the familiar figure, the recognizable gait. His concern is the son who wears his name, the child who bears his image. You.

He wants you home.

God wants you to be free of yesterday's guilt. He wants you free of today's fears. He wants you free of tomorrow's grave. Sin, fear, and death. These are the mountains he has moved by the power of the cross. These are the prayers he will answer through the gift of his love.

The message is simple: God gave up his Son in order to rescue all his sons and daughters. To bring his children home. He's listening for your answer.

# TOO GOOD TO BE TRUE?

✦

When does salvation come? When we look to Christ. When we embrace him as Savior. Astonishingly simple, isn't it? Claim the great promise of John 3:16: "God loved the world so much that he gave his one and only Son so that whoever believes in him may not be lost, but have eternal life."

God, the Lover. God, the Giver. God, the Savior.

And man, the believer. And for those who believe, he has promised a new birth.

But despite the simplicity, there are still those who don't believe. They don't trust the promise. They can't imagine how God could forgive their sins. It's almost too good to be true.

If only they would try. If only they would test it. But God is as polite as he is passionate. He never forces his way in. The choice is theirs.

And for those who do come, he has promised a new birth.

Does that mean the old nature will never rear its ugly head? Does that mean you will instantly be able to resist any temptation?

To answer that question, compare your new birth in Christ to a newborn baby. Can a newborn walk? Can he feed himself?

Can he sing or read or speak? No, not yet. But someday he will.

It takes time to grow. But is the parent in the delivery room ashamed of the baby? Is the mom embarrassed that the infant can't spell...that the baby can't walk...that the newborn can't give a speech?

Of course not. The parents aren't ashamed; they are proud. They know that growth will come with time. So does God. "God is being patient with you. He does not want anyone to be lost, but he wants all people to change their hearts and lives" (2 Peter 3:9).

God is often more patient with us than we are with ourselves. We assume that if we fall, we aren't born again. If we stumble, then we aren't truly converted. If we have the old desires, then we must not be a new creation.

Please remember: "God began doing a good work in you, and I am sure he will continue it until it is finished when Jesus Christ comes again" (Philippians 1:6).

In many ways, your new birth in Christ is like your first: In your new birth, God provides what you need and someone else does the work. And just as parents are patient with their newborn, so God is patient with you. But there is one difference. The first time you had no choice about being born; this time you do. The power is God's. The effort is God's. The pain is God's.

But the choice is yours.

# WHO'S TO CHOOSE?

✦

To whom does God offer his gift? To the brightest? The most beautiful or the most charming? No. His gift is for us all—beggars and bankers, clergy and clerks, judges and janitors. All God's children.

And he wants us so badly, he'll take us in any condition— "as is" reads the tag on our collars. He's not about to wait for us to reach perfection (he knows we'll never get there!). Do you think he's waiting for us to overcome all temptations? Hardly. When we master the Christian walk? Far from it. Remember, Christ died for us when we were still sinners. His sacrifice, then, was not dependent on our performance.

He wants us *now.* And he'll do whatever it takes to bring his children home.

Christ's love has no strings, no expectations, no hidden agendas, no secrets. His love for us is up front and clear. "I love you," he says. "Even if you let me down. I love you in spite of your failures."

Why did God choose you? Why did he choose me? Honestly. Why? What do we have that he needs?

*Intellect?* Do we honestly think for one minute that we have—or ever will have—a thought he hasn't had?

*Willpower?* I can respect that. Some of us are stubborn enough to walk on water if we felt called to do so...but to think God's kingdom would have done a belly-up without our determination?

Beauty, talent, charm? Right. All those came from him in the first place. Why then? Why would he choose you?

The answer is at once simple and profound. He chose you because he wanted to. After all, you are his. He made you. He brought you home. He owns you. And if you've never heard him assuring you of that simple fact, be reminded by the words on this page. Let these words resonate in your heart: the God who created you loves you. He made the ultimate sacrifice because of *you.* No, God doesn't need you. He *wants* you. So, what do we do with this gift? What does it have to do with our daily existence?

It has *everything* to do with it. Our task on earth is singular—to choose our eternal home. You can afford many wrong choices in life. You can choose the wrong career and survive, the wrong city and survive, the wrong house and survive. You can even choose the wrong mate and survive. But there is one choice that must be made correctly and that is your eternal destiny.

# PURSUED BY GOD

✦

How far do you want God to go in getting your attention? If God has to choose between your eternal safety and your earthly comfort, which do you hope he chooses?

What if he moved you to another land? (As he did Abraham.) What if he called you out of retirement? (Remember Moses?) How about the voice of an angel or the bowel of a fish? (A la Gideon and Jonah.) How about a promotion like Daniel's or a demotion like Samson's?

God does what it takes to get our attention. Isn't that the message of the Bible? The relentless pursuit of God. God on the hunt. God in the search. Peeking under the bed for hiding kids, stirring the bushes for lost sheep. Cupping hand to mouth and shouting into the canyon. Wrestling with us Jacobs in the muddy Jabboks of life.

For all its peculiarities and unevenness, the Bible has a simple story. God made man. Man rejected God. God won't give up until he wins him back. From Moses in Moab to John on Patmos, God is as creative as he is relentless. The same hand that sent manna to Israel sent Uzzah to his death. The same hand that set the children free from Israel also sent them captive to Babylon. Both kind and stern. Tender and tough. Faithfully firm. Patiently urgent. Eagerly tolerant. Softly shouting.

God's voice gently thundering, "I want you."

And your response?

Jesus said, "I am the bread that gives life. I am the light of the world. I am the resurrection and the life. I am the door. I am the way, the truth, and the life. I will come back and take you with me" (John 6:48, 8:12, 11:25, 10:9, 14:6, 14:3).

Jesus proclaiming—ever offering but never forcing: Standing over the crippled man: "Do you want to be well?" John 5:6

Eye to eye with the blind man, now healed: "Do you believe in the Son of Man?" John 9:35

Near the tomb of Lazarus, probing the heart of Martha: "Everyone who lives and believes in me will never die. Martha, do you believe this?" John 11:26

Honest questions. Thundering claims. Gentle touch. Never going where not invited, but once invited never stopping until he's finished, until a choice has been made.

God will whisper. He will shout. He will touch and tug. He will take away our burdens; he'll even take away our blessings. If there are a thousand steps between us and him, he will take all but one. But he will leave the final one for us.

The choice is ours.

# A DEMONSTRATION OF DEVOTION

✦

Does this sound like you? You have nothing to give God but problems. All you have to offer him is your hurt. You want to accept his gift of grace, but you feel unworthy of his sacrifice.

Maybe that has kept you from coming to God. Oh, you've taken a step or two in his direction. But then you saw the other people who follow him. They seemed so clean, so neat, so trim and fit in their faith. So you hesitated.

If that description fits, read the story of the nameless woman in Mark 5. She, considered unclean by her culture, demonstrated her devotion to Jesus by touching the hem of the Savior's garment. And that slight gesture moved Jesus to heal her. She was a shame-struck, penniless outcast who clutched onto her hunch that he could and her hope that he would.

Isn't that what faith is all about? A conviction that he can and that he will. Sounds similar to the definition of faith given by the Bible: "Without faith no one can please God. Anyone who comes to God must believe that he is real and that he rewards those who truly want to find him" (Hebrews 11:6).

Not too complicated, is it? Faith is the belief that God is real and that God is good. Faith is not a mystical experience or a midnight vision or a voice in the forest…it is a choice to believe that the One who made it all hasn't left it all and that he still sends light into shadows and responds to gestures of faith.

Faith is not the belief that God will do what you want. Faith is the belief that God will do what is right. God is always near and always available. Just waiting for your touch. So let him know. Demonstrate your devotion:

Write a letter.
Ask forgiveness.
Confess.
Be baptized.
Feed a hungry person.
Pray.
Teach.
Go.

Do something that reveals your faith. For faith with no effort is no faith at all. God will respond. He has never rejected a genuine gesture of faith. Never.

God honors radical, risk-taking faith. When arks are built, lives are saved. When soldiers march, Jerichos tumble. When staffs are raised, seas still open. When a lunch is shared, thousands are fed. And when a garment is touched—whether by the hand of an anemic woman in Galilee or by the prayers of a beggar in Bangladesh—Jesus stops. So make your choice, announce your faith to God, and demonstrate your devotion.

# YOUR ABBA'S ARMS

✦

Some time back, my daughter Jenna and I spent several days in the old city of Jerusalem. One afternoon, as we were exiting the Jaffa gate, we found ourselves behind an Orthodox Jewish family—a father and his three small girls.

One of the daughters, perhaps four or five years of age, fell a few steps behind and couldn't see her father.

*"Abba!"* she called to him. He stopped and looked. Only then did he realize he was separated from his daughter.

*"Abba!"* she called again. He spotted her and immediately extended his hand. She took it and I took mental notes as they continued. I wanted to see the actions of an *abba*.

He held her hand tightly in his as they descended the ramp. When he stopped at a busy street, she stepped off the curb, so he pulled her back. When the signal changed, he led her and her sisters through the intersection. In the middle of the street, he reached down and swung her up into his arms and continued their journey.

Isn't that what we all need? An *abba* who will hear when we call? Who will take our hand when we're weak? Who will guide us through the hectic intersections of life? Don't we all need an *abba* who will swing us up into his arms and carry us home? We all need a father.

There's a God in heaven who wants you to call him your *abba.*

Choosing God as Lord is to acknowledge that he is sovereign and supreme in the universe. To accept him as Savior is to accept his gift of salvation offered on the cross. But to regard him as Abba—Father—is to go one step further. Ideally, a father is the one in your life who provides and protects. That is exactly what God has done.

He has provided for your needs (Matthew 6:25–34). He has protected you from harm (Psalm 139:5). He has adopted you (Ephesians 1:5). And he has given you his name (1 John 3:1).

God has proven himself as a faithful father. Now it falls to us to be trusting children. Let God give you what the world cannot. Rely on him alone for your affirmation and encouragement. Hold onto these glorious words: "You are God's child, and God will give you the blessing he promised, because you are his child" (Galatians 4:7).

Turn to God. Your abba is waiting for you, with arms open wide.

# GOD'S DESTINY FOR YOUR LIFE

I can remember, as a seven-year-old, going to my grandparents' house for a week. Mom and Dad bought a ticket, gave me some spending money, put me on a Greyhound bus, and told me not to talk to strangers or get off the bus until I saw my grandma out the window. They made it very clear to me that my destination was Ralls, Texas.

God has done the same for you. He has placed you on a journey. He has a destiny for your life (and you'll be glad to know it's not Ralls, Texas.)

*For God has not destined us for wrath,*
*but to obtain salvation through our Lord Jesus.*
1 THESSALONIANS 5:9

According to the Bible, God's destiny for your life is salvation. Your intended destination is heaven. God has done exactly what my parents did. He has purchased our passage. He has equipped us for the journey. God loves you so much that he wants you to be with him forever.

The choice, however, is up to you. Even though he stands at

the door with ticket paid and pocket money for the trip, many choose to go in other directions than the one God intends. That is our problem.

*Our Problem: Sin*
*(We're on the wrong bus.)*

When my parents gave me the ticket and told me which bus to board, I believed them and did what they said. I trusted them. I knew they loved me and I knew they knew more than I did...so I got on board.

Becoming a Christian is getting on board with Christ. Jesus stands at the door of the bus and says, "I am the way, the truth, and the life. No one comes to the Father but by me" (John 14:6). Unfortunately, not all accept his invitation. I know I didn't the first time he invited. I spent some time on the wrong bus.

There are many buses, each of them promising to take you to happiness. There are the buses of pleasure, possessions, power, passion. I saw a bus called party and got on board. It was full of people laughing and carousing; they seemed to be enjoying a nonstop party. It was quite some time before I learned they had to be loud to cover up all the pain inside.

The word for getting on the wrong bus is sin. Sin is when we say, "I'll go my way instead of God's way." Right in the middle of the word *sin* is the word *I.* Sin is when we say, *I'll do what I want, no matter what God says.* Only God can fulfill our needs. Sin is the act of going to everyone but God for what only God can give. Am I the only one who has spent time on the wrong bus? No. Some buses are more violent than others. Some rides are more lengthy than others, but:

*All of us, like sheep, have gone astray, and*
*each of us has turned to his own way.*

ISAIAH 53:6

*If we say we never sin, we are only fooling ourselves, and refuse to accept the truth.*
1 JOHN 1:8

*We're sinners, every one of us in the same sinking boat with everyone else.*
ROMANS 3:20, THE MESSAGE

To board the wrong bus is a serious mistake. Sin breaks our relationship with God. We were intended to journey with him. But when we are on a different bus headed the wrong direction, we feel far from God. This is why life can seem so cruddy. We aren't fulfilling our destiny.

Sin not only breaks our relationship with God; it hampers our relationship with others. Can you imagine taking a long trip to the wrong place with a busload of people? With time, everyone gets cranky. Nobody likes the trip. The journey is miserable.

We try to cope with the problems by therapy or recreation or prescriptions. But nothing helps. The Bible says:

*There are ways that seem right to a man, but they only end in death.*
PROVERBS 16:25

You see, the end result of sin is death...spiritual death. "The wages of sin," Paul writes, "is death..." (Romans 6:23).

Spend a lifetime on the wrong bus headed in the wrong direction and you'll end up in the wrong place. You'll end up in hell. Not because God wants you in hell. His plan for you is heaven. Your destiny is heaven. He'll do anything to get you to heaven, with one exception. There is one thing he won't do. He won't force you. The decision is yours. But he has done everything else. Let me show you what I mean.

## *The Solution: GRACE*
## *(Go to the right bus.)*

If the problem is sin and all have sinned, what can I do? Well, you can go to church, but that won't make you a Christian. Just as going to a rodeo doesn't make you a cowboy, going to church doesn't make you a Christian. You could work hard to please God. You could do a lot of good stuff, give away a lot of things...the only problem with that is that you don't know how many good things you have to do. Or you could compare yourself with others. "I may be bad, but at least I'm better than Hitler." The problem with comparisons is that other people aren't the standard; God is!

So what are you going to do? If you aren't saved by going to church or doing good works or comparing yourself to others, how are you saved? The answer is simple: go to the right bus.

*For God so loved the world that he gave his one and only Son,*
*that whoever believes in him shall not perish but have eternal life.*

JOHN 3:16

Note what God did: "He gave his only Son." This is how he dealt with your sin. Imagine it this way: Suppose you are found guilty of a crime. You are in a courtroom in front of the judge and he sentences you to death for your crime. His sentence is just. You are guilty and the punishment for your crime is death. But suppose that the judge is your father. He knows the law; he knows that your crime demands a death. But he knows love; he knows that he loves you too much to let you die. So in a wonderful act of love he steps down from the bench and removes his robe and stands by your side and says, "I'm going to die in your place."

That is what God did for you. The wages of sin is death. Heaven's justice demands a death for your sin. Heaven's love, however, can't bear to see you die. So here is what God did. He stood and removed his heavenly robes. He came to earth to tell us that he would die for us. He would be our Savior. And that is what he did.

*God put the world square with himself through the Messiah,*
*giving the world a fresh start by offering the forgiveness of sins...*
*God put on him the wrong who never did anything wrong,*
*so we could be put right with God.*

2 CORINTHIANS 5:21, THE MESSAGE

*The Response:* TRUST
*(Getting on the right bus.)*

What does God want you to do? He wants you to get on his bus. How is this done? Three simple steps: admit, agree, accept.

1. Admit that God has not been first place in your life and ask him to forgive your sins.

*If we confess our sins, he is faithful and just*
*and will forgive our sins and cleanse us from every wrong.*

1 JOHN 1:9

2. Agree that Jesus died to pay for your sins and that he rose from the dead and is alive today.

*If you confess that Jesus is your Lord,*
*and you believe in your heart that God raised him from the dead,*
*you will be saved.*

ROMANS 10:9

*Salvation is found in no one else, for there is*
*no other name [Jesus] by which we must be saved.*

ACTS 4:12

3. Accept God's free gift of salvation. Don't try to earn it.

*For it is by grace that you have been saved,*
*through faith—and this is not from yourselves, it is the gift of God—*
*not by works, so that no one can boast.*

EPHESIANS 2:8–9

*To all who received him, he gave the right*
*to become children of God. All they needed to do was to*
*trust him to save them. All those who believe this are reborn!—*
*not a physical rebirth...but from the will of God.*

JOHN 1:12–13

*Jesus says, Listen, I stand at the door and knock.*
*If anyone hears my voice and opens the door, I will come in...*

REVELATION 3:20

With all of my heart, I urge you to accept God's destiny for your life. I urge you to get on board with Christ. According to the Bible, "Jesus is the only one who can save people. His name is the only power in the world that has been given to save people. We must be saved through him" (Acts 4:12).

Would you let him save you? This is the most important decision you will ever make. Why don't you give your heart to him right now? *Admit* your need. *Agree* with his work. *Accept* his gift. Go to God in prayer and tell him, "I am a sinner in need of grace. I believe that Jesus died for me on the cross. I accept your offer of salvation." It's a simple prayer with eternal results.

Once you've placed your faith in Christ, I urge you to take three steps. You'll find them easy to remember. Just think of these three words (they each start with *b*): baptism, Bible, and belong.

*Baptism* demonstrates and celebrates our decision to follow Jesus. Our immersion into water symbolizes our immersion into God's grace. Just as water cleanses the body, so grace cleanses the soul. Jesus said, "Anyone who believes and is baptized will be saved" (Mark 16:16). When the apostle Paul became a believer, he was asked this question: "Now, why wait any longer? Get up, be baptized, and wash your sins away, trusting in him to save you" (Acts 22:16). Paul responded by being baptized immediately. You can, too.

*Bible* reading brings us face-to-face with God. God reveals himself to us through his Word by the Holy Spirit. "Let the teaching of Christ live in you richly" (Colossians 3:16).

*Belonging* to a church reinforces your faith. A Christian without a church is like a baseball player without a team or a soldier without an army. You aren't strong enough to survive alone. "You should not stay away from the church meetings as some are in the habit of doing, but you should meet together and encourage each other" (Hebrews 10:25).

These three steps—baptism, Bible reading, and belonging to a church—are essential steps in your faith.

I pray that you'll accept this great gift of salvation. Believe me, this is not only the most important decision you'll ever make; it's the greatest decision you'll ever make. There's no higher treasure than God's gift of salvation. It's God's wonderful destiny for your life.

# REFERENCES



"It Began in a Manger" is taken from *God Came Near* (Sisters, Ore.: Multnomah Publishers, Inc., 1987), 23, 25–26.

"A Day for Good-bye" is taken from *God Came Near* (Sisters, Ore.: Multnomah Publishers, Inc., 1987), 49–52.

"God in the Flesh" is taken from *God Came Near* (Sisters, Ore.: Multnomah Publishers, Inc., 1987), 55–56.

"Compassionate Savior" is taken from *In the Eye of the Storm* (Nashville, Tenn.: Word Publishing, 1991), 53–54, 58.

"Jesus Knows How You Feel" is taken from *In the Eye of the Storm* (Nashville, Tenn.: Word Publishing, 1991), 48–49.

"Faith Beheld, Faith Blessed" is taken from *In the Eye of the Storm* (Nashville, Tenn.: Word Publishing, 1993), 119–121.

"The Great Exchange" is taken from *A Gentle Thunder* (Nashville, Tenn.: Word Publishing, 1995), 86–87.

"Eyes on the Savior" is taken from *God Came Near* (Sisters, Ore.: Multnomah Publishers, Inc., 1987), 160–162.

"Come and See" is taken from *A Gentle Thunder* (Nashville, Tenn.: Word Publishing, 1995), 21–23.

"Road to Calvary" is taken from *The Applause of Heaven* (Nashville, Tenn.: Word Publishing, 1990), 7–8.

"The Fog of a Broken Heart" is taken from *No Wonder They Call Him the Savior* (Sisters, Ore.: Multnomah Publishers, Inc., 1986), 131–133.

"Partner in the Plan" is taken from *God Came Near* (Sisters, Ore.: Multnomah Publishers, Inc., 1987), 79–81.

"He Saw You" is taken from *And the Angels Were Silent* (Sisters, Ore.: Multnomah Publishers, Inc., 1992), 154–155.

"Heaven's Silence" is taken from *Just Like Jesus* (Nashville, Tenn.: Word Publishing, 1998), 131–134.

"At Any Cost" is taken from *Six Hours One Friday* (Sisters, Ore.: Multnomah Publishers, Inc., 1989), 56–57.

"Right or Righteous" is taken from *The Applause of Heaven* (Nashville, Tenn.: Word Publishing, 1990), 178.

"Heartbroken for You" is taken from *No Wonder They Call Him the Savior* (Sisters, Ore.: Multnomah Publishers, Inc., 1986), 47–48.

"It Is Finished!" is taken from *No Wonder They Call Him the Savior* (Sisters, Ore.: Multnomah Publishers, Inc., 1986), 61, 65–66.

Introduction to "Bounteous Grace" is taken from *In the Grip of Grace* (Nashville, Tenn.: Word Publishing, 1996), 55.

"Gracious Promises" is taken from *The Applause of Heaven* (Nashville, Tenn.: Word Publishing, 1990), 85.

"Pardon and Peace" is taken from *In the Grip of Grace* (Nashville, Tenn.: Word Publishing, 1996), 91–92.

"Grasping Grace" is taken from *In the Eye of the Storm* (Nashville, Tenn.: Word Publishing, 1991), 202–203.

"Grace Means" is taken from *In the Grip of Grace* (Nashville, Tenn.: Word Publishing, 1996), 173–174.

"With Towel and Basin" is taken from *Just Like Jesus* (Nashville, Tenn.: Word Publishing, 1998), 19–20.

"Adoption of the Heart" is taken from *In the Grip of Grace* (Nashville, Tenn.: Word Publishing, 1996), 97–98.

"The Source of My Strength" is taken from *In the Grip of Grace* (Nashville, Tenn.: Word Publishing, 1996), 103–106.

"The God Who Invites" is taken from *And the Angels Were Silent* (Sisters, Ore.: Multnomah Publishers, Inc., 1992), 83, 85–86.

"Leaving the Porch Light On" is taken from *And the Angels Were Silent* (Sisters, Ore.: Multnomah Publishers, Inc., 1992), 71–72.

"Too Good to Be True?" is taken from *A Gentle Thunder* (Nashville, Tenn.: Word Publishing, 1995), 110–111.

"Who's to Choose?" is taken from *No Wonder They Call Him the Savior* (Sisters, Ore.: Multnomah Publishers, Inc., 1986), 156, and *And the Angels Were Silent* (Sisters, Ore.: Multnomah Publishers, Inc., 1992), 18, 137.

"Pursued by God" is taken from *A Gentle Thunder* (Nashville, Tenn.: Word Publishing, 1995), 4–5.

"A Demonstration of Devotion" is taken from *He Still Moves Stones* (Nashville, Tenn.: Word Publishing, 1993), 67–69.

"Your Abba's Arms" is taken from *The Great House of God* (Nashville, Tenn.: Word Publishing, 1993), 136–137, and *He Still Moves Stones* (Nashville, Tenn.: Word Publishing, 1993), 44.

# GOD CAME NEAR

## CHRONICLES OF THE CHRIST

Max Lucado

Multnomah Publishers *Sisters, Oregon*

GOD CAME NEAR
published by Multnomah Publishers, Inc.


*International Standard Book Number:* *1-59052-233-8 (3-in-1 ABA)*

Printed in the United States of America
Cover photograph by: Marc Norberg
Cover design by: Stephen Gardner



Library of Congress Cataloging-in-Publication Data

Lucado, Max
God came near.
1. Incarnation—Meditations. I. Title.
BT220.L82 1987 232.'1 87-12502
ISBN 1-57673-387-4 (hd)
ISBN 1-57673-386-6 (pa)

03 04 05 06 — 57 56 55 54

*To Steve and Cheryl Green*
*"A faithful friend is a sure shelter,*
*whoever finds one has found a rare treasure."*

ECCLESIASTICUS 6:14

*"Sir," they said, "we would like to see Jesus."*

JOHN 12:21

*"We were eyewitnesses of his majesty."*

2 PETER 1:16

# CONTENTS

Part II

## OUR IMITATION

*"A student...who is fully trained will be like his teacher."*

# Acknowledgments

My deepest thanks to:
Liz Heaney and the Multnomah staff:
they don't come any better.

Jim Woodroof, Rubel Shelley, Richard Rogers and
Joan Carrigan (my sister):
your encouragement and suggestions were invaluable.

Carl Cope:
what would I do without your eleventh hour aid and
twenty-four hour friendship?

The Rio team:
amigos queridos!

Stanley Shipp:
you're one of the finest men on earth.

The elders of the Highland Church of Christ:
I appreciate the pastoral care and prayers.

And most tenderly, thank you, Denalyn:
If a star fell each time I thought of you, the sky would be empty.

# Eyewitnesses of His Majesty

*Christianity, in its purest form, is nothing*
*more than seeing Jesus.*
*Christian service, in its purest form, is nothing*
*more than imitating him who we see.*
*To see His Majesty and to imitate him,*
*that is the sum of Christianity.*

For fifty-one years Bob Edens was blind. He couldn't see a thing. His world was a black hall of sounds and smells. He felt his way through five decades of darkness.

And then, he could see.

A skilled surgeon performed a complicated operation and, for the first time, Bob Edens had sight. He found it overwhelming. "I never would have dreamed that yellow is so…yellow," he exclaimed. "I don't have the words. I am amazed by yellow. But red is my favorite color. I just can't believe red.

"I can see the shape of the moon—and I like nothing better than seeing a jet plane flying across the sky leaving a vapor trail. And of course, sunrises and sunsets. And at night I look at the stars in the sky and the flashing light. You could never know how wonderful everything is."

He's right. Those of us who have lived a lifetime with vision can't know how wonderful it must be to be given sight.

But Bob Edens isn't the only one who has spent a lifetime near something without seeing it. Few are the people who don't suffer from some form of blindness. Amazing, isn't it? We can live next to something for a lifetime, but unless we take time to focus on it, it doesn't become a part of our life. Unless we somehow have our blindness lifted, our world is but a black cave.

Think about it. Just because one has witnessed a thousand rainbows doesn't mean he's seen the grandeur of one. One can live near a garden and fail to focus on the splendor of the flower. A man can spend a lifetime with a woman and never pause to look into her soul.

And a person can be all that goodness calls him to be and still never see the Author of life.

Being honest or moral or even religious doesn't necessarily mean we will see him. No. We may see what others see in him. Or we may hear what some say he said. But until we see him for ourselves, until our own sight is given, we may think we see him, having in reality seen only a hazy form in the gray semidarkness.

Have you seen him?

Have you caught a glimpse of His Majesty? A word is placed in a receptive crevice of your heart that causes you, ever so briefly, to see his face. You hear a verse read in a tone you'd never heard, or explained in a way you'd never thought and one more piece of the puzzle falls into place. Someone touches your painful spirit as only one sent from him could do...and there he is.

Jesus.

The man. The bronzed Galilean who spoke with such thunderous authority and loved with such childlike humility.

The God. The one who claimed to be older than time and greater than death.

Gone is the pomp of religion; dissipated is the fog of theology. Momentarily lifted is the opaque curtain of controversy and opinion. Erased are our own blinding errors and egotism. And there he stands.

Jesus.

Have you seen him?

Those who first did were never the same.

"My Lord and my God!" cried Thomas.

"I have seen the Lord," exclaimed Mary Magdalene.

"We have seen his glory," declared John.

"Were not our hearts burning within us while he talked?" rejoiced the two Emmaus-bound disciples.

But Peter said it best. "We were eyewitnesses of his majesty."

His Majesty. The emperor of Judah. The soaring eagle of eternity. The noble admiral of the Kingdom. All the splendor of heaven revealed in a human body. For a period ever so brief, the doors to the throne room were open and God came near. His Majesty was seen. Heaven touched the earth and, as a result, earth can know heaven. In astounding tandem a human body housed divinity. Holiness and earthliness intertwined.

This is no run-of-the-mill messiah. His story was extraordinary. He called himself divine, yet allowed a minimum-wage Roman soldier to drive a nail into his wrist. He demanded purity, yet stood for the rights of a repentant whore. He called men to march, yet refused to allow them to call him King. He sent men into all the world, yet equipped them with only bended knees and memories of a resurrected carpenter.

We can't regard him as simply a good teacher. His claims are too outrageous to limit him to the company of Socrates or Aristotle. Nor can we categorize him as one of many prophets sent to reveal eternal truths. His own claims eliminate that possibility.

Then who is he?

Let's try to find out. Let's follow his sandalprints. Let's sit on the cold, hard floor of the cave in which he was born. Let's smell the sawdust of the carpentry shop. Let's hear his sandals slap the hard trails of Galilee. Let's sigh as we touch the healed sores of the leper. Let's smile as we see his compassion with the woman at the well. Let's cringe as we hear the hissing of hell's Satan. Let's let our voices soar with the praises of the multitudes. Let's try to see him.

Has it been a while since you have seen him? If your prayers seem stale, it probably has. If your faith seems to be trembling, perhaps your vision of him has blurred. If you can't find power to face your problems, perhaps it is time to face him.

One warning. Something happens to a person who has witnessed His Majesty. He becomes addicted. One glimpse of the King and you are consumed by a desire to see more of him and say more about him.

Pew-warming is no longer an option. Junk religion will no longer suffice. Sensation-seeking is needless. Once you have seen his face you will forever long to see it again.

My prayer for this book—without apologies—is that the Divine Surgeon will use it as a delicate surgical tool to restore sight. That blurriness will be focused and darkness dispersed. That the Christ will emerge from a wavy figure walking out of a desert mirage to become the touchable face of a best friend. That we will lay our faces at the pierced feet and join Thomas in proclaiming, "My Lord and my God." And, most supremely, that we will whisper the secret of the universe, "We were eyewitnesses of his majesty."

PART ONE

# HIS INCARNATION

*And the Word became flesh and dwelt among us, and we beheld His glory,...full of grace and truth.*

JOHN 1:14

CHAPTER 1

# THE ARRIVAL

The noise and the bustle began earlier than usual in the village. As night gave way to dawn, people were already on the streets. Vendors were positioning themselves on the corners of the most heavily traveled avenues. Store owners were unlocking the doors to their shops. Children were awakened by the excited barking of the street dogs and the complaints of donkeys pulling carts.

The owner of the inn had awakened earlier than most in the town. After all, the inn was full, all the beds taken. Every available mat or blanket had been put to use. Soon all the customers would be stirring and there would be a lot of work to do.

One's imagination is kindled thinking about the conversation of the innkeeper and his family at the breakfast table. Did anyone mention the arrival of the young couple the night before? Did anyone ask about their welfare? Did anyone comment on the pregnancy of the girl on the donkey? Perhaps. Perhaps someone raised the subject. But, at best, it was raised, not discussed. There was nothing *that* novel about them. They were, possibly, one of several families turned away that night.

Besides, who had time to talk about them when there was so much excitement in the air? Augustus did the economy of Bethlehem a favor when he decreed that a census should be taken. Who could remember when such commerce had hit the village?

No, it is doubtful that anyone mentioned the couple's arrival or wondered about the condition of the girl. They were too busy. The day was upon them. The day's bread had to be made. The morning's chores had to be done. There was too much to do to imagine that the impossible had occurred.

God had entered the world as a baby.

Yet, were someone to chance upon the sheep stable on the outskirts of Bethlehem that morning, what a peculiar scene they would behold.

The stable stinks like all stables do. The stench of urine, dung, and sheep reeks pungently in the air. The ground is hard, the hay scarce. Cobwebs cling to the ceiling and a mouse scurries across the dirt floor.

A more lowly place of birth could not exist.

Off to one side sit a group of shepherds. They sit silently on the floor; perhaps perplexed, perhaps in awe, no doubt in amazement. Their night watch had been interrupted by an explosion of light from heaven and a symphony of angels. God goes to those who have time to hear him—so on this cloudless night he went to simple shepherds.

Near the young mother sits the weary father. If anyone is dozing, he is. He can't remember the last time he sat down. And now that the excitement has subsided a bit, now that Mary and the baby are comfortable, he leans against the wall of the stable and feels his eyes grow heavy. He still hasn't figured it all out. The mystery of the event puzzles him. But he hasn't the energy to wrestle with the questions. What's important is that the baby is fine and that Mary is safe. As sleep comes he remembers the name the angel told him to use…Jesus. "We will call him Jesus."

Wide awake is Mary. My, how young she looks! Her head rests on the soft leather of Joseph's saddle. The pain has been eclipsed by wonder. She looks into the face of the baby. Her son. Her Lord. His Majesty. At this point in history, the human being who best understands who God is and what he is doing is a teenage girl in a smelly stable. She can't take her eyes off him. Somehow Mary knows she is holding God. *So this is he.* She remembers the words of the angel. "His kingdom will never end."[1]

He looks like anything but a king. His face is prunish and red. His cry, though strong and healthy, is still the helpless and piercing cry of a baby. And he is absolutely dependent upon Mary for his well-being.

Majesty in the midst of the mundane. Holiness in the filth of sheep manure and sweat. Divinity entering the world on the floor of a stable, through the womb of a teenager and in the presence of a carpenter.

She touches the face of the infant-God. *How long was your journey!*

This baby had overlooked the universe. These rags keeping him warm were the robes of eternity. His golden throne room had been abandoned in favor of a dirty sheep pen. And worshiping angels had been replaced with kind but bewildered shepherds.

Meanwhile, the city hums. The merchants are unaware that God has visited their planet. The innkeeper would never believe that he had just sent God into the cold. And the people would scoff at anyone who told them the Messiah lay in the arms of a teenager on the outskirts of their village. They were all too busy to consider the possibility.

Those who missed His Majesty's arrival that night missed it not because of evil acts or malice; no, they missed it because they simply weren't looking.

Little has changed in the last two thousand years, has it?

CHAPTER 2

# "JUST A MOMENT..."

It all happened in a moment, a most remarkable moment.

As moments go, that one appeared no different than any other. If you could somehow pick it up off the timeline and examine it, it would look exactly like the ones that have passed while you have read these words. It came and it went. It was preceded and succeeded by others just like it. It was one of the countless moments that have marked time since eternity became measurable.

But in reality, that particular moment was like none other. For through that segment of time a spectacular thing occurred. God became a man. While the creatures of earth walked unaware, Divinity arrived. Heaven opened herself and placed her most precious one in a human womb.

The omnipotent, in one instant, made himself breakable. He who had been spirit became pierceable. He who was larger than the universe became an embryo. And he who sustains the world with a word chose to be dependent upon the nourishment of a young girl.

God as a fetus. Holiness sleeping in a womb. The creator of life being created.

God was given eyebrows, elbows, two kidneys, and a spleen. He stretched against the walls and floated in the amniotic fluids of his mother.

God had come near.

He came, not as a flash of light or as an unapproachable conqueror, but as one whose first cries were heard by a peasant girl and a sleepy carpenter. The hands that first held him were unmanicured, calloused, and dirty.

No silk. No ivory. No hype. No party. No hoopla.

Were it not for the shepherds, there would have been no reception. And were it not for a group of star-gazers, there would have been no gifts.

Angels watched as Mary changed God's diaper. The universe watched with wonder as The Almighty learned to walk. Children played in the street with him. And had the synagogue leader in Nazareth known who was listening to his sermons…

Jesus may have had pimples. He may have been tone-deaf. Perhaps a girl down the street had a crush on him or vice-versa. It could be that his knees were bony. One thing's for sure: He was, while completely divine, completely human.

For thirty-three years he would feel everything you and I have ever felt. He felt weak. He grew weary. He was afraid of failure. He was susceptible to wooing women. He got colds, burped, and had body odor. His feelings got hurt. His feet got tired. And his head ached.

To think of Jesus in such a light is—well, it seems almost irreverent, doesn't it? It's not something we like to do; it's uncomfortable. It is much easier to keep the humanity out of the incarnation. Clean the manure from around the manger. Wipe the sweat out of his eyes. Pretend he never snored or blew his nose or hit his thumb with a hammer.

He's easier to stomach that way. There is something about keeping him divine that keeps him distant, packaged, predictable.

But don't do it. For heaven's sake, don't. Let him be as human as he intended to be. Let him into the mire and muck of our world. For only if we let him in can he pull us out.

Listen to him.

"Love your neighbor" was spoken by a man whose neighbors tried to kill him.[1]

The challenge to leave family for the gospel was issued by one who kissed his mother good-bye in the doorway.[2]

"Pray for those who persecute you" came from the lips that would soon be begging God to forgive his murderers.[3]

"I am with you always" are the words of a God who in one instant did the impossible to make it all possible for you and me.[4]

It all happened in a moment. In one moment…a most remarkable moment. The Word became flesh.

There will be another. The world will see another instantaneous transformation. You see, in becoming man, God made it possible for man to see God. When Jesus went home he left the back door open. As a result, "we will all be changed—in a moment, in the twinkling of an eye."[5]

The first moment of transformation went unnoticed by the world. But you can bet your sweet September that the second one won't. The next time you use the phrase "just a moment,…" remember that's all the time it will take to change this world.

CHAPTER 3

# ABSURDITY IN THE FLESH

"*You mean to tell me God became a baby...*"

The one posing the questions was puzzled. His thick eyebrows furrowed in doubt and his eyes squinted in caution. Though there were places to sit, he opted not to do so. He preferred to stand safely behind the crowd, unsure, yet intrigued by what he was hearing. Throughout the lecture he had listened intently, occasionally uncrossing his arms to stroke his whiskered chin. Now, however, he stood upright, punching the air with his finger as he queried.

*"and that he was born in a sheep stable?"*

He looked as though he'd walked down from one of the adjacent Colorado mountains: stocking hat, down vest, nylon leggings, hiking boots. And he sounded as though he honestly didn't know if the story he was hearing was a mountain legend or the gospel truth.

*"Yes, that is what I mean to say,"* the lecturer responded.

*"And then, after becoming a baby, he was raised in a blue-collar home? He never wrote any books or held any offices, yet he called himself the Son of God?"*

*"That is right."*

The lecturer being questioned was Landon Saunders; the voice of the Heartbeat Radio program. I've never heard anybody tell the story of the Nazarene like Landon can.

*"He never traveled outside of his own country, never studied at a university, never lived in a palace, and yet asked to be regarded as the creator of the universe?"*

*"That's correct."*

I was a bit unnerved by the dialogue. I was fresh out of college, gung ho, enthusiastic. As a volunteer helper in the lecture series, I had come with memorized verses and responses loaded in the chamber of my evangelistic six-shooter. However, I came prepared to defend a lifestyle, not a Savior. I was ready to argue morality, doctrine, heaven and hell. I wasn't ready to argue a man. Jesus had always been someone I just accepted. These questions were a bit too aggressive for my virgin faith.

*"And this crucifixion story...he was betrayed by his own people? No followers came to his defense? And then he was executed like a common junkyard thief?"*

*"That's the gist of it."*

The authenticity of the questioner didn't allow you to regard him as a cynic nor to dismiss him as a show-off. To the contrary, he seemed nervous about commanding such attention. His awkwardness betrayed his inexperience in public speaking. But his desire to know was just an ounce or two heavier than his discomfort, so he continued.

*"And after the killing he was buried in a borrowed grave?"*

*"Yes, he had no grave of his own, nor money with which to purchase one."*

The honesty of the dialogue kept the audience spellbound. I realized I was witnessing one of those rare times when two people were willing to question the holy. Here were two men standing on opposite sides of a deep chasm, one asking the other if the bridge that stretched between them could actually be trusted.

There was a hint of emotion in the student's voice as he carefully worded the next question.

*"And according to what's written, after three days in the grave he was resurrected and made appearances to over five hundred people?"*

*"Yes."*

*"And all this was to prove that God still loves his people and provides a way for us to return to him?"*

*"Right."*

I knew which question was coming next. Every one in the room knew it. It could have gone without being asked. In my heart of hearts, I was hoping that it wouldn't be asked.

*"Doesn't that all sound rather..."* He paused a second, searching for the right adjective. *"Doesn't that all sound rather absurd?"*

All the heads turned in perfect sync and looked at Landon. All the heads, that is, except mine. My head was spinning as I was forced to look at Jesus from a new angle. Christianity...absurd? Jesus on a cross...absurd? The Incarnation...absurd? The Resurrection...absurd? My Sunday school Jesus had been taken down from the flannel board.

Landon's response was simple. *"Yes. Yes, I suppose it does sound absurd, doesn't it?"*

I didn't like that answer. I didn't like it at all. Tell the fellow how it made sense! Diagram the dispensations. Present fulfilled prophecies. Explain the fulfillment of the Old Law. Covenant. Reconciliation. Redemption. Sure it made sense. Don't let him describe God's actions as absurd!

Then it began to dawn on me: *What* God did makes sense. It makes sense that Jesus would be our sacrifice because a sacrifice was needed to justify man's presence before God. It makes sense that God would use the Old Law to tutor Israel on their need for grace. It makes sense that Jesus would be our High Priest. *What* God did makes sense. It can be taught, charted, and put in books on systematic theology.

However, *why* God did it is absolutely absurd. When one leaves the method and examines the motive, the carefully stacked blocks of logic begin to tumble. That type of love isn't logical; it can't be neatly outlined in a sermon or explained in a term paper.

Think about it. For thousands of years, using his wit and charm, man had tried to be friends with God. And for thousands of years he had let God down more than he had lifted him up. He'd done the very thing he promised he'd never do. It was a fiasco. Even the holiest of the heroes sometimes forgot whose side they were on. Some of the scenarios in the Bible look more like the adventures of Sinbad the Sailor than stories for vacation Bible school. Remember these characters?

Aaron. Right-hand man to Moses. Witness of the plagues. Member of the "Red Sea Riverbed Expedition." Holy priest of God. But if he was so saintly, what is he doing leading the Israelites in fireside aerobics in front of the golden calf?

The sons of Jacob. The fathers of the tribes of Israel. Great-grandsons of Abraham. Yet, if they were so special, why were they gagging their younger brother and sending him to Egypt?

David. The man after God's own heart. The King's king. The giant-slayer and songwriter. He's also the guy whose glasses got steamy as a result of a bath on a roof. Unfortunately, the water wasn't his, nor was the woman he was watching.

And Samson. Swooning on Delilah's couch, drunk on the wine, perfume, and soft lights. He's thinking, *She's putting on something more comfortable.* She's thinking, *I know I put those shears in here somewhere.*

Adam adorned in fig leaves and stains of forbidden fruit. Moses throwing both a staff and a temper tantrum. King Saul looking into a crystal ball for the will of God. Noah, drunk and naked in his own tent.

These are the chosen ones of God? This is the royal lineage of the King? These are the ones who were to carry out God's mission?

It's easy to see the absurdity.

Why didn't he give up? Why didn't he let the globe spin off its axis?

Even after generations of people had spit in his face, he still loved them. After a nation of chosen ones had stripped him naked and ripped his incarnated flesh, he still died for them. And even today, after billions have chosen to prostitute themselves before the pimps of power, fame, and wealth, he still waits for them.

It *is* inexplicable. It doesn't have a drop of logic nor a thread of rationality.

And yet, it is that very irrationality that gives the gospel its greatest defense. For only God could love like that.

I don't know what happened to that inquisitive fellow in Colorado. He disappeared as quickly as he came. But I'm in his debt. He forced me to see Jesus as I'd never seen him.

At first I didn't recognize him. I guess I was expecting someone in a flowing frock with silky-white hands. But it was he. The lion. The Judean Lion. He walked out from among the dense trees of theology and ritual and lay down in a brief clearing. In his paw was a wound and in his mane were stains of blood. But there was a royalty about him that silenced even the breeze in the trees.

Bloodstained royalty. A God with tears. A creator with a heart. God became earth's mockery to save his children.

How absurd to think that such nobility would go to such poverty to share such a treasure with such thankless souls.

But he did.

In fact, the only thing more absurd than the gift is our stubborn unwillingness to receive it.

CHAPTER 4

# MARY'S PRAYER

God. O infant-God. Heaven's fairest child. Conceived by the union of divine grace with our disgrace. Sleep well.

Sleep well. Bask in the coolness of this night bright with diamonds. Sleep well, for the heat of anger simmers nearby. Enjoy the silence of the crib, for the noise of confusion rumbles in your future. Savor the sweet safety of my arms, for a day is soon coming when I cannot protect you.

Rest well, tiny hands. For though you belong to a king, you will touch no satin, own no gold. You will grasp no pen, guide no brush. No, your tiny hands are reserved for works more precious:

> to touch a lepers open wound,
> to wipe a widow's weary tear,
> to claw the ground of Gethsemane.

Your hands, so tiny, so tender, so white—clutched tonight in an infant's fist. They aren't destined to hold a scepter nor wave from a palace balcony. They are reserved instead for a Roman spike that will staple them to a Roman cross.

Sleep deeply, tiny eyes. Sleep while you can. For soon the blurriness will clear and you will see the mess we have made of your world.

You will see our nakedness, for we cannot hide.

You will see our selfishness, for we cannot give.
You will see our pain, for we cannot heal.

O eyes that will see hell's darkest pit and witness her ugly prince...sleep, please sleep; sleep while you can.

Lay still, tiny mouth. Lay still mouth from which eternity will speak.
Tiny tongue that will soon summon the dead,

that will define grace,
that will silence our foolishness.

Rosebud lips—upon which ride a starborn kiss of forgiveness to those who believe you, and of death to those who deny you—lay still.

And tiny feet cupped in the palm of my hand, rest. For many difficult steps lie ahead for you.

Do you taste the dust of the trails you will travel?
Do you feel the cold sea water upon which you will walk?
Do you wrench at the invasion of the nail you will bear?
Do you fear the steep descent down the spiral staircase into Satan's domain?

Rest, tiny feet. Rest today so that tomorrow you might walk with power. Rest. For millions will follow in your steps.

And little heart...holy...pumping the blood of life through the universe: How many times will we break you?

You'll be torn by the thorns of our accusations.
You'll be ravaged by the cancer of our sin.
You'll be crushed under the weight of your own sorrow.
And you'll be pierced by the spear of our rejection.

Yet in that piercing, in that ultimate ripping of muscle and membrane, in that final rush of blood and water, you will find rest. Your hands will be freed, your eyes will see justice, your lips will smile, and your feet will carry you home.

And there you'll rest again—this time in the embrace of your Father.

CHAPTER 5

# LIMB-CLIMBER OR BRANCH-SITTER

Joseph was perched firmly on his branch in the tree. It was thick, reliable, and perfect for sitting. It was so strong that he didn't tremble when the storms came, nor did he shake when the winds blew. No, this branch was predictable and solid and Joseph had no intention of leaving it.

That is, until he was told to go out on a limb.

As he sat securely on his branch, he looked up at the limb God wanted him to climb. He'd never seen one so thin! "That's no place for a man to go!" he said to himself. "There's no place to sit. There's no protection from the weather. And how could you sleep dangling from that quivering twig?" He inched back a bit, leaned against the trunk, and pondered the situation.

Common sense told him not to go out on the limb. "Conceived by the Holy Spirit? Come on!"

Self-defense told him not to do it. "Who will believe me? What will our families think?"

Convenience told him not to do it. "Just when I was hoping to settle down and raise a family."

Pride told him not to do it. "If she expects me to buy a tale like that..."

But God had told him to do it. And that's what bothered him.

It bothered him because he was happy where he was. Life next to the trunk was good. His branch was big enough to allow him to sit in comfort. He was near scores of other branch-sitters and had made some valid contributions to the tree community. After all, didn't he make regular visits to the sick at the North Branch Medical Center? And wasn't he the best tenor in the Treedom Singers Chorale? And what about the class he taught on religious heritage, appropriately entitled "Our Family Tree"? Surely God wouldn't want him to leave. He had…well, you could say that he had roots here.

Besides, he knew the kind of fellow who goes out on a limb. Radical. Extremist. Liberal. Always going overboard. Always stirring the leaves. Guys with their heads full of strange ideas in search of foreign fruit. Why, the stable ones are the ones who know how to stay close to home and leave well enough alone.

I have a feeling some of you can relate to Joseph. You know how he feels, don't you? You've been there. You're smiling because you, too, have been called to go out on a limb a time or two. You know the imbalance that comes from having one foot in your will and one foot in his. You, too, have sunk your fingernails into the bark to get a better grip. You know too well the butterflies that swarm in the pit of your stomach when you realize changes are in the air.

Perhaps changes are in the air right now. Maybe you're in the midst of a decision. It's disrupting, isn't it? You like your branch. You've grown accustomed to it and it to you. And, like Joseph, you've been a pretty good branch-sitter. And then you hear the call. "I need you to go out on the limb and

> …take a stand. Some of the local churches are organizing an anti-pornography campaign. They need some volunteers."
>
> …move. Take your family and move overseas; I have a special work for you."
>
> …forgive. It doesn't matter who hurt who first. What matters is that you go and build the bridge."
>
> …evangelize. That new family down the block? They don't know anyone in town. Go meet them."

> ...sacrifice. The orphanage has a mortgage payment due this month. They can't meet it. Remember the bonus you received last week?"

Regardless of the nature of the call, the consequences are the same: civil war. Though your heart may say yes, your feet say no. Excuses blow as numerously as golden leaves in an autumn wind. "That's not my talent." "It's time for someone else to take charge." "Not now. I'll get to it tomorrow."

But eventually you're left staring at a bare tree and a hard choice: His will or yours?

Joseph chose his. After all, it was really the only option. Joseph knew that the only thing worse than a venture into the unknown was the thought of denying his Master. So, resolute, he grasped the smaller limb. With tight lips and a determined glint in his eye, he placed one hand in front of the other until he dangled in the air with only his faith in God as a safety net.

As things turned out, Joseph's fears were justified. Life wasn't as comfortable as it had been. The limb he grasped was, indeed, a slender one: The Messiah was to be born to Mary and to be raised in his home. He took cold showers for nine months so the baby could be born of a virgin. He had to push away the sheep and clear out the cow patties so his wife would have a place to give birth. He became a fugitive of the law. He spent two years trying to understand Egyptian.

At times that limb must have bounced furiously in the wind. But Joseph just shut his eyes and held on. But you can be sure of one thing. He never regretted it. Sweet was the reward for his courage. One look in the face of that heavenly toddler and he knew he would do it again in a heartbeat.

Have you been called to go out on a limb for God? You can bet it won't be easy. Limb-climbing has never been easy. Ask Joseph. Or, better yet, ask Jesus.

He knows better than anyone the cost of hanging on a tree.

CHAPTER 6

# TWENTY-FIVE QUESTIONS FOR MARY

What was it like watching him pray?

How did he respond when he saw other kids giggling during the service at the synagogue?

When he saw a rainbow, did he ever mention a flood?

Did you ever feel awkward teaching him how he created the world?

When he saw a lamb being led to the slaughter, did he act differently?

Did you ever see him with a distant look on his face as if he were listening to someone you couldn't hear?

How did he act at funerals?

Did the thought ever occur to you that the God to whom you were praying was asleep under your own roof?

Did you ever try to count the stars with him…and succeed?

Did he ever come home with a black eye?

How did he act when he got his first haircut?

Did he have any friends by the name of Judas?

Did he do well in school?

Did you ever scold him?

Did he ever have to ask a question about Scripture?

What do you think he thought when he saw a prostitute offering to the highest bidder the body he made?

Did he ever get angry when someone was dishonest with him?

Did you ever catch him pensively looking at the flesh on his own arm while holding a clod of dirt?

Did he ever wake up afraid?

Who was his best friend?

When someone referred to Satan, how did he act?
Did you ever accidentally call him Father?
What did he and his cousin John talk about as kids?
Did his other brothers and sisters understand what was happening?
Did you ever think, *That's God eating my soup*?

CHAPTER 7

# CHRISTMAS NIGHT

It's Christmas night. The house is quiet. Even the crackle is gone from the fireplace. Warm coals issue a lighthouse glow in the darkened den. Stockings hang empty on the mantle. The tree stands naked in the corner. Christmas cards, tinsel, and memories remind Christmas night of Christmas Day.

It's Christmas night. What a day it has been! Spiced tea. Santa Claus. Cranberry sauce. "Thank you so much." "You shouldn't have!" "Grandma is on the phone." Knee-deep wrapping paper. "It just fits." Flashing cameras.

It's Christmas night. The girls are in bed. Jenna dreams of her talking Big Bird and clutches her new purse. Andrea sleeps in her new Santa pajamas.

It's Christmas night. The tree that only yesterday grew from soil made of gifts, again grows from the Christmas tree stand. Presents are now possessions. Wrapping paper is bagged and in the dumpster. The dishes are washed and leftover turkey awaits next week's sandwiches.

It's Christmas night. The last of the carolers appeared on the ten o'clock news. The last of the apple pie was eaten by my brother-in-law. And the last of the Christmas albums have been stored away having dutifully performed their annual rendition of chestnuts, white Christmases, and red-nosed reindeers.

It's Christmas night.

The midnight hour has chimed and I should be asleep, but I'm awake. I'm kept awake by one stunning thought. The world was different this week. It was temporarily transformed.

The magical dust of Christmas glittered on the cheeks of humanity ever so briefly, reminding us of what is worth having and what we were intended to be. We forgot our compulsion with winning, wooing, and warring. We put away our ladders and ledgers, we hung up our stop-watches and weapons. We stepped off our race tracks and roller coasters and looked outward toward the star of Bethlehem.

It's the season to be jolly because, more than at any other time, we think of him. More than in any other season, his name is on our lips.

And the result? For a few precious hours our heavenly yearnings intermesh and we become a chorus. A ragtag chorus of longshoremen, Boston lawyers, illegal immigrants, housewives, and a thousand other peculiar persons who are banking that Bethlehem's mystery is in reality, a reality. "Come and behold him" we sing, stirring even the sleepiest of shepherds and pointing them toward the Christ-child.

For a few precious hours, he is beheld. Christ the Lord. Those who pass the year without seeing him, suddenly see him. People who have been accustomed to using his name in vain, pause to use it in praise. Eyes, now free of the blinders of self, marvel at his majesty.

All of a sudden he's everywhere.

In the grin of the policeman as he drives the paddy wagon full of presents to the orphanage.

In the twinkle in the eyes of the Taiwanese waiter as he tells of his upcoming Christmas trip to see his children.

In the emotion of the father who is too thankful to finish the dinner table prayer.

He's in the tears of the mother as she welcomes home her son from overseas.

He's in the heart of the man who spent Christmas morning on skid row giving away cold baloney sandwiches and warm wishes.

And he's in the solemn silence of the crowd of shopping mall shoppers as the elementary school chorus sings "Away in a Manger."

Emmanuel. He is with us. God came near.

It's Christmas night. In a few hours the cleanup will begin—lights will come down, trees will be thrown out. Size 36 will be exchanged for size 40, eggnog will be on sale for half price. Soon life will be normal again. December's generosity will become January's payments and the magic will begin to fade.

But for the moment, the magic is still in the air. Maybe that's why I'm still awake. I want to savor the spirit just a bit more. I want to pray that those who beheld him today will look for him next August. And I can't help but linger on one fanciful thought: If he can do so much with such timid prayers lamely offered in December, how much more could he do if we thought of him every day?

CHAPTER 8

# OUT OF THE CARPENTRY SHOP

The heavy door creaked on its hinges as he pushed it open. With a few strides he crossed the silent shop and opened the wooden shutters to a square shaft of sunshine that pierced the darkness, painting a box of daylight on the dirt floor.

He looked around the carpentry shop. He stood a moment in the refuge of the little room that housed so many sweet memories. He balanced the hammer in his hand. He ran his fingers across the sharp teeth of the saw. He stroked the smoothly worn wood of the sawhorse. He had come to say good-bye.

It was time for him to leave. He had heard something that made him know it was time to go. So he came one last time to smell the sawdust and lumber.

Life was peaceful here. Life was so…safe.

Here he had spent countless hours of contentment. On this dirt floor he had played as a toddler while his father worked. Here Joseph had taught him how to grip a hammer. And on this workbench he had built his first chair.

I wonder what he thought as he took one last look around the room. Perhaps he stood for a moment at the workbench looking at the tiny shadows cast by the chisel and shavings. Perhaps he listened as voices from the past filled the air.

"Good job, Jesus."

"Joseph, Jesus—come and eat!"

"Don't worry, sir, we'll get it finished on time. I'll get Jesus to help me."

I wonder if he hesitated. I wonder if his heart was torn. I wonder if he rolled a nail between his thumb and fingers, anticipating the pain.

It was in the carpentry shop that he must have given birth to his thoughts. Here concepts and convictions were woven together to form the fabric of his ministry.

You can almost see the tools of the trade in his words as he spoke. You can see the trueness of a plumb line as he called for moral standards. You can hear the whistle of the plane as he pleads for religion to shave away unnecessary traditions. You can picture the snugness of a dovetail as he demands loyalty in relationships. You can imagine him with a pencil and a ledger as he urges honesty.

It was here that his human hands shaped the wood his divine hands had created. And it was here that his body matured while his spirit waited for the right moment, the right day.

And now that day had arrived.

It must have been difficult to leave. After all, life as a carpenter wasn't bad. It wasn't bad at all. Business was good. The future was bright and his work was enjoyable.

In Nazareth he was known only as Jesus, the son of Joseph. You can be sure he was respected in the community. He was good with his hands. He had many friends. He was a favorite among the children. He could tell a good joke and had a habit of filling the air with contagious laughter.

I wonder if he wanted to stay. "I could do a good job here in Nazareth. Settle down. Raise a family. Be a civic leader."

I wonder because I know he had already read the last chapter. He knew that the feet that would step out of the safe shadow of the carpentry shop would not rest until they'd been pierced and placed on a Roman cross.

You see, he didn't have to go. He had a choice. He could have stayed. He could have kept his mouth shut. He could have ignored the call or at least postponed it. And had he chosen to stay, who would've known? Who would have blamed him?

He could have come back as a man in another era when society wasn't so volatile, when religion wasn't so stale, when people would listen better.

He could have come back when crosses were out of style.

But his heart wouldn't let him. If there was hesitation on the part of his humanity, it was overcome by the compassion of his divinity. His divinity heard the voices. His divinity heard the hopeless cries of the poor, the bitter accusations of the abandoned, the dangling despair of those who are trying to save themselves.

And his divinity saw the faces. Some wrinkled. Some weeping. Some hidden behind veils. Some obscured by fear. Some earnest with searching. Some blank with boredom. From the face of Adam to the face of the infant born somewhere in the world as you read these words, he saw them all.

And you can be sure of one thing. Among the voices that found their way into that carpentry shop in Nazareth was your voice. Your silent prayers uttered on tearstained pillows were heard before they were said. Your deepest questions about death and eternity were answered before they were asked. And your direst need, your need for a Savior, was met before you ever sinned.

And not only did he hear you, he saw you. He saw your face aglow the hour you first knew him. He saw your face in shame the hour you first fell. The same face that looked back at you from this morning's mirror, looked at him. And it was enough to kill him.

He left because of you.

He laid his security down with his hammer. He hung tranquillity on the peg with his nail apron. He closed the window shutters on the sunshine of his youth and locked the door on the comfort and ease of anonymity.

Since he could bear your sins more easily than he could bear the thought of your hopelessness, he chose to leave.

It wasn't easy. Leaving the carpentry shop never has been.

CHAPTER 9

# "JUST CALL ME JESUS"

Many of the names in the Bible that refer to our Lord are nothing less than palatial and august: Son of God, The Lamb of God, The Light of the World, The Resurrection and the Life, The Bright and Morning Star, He that Should Come, Alpha and Omega.

They are phrases that stretch the boundaries of human language in an effort to capture the uncapturable, the grandeur of God. And try as they might to draw as near as they may, they always fall short. Hearing them is somewhat like hearing a Salvation Army Christmas band on the street corner play Handel's *Messiah.* Good try, but it doesn't work. The message is too majestic for the medium.

And such it is with language. The phrase "There are no words to express..." is really the only one that can honestly be applied to God. No names do him justice.

But there is one name which recalls a quality of the Master that bewildered and compelled those who knew him. It reveals a side of him that, when recognized, is enough to make you fall on your face.

It is not too small, nor is it too grand. It is a name that fits like the shoe fit Cinderella's foot.

Jesus.

In the gospels it's his most common name—used almost six hundred times. And a common name it was. Jesus is the Greek form of Joshua, Jeshua, and Jehoshua—all familiar Old Testament names. There were at least five high priests known as Jesus. The writings of the historian Josephus refer to about twenty people called Jesus. The New Testament speaks of Jesus Justus, the friend of Paul,[1] and the sorcerer of Paphos is called Bar-Jesus.[2] Some manuscripts give Jesus as the first name of Barabbas. "Which would you like me to release to you—Jesus Barabbas or Jesus called the Messiah?"[3]

What's the point? Jesus could have been a "Joe." If Jesus came today, his name might have been John or Bob or Jim. Were he here today, it is doubtful he would distance himself with a lofty name like Reverend Holiness Angelic Divinity III. No, when God chose the name his son would carry, he chose a human name.[4] He chose a name so typical that it would appear two or three times on any given class roll.

"The Word became flesh," John said, in other words.

He was touchable, approachable, reachable. And, what's more, he was ordinary. If he were here today you probably wouldn't notice him as he walked through a shopping mall. He wouldn't turn heads by the clothes he wore or the jewelry he flashed.

"Just call me Jesus," you can almost hear him say.

He was the kind of fellow you'd invite to watch the Rams-Giants game at your house. He'd wrestle on the floor with your kids, doze on your couch, and cook steaks on your grill. He'd laugh at your jokes and tell a few of his own. And when you spoke, he'd listen to you as if he had all the time in eternity.

And one thing's for sure, you'd invite him back.

It is worth noting that those who knew him best remembered him as Jesus. The titles Jesus Christ and Lord Jesus are seen only six times. Those who walked with him remembered him not with a title or designation, but with a name—Jesus.

Think about the implications. When God chose to reveal himself to mankind, what medium did he use? A book? No, that was secondary. A church? No. That was consequential. A moral code? No. To limit God's revelation to a cold list of do's and don'ts is as tragic as looking at a Colorado road map and saying that you'd seen the Rockies.

When God chose to reveal himself, he did so (surprise of surprises) through a human body. The tongue that called forth the dead was a human one. The hand that touched the leper had dirt under its nails. The feet upon which the woman wept were calloused and dusty. And his tears...oh, don't miss the tears...they came from a heart as broken as yours or mine ever has been.

"For we do not have a high priest who is unable to sympathize with our weaknesses."[5]

So, people came to him. My, how they came to him! They came at night; they touched him as he walked down the street; they followed him around the sea; they invited him into their homes and placed their children at his feet. Why? Because he refused to be a statue in a cathedral or a priest in an elevated pulpit. He chose instead to be Jesus.

There is not a hint of one person who was afraid to draw near him. There were those who mocked him. There were those who were envious of him. There were those who misunderstood him. There were those who revered him. But there was not one person who considered him too holy, too divine, or too celestial to touch. *There was not one person who was reluctant to approach him for fear of being rejected.*

Remember that.

Remember that the next time you find yourself amazed at your own failures.

Or the next time acidic accusations burn holes in your soul.

Or the next time you see a cold cathedral or hear a lifeless liturgy.

Remember. It is man who creates the distance. It is Jesus who builds the bridge.

"Just call me Jesus."

CHAPTER 10

# WOMEN OF WINTER

## I

The mourners didn't cause him to stop. Nor did the large crowd, or even the body of the dead man on the stretcher. It was the woman—the look on her face and the redness in her eyes. He knew immediately what was happening. It was her son who was being carried out, her only son. And if anyone knows the pain that comes from losing your only son, God does.

So he did it; he went into action. "Don't cry" he told the mother. "Arise!" he told the boy. The dead man spoke, the devil ran, and the people were reminded of this truth: For those who know the Author of Life, death is nothing more than Satan's dead-man's-bluff.[1]

## II

His plan was to catch a few winks while the boys went to town for food. And what better place to rest than a well at noon. No one comes for water at this hour. So he sat down, stretched his arms, and leaned against the wall of the well. But his nap was soon interrupted. He opened one eye just wide enough to see her trudging up the trail with a heavy jar on her shoulder. Behind her came half a dozen kids, each one looking like a different daddy.

She didn't have to say a word. Her life story was written in the wrinkles on her face. The wounds of five broken romances were gaping and festered. Each man who had left her had taken a piece of her heart. Now she wasn't sure there was anything left.

"And the man you now live with won't even give you his name." Jesus said it for her. He understood her pain too well. Far more than five men had broken commitments to him.

Silently the Divine Surgeon reached into his kit and pulled out a needle of faith and a thread of hope. In the shade of Jacob's well he stitched her wounded soul back together. "There will come a day..." he whispered.[2]

## III

By the time she got to Jesus, she had nothing left. The doctors had taken her last dime. The diagnosis had stolen her last hope. And the hemorrhage had robbed her of her last drop of energy. She had no more money, no more friends, and no more options. With the end of her rope in one hand and a wing and a prayer in her heart, she shoved her way through the crowd.

When her hand touched his garment a transfusion occurred. He let it go out and she let it go in.

It didn't bother Jesus that the woman came to him as a last resort. To him it mattered only that she came. He knows that with some of us it takes a lot of reality to snap us to our senses, so he doesn't keep a time clock. Those who scramble in at quitting time get the same wage as those who beat the morning whistle. I guess that's what makes grace, grace.[3]

Three women. One bereaved. One rejected. One dying. All alone.

Alone in the winter of life.

Though we don't know what they looked like, it would be fair to assume they had passed the peak of their desirability. The only heads that turned as they walked down the street were heads shaking with pity. One of the three was widowed and childless; another had lost her innocence six bedrooms back; and the third was broke, desperate, and dying.

Had Jesus ignored them, who would have noticed? In a culture where women were only a grade or two above farm animals no one would've thought any less had he walked silently past the funeral or closed his eyes and leaned back against the well or ignored the tug on his robe. After all, they were only women!

Worn,<br>
    wrinkled,<br>
        weary women.<br>
            Winter women.

Let them alone, Jesus, one could reason. Find someone with a bit of springtime about them.

By the world's standards these three could give nothing in return. They'd served their purpose: borne their children, fed their families, pleased their men. Now it was time to push them out into the cold until they died, making room for the young and spotless.

That's where Jesus found them. Shivering in the icy sleet of uselessness.

The raw winter of life.

Sound familiar? Sure it does. We have our own people of winter. People who for the lack of good looks or sufficient earning power wander around like porcupines at a picnic, unwanted and unapproachable.

Hard to believe?

Visit a high school sometime and look for the teenagers already feeling the chilly winds of rejection. They are easy to find. They're the ones with acne, or greasy hair, or holes in their shoes; they sit alone at lunch and stay at home on weekends. They orbit around the class stars, longing for acceptance yet increasingly convinced they don't deserve it.

Or try Miami Beach. I don't mean the north beach where tourists pay $150 a day to get sunburned. I mean the south beach, a city deliberately built for the exhausted. Watch them shuffle aged feet down the sidewalk. They have come to their burial ground. They have fulfilled their function and now fill their days with dominoes, dogs, and doctor visits. They fill their nights with dreams of the granddaughter who might come next Christmas. And though the Gold Coast is warm, in their souls blow the winds of winter.

Or consider the unborn. Every twenty seconds one is taken from the warmth of the womb and cast into the cold lake of selfishness. In spite of the clinical phrases used to make the act more palatable—"termination of pregnancy" rather than "abortion," "fetus" instead of "unborn child," "conceptus" as opposed to "baby"—the act is deplorable. The bottom line is still a denial of the inherent value of a human being.

The paragraphs could go on and on. Paragraphs about quadriplegics, AIDS victims, or the terminally ill. Single parents. Alcoholics. Divorcées. The blind. All are social outcasts. Lepers, mutations. All, to one degree or another, shunned by the "normal world."

Society doesn't know what to do with them. And, sadly, even the Church doesn't know what to do with them. They often would find a warmer reception at the corner bar than in a Sunday school class.

But Jesus would find a place for them. He would find a place for them because he cares. And he cares unconditionally.

No, no one would have blamed Jesus for ignoring the three women. To have turned his head would have been much easier, less controversial, and not nearly as risky. But God, who made them, couldn't do that. And we, who follow him, can't either.

CHAPTER 11

# WHEN GOD SIGHED

Two days ago I read a word in the Bible that has since taken up residence in my heart.

To be honest, I didn't quite know what to do with it. It's only one word, and not a very big one at that. When I ran across the word, (which, by the way, is exactly what happened; I was running through the passage and this word came out of nowhere and bounced me like a speed bump) I didn't know what to do with it. I didn't have any hook to hang it on or category to file it under.

It was an enigmatic word in an enigmatic passage. But now, forty-eight hours later, I have found a place for it, a place all its own. My, what a word it is. Don't read it unless you don't mind changing your mind, because this little word might move your spiritual furniture around a bit.

Look at the passage with me.

> Then Jesus left the vicinity of Tyre and went through Sidon, down to the Sea of Galilee and into the region of the Decapolis. There some people brought a man to him who was deaf and could hardly talk, and they begged him to place his hand on the man.
>
> After he took him aside, away from the crowd, Jesus put his fingers into the man's ears. Then he spit and touched the man's tongue. He looked up to heaven and with a deep sigh said to him, "*Ephphatha!*" (which means, "Be opened!"). At this, the man's ears were opened, his tongue was loosened and he began to speak plainly.[1]

Quite a passage, isn't it?

Jesus is presented with a man who is deaf and has a speech impediment. Perhaps he stammered. Maybe he spoke with a lisp. Perhaps, because of his deafness, he never learned to articulate words properly.

Jesus, refusing to exploit the situation, took the man aside. He looked him in the face. Knowing it would be useless to talk, he explained what he was about to do through gestures. He spat and touched the man's tongue, telling him that whatever restricted his speech was about to be removed. He touched his ears. They, for the first time, were about to hear.

But before the man said a word or heard a sound, Jesus did something I never would have anticipated.

He sighed.

I might have expected a clap or a song or a prayer. Even a "Hallelujah!" or a brief lesson might have been appropriate. But the Son of God did none of these. Instead, he paused, looked into heaven, and sighed. From the depths of his being came a rush of emotion that said more than words.

*Sigh.* The word seemed out of place.

I'd never thought of God as one who sighs. I'd thought of God as one who commands. I'd thought of God as one who weeps. I'd thought of God as one who called forth the dead with a command or created the universe with a word…but a God who sighs?

Perhaps this phrase caught my eye because I do my share of sighing.

I sighed yesterday when I visited a lady whose invalid husband had deteriorated so much he didn't recognize me. He thought I was trying to sell him something.

I sighed when the dirty-faced, scantily dressed, six-year-old girl in the grocery store asked me for some change.

And I sighed today listening to a husband tell how his wife won't forgive him.

No doubt you've done your share of sighing.

If you have teenagers, you've probably sighed. If you've tried to resist temptation, you've probably sighed. If you've had your motives questioned or your best acts of love rejected, you have been forced to take a deep breath and let escape a painful sigh.

I realize there exists a sigh of relief, a sigh of expectancy, and even a sigh of joy. But that isn't the sigh described in Mark 7. The sigh described is a hybrid of frustration and sadness. It lies somewhere between a fit of anger and a burst of tears.

The apostle Paul spoke of this sighing. Twice he said that Christians will sigh as long as we are on earth and long for heaven. The creation sighs as if she were giving birth. Even the Spirit sighs as he interprets our prayers.[2]

All these sighs come from the same anxiety; a recognition of pain that was never intended, or of hope deferred.

Man was not created to be separated from his creator; hence he sighs, longing for home. The creation was never intended to be inhabited by evil; hence she sighs, yearning for the Garden. And conversations with God were never intended to depend on a translator; hence the Spirit groans on our behalf, looking to a day when humans will see God face to face.

And when Jesus looked into the eyes of Satan's victim, the only appropriate thing to do was sigh. "It was never intended to be this way," the sigh said. "Your ears weren't made to be deaf, your tongue wasn't made to stumble." The imbalance of it all caused the Master to languish.

So, I found a place for the word. You might think it strange, but I placed it beside the word *comfort,* for in an indirect way, God's pain is our comfort.

And in the agony of Jesus lies our hope. Had he not sighed, had he not felt the burden for what was not intended, we would be in a pitiful condition. Had he simply chalked it all up to the inevitable or washed his hands of the whole stinking mess, what hope would we have?

But he didn't. That holy sigh assures us that God still groans for his people. He groans for the day when all sighs will cease, when what was intended to be will be.

CHAPTER 12

# THE QUESTION FOR THE CANYON'S EDGE

*"How was the night?" asked the nurse.*

*The young man's weary eyes answered the question before his lips could. It had been long and hard. Vigils always are. But even more so when they are with your own father.*

*"He didn't wake up."*

*The son sat by the bed and held the bony hand that had so often held his own. He was afraid to release it for fear that doing so might allow the man he so dearly loved to tumble over the brink. He had held it all night as the two stood on the canyon's edge, aware of the final step that was only hours away.*

*With words painted black with confusion, he summarized the fears that had been his companions during the darkness. "I know it has to happen," the son yearned, looking at his father's ashen face; "I just don't know why."*

The canyon of death.

It is a desolate canyon. The dry ground is cracked and lifeless. A blistering sun heats the wind that moans eerily and stings mercilessly. Tears burn and words come slowly as visitors to the canyon are forced to stare into the ravine. The bottom of the crevice is invisible, the other side unreachable. You can't help but wonder what is hidden in the darkness. And you can't help but long to leave.

Have you been there? Have you been called to stand at the thin line that separates the living from the dead? Have you lain awake at night listening to machines pumping air in and out of your lungs? Have you watched sickness corrode and atrophy the body of a friend? Have you lingered behind at the cemetery long after the others have left, gazing in disbelief at the metal casket that contains the body that contained the soul of the one you can't believe is gone?

If so, then this canyon is not unfamiliar to you. You've heard the lonesome whistle of the winds. You've heard the painful questions Why? What for? ricochet answerless off the canyon walls. And you've kicked loose rocks off the edge and listened for the sound of their crashing, which never comes.

*The young father crushed the cigarette into the plastic ashtray. He was alone in the hospital waiting room. How long will it take? It all had happened so quickly! First came the news from the hospital, then the frantic drive to the emergency room and then the explanation of the nurse. "Your son was hit by a car. He has some serious head wounds. He is in surgery. The doctors are doing the best they can."*

*Another cigarette. "My God." The words of the father were almost audible. "He's only five years old."*

Standing on the edge of the canyon draws all of life into perspective. What matters and what doesn't are easily distinguished. Above the canyon wall no one is concerned about salaries or positions. No one asks about the car you drive or what part of town you live in. As aging humans stand beside this ageless chasm, all the games and disguises of life seem sadly silly.

*It happened in one fiery instant.*

*"Where is the bird?" shouted a space engineer at Cape Canaveral.*

*"Oh, my God!" cried a teacher from the viewing stands nearby. "Don't let happen what I think just happened."*

*Confusion and horror raced through the nation as we stood on the edge of the canyon watching seven of our best disintegrate before our eyes as the shuttle exploded into a white and orange fireball.*

*Once again we were reminded that even at our technological finest, we are still frighteningly frail.*

It is possible that I'm addressing someone who is walking the canyon wall. Someone you love dearly has been called into the unknown and you are alone. Alone with your fears and alone with your doubts. If this is the case, please read the rest of this piece very carefully. Look carefully at the scene described in John 11.

In this scene there are two people: Martha and Jesus. And for all practical purposes they are the only two people in the universe.

Her words were full of despair. "If you had been here..." She stares into the Master's face with confused eyes. She'd been strong long enough; now it hurt too badly. Lazarus was dead. Her brother was gone. And the one man who could have made a difference didn't. He hadn't even made it for the burial. Something about death makes us accuse God of betrayal. "If God were here there would be no death!" we claim.

You see, if God is God anywhere, he has to be God in the face of death. Pop psychology can deal with depression. Pep talks can deal with pessimism. Prosperity can handle hunger. But only God can deal with our ultimate dilemma—death. And only the God of the Bible has dared to stand on the canyon's edge and offer an answer. He has to be God in the face of death. If not, he is not God anywhere.

Jesus wasn't angry at Martha. Perhaps it was his patience that caused her to change her tone from frustration to earnestness. "Even now God will give you whatever you ask."

Jesus then made one of those claims that place him either on the throne or in the asylum: "Your brother will rise again."

Martha misunderstood. (Who wouldn't have?) "I know he will rise again in the resurrection at the last day."

That wasn't what Jesus meant. Don't miss the context of the next words. Imagine the setting: Jesus has intruded on the enemy's turf; he's standing in Satan's territory, Death Canyon. His stomach turns as he smells the sulfuric stench of the ex-angel, and he winces as he hears the oppressed wails of those trapped in the prison. Satan has been here. He has violated one of God's creations.

With his foot planted on the serpent's head, Jesus speaks loudly enough that his words echo off the canyon walls.

"I am the resurrection and the life. He who believes in me will live, even though he dies; and whoever lives and believes in me will never die" (John 11:25).

It is a hinge point in history. A chink has been found in death's armor. The keys to the halls of hell have been claimed. The buzzards scatter and the scorpions scurry as Life confronts death—and wins! The wind stops. A cloud blocks the sun and a bird chirps in the distance while a humiliated snake slithers between the rocks and disappears into the ground.

The stage has been set for a confrontation at Calvary.

But Jesus isn't through with Martha. With eyes locked on hers he asks the greatest question found in Scripture, a question meant as much for you and me as for Martha.

"Do you believe this?"

Wham! There it is. The bottom line. The dimension that separates Jesus from a thousand gurus and prophets who have come down the pike. The question that drives any responsible listener to absolute obedience to or total rejection of the Christian faith.

"Do you believe this?"

Let the question sink into your heart for a minute. Do you believe that a young, penniless itinerant is larger than your death? Do you truly believe that death is nothing more than an entrance ramp to a new highway?

"Do you believe this?"

Jesus didn't pose this query as a topic for discussion in Sunday schools. It was never intended to be dealt with while basking in the stained glass sunlight or while seated on padded pews.

No. This is a canyon question. A question which makes sense only during an all-night vigil or in the stillness of smoke-filled waiting rooms. A question that makes sense when all of our props, crutches, and costumes are taken away. For then we must face ourselves as we really are: rudderless humans tailspinning toward disaster. And we are forced to see him for what he claims to be: our only hope.

As much out of desperation as inspiration, Martha said yes. As she studied the tan face of that Galilean carpenter, something told her she'd probably never get closer to the truth than she was right now. So she gave him her hand and let him lead her away from the canyon wall.

"I am the resurrection and the life.... Do you believe this?"

CHAPTER 13

# A TALE OF TWO TREES

## I

Formless masses. Floating. Disconnected.

Divine artist. Earthly dream.

Light! Sun rays piercing through jungle trees. Sunsets volcanic with explosions of gold. Soft sheets of moonlight soothing a weary ocean.

Beings! Snorting. Flying. Splashing. Bleating. Gnawing. Clawing. Digging.

Sound! Horse's hoof beats. Cawing crows. Hyena laughter. Cannoning thunder. Chirping chicks. Rat-tat-tatting rain.

Nothingness converted.

Then silence…as an unseen Sculptor molds mud and dust. Lions motionlessly watching. Sparrows perched, peering downward. Clouds hovering. Inquisitive kangaroos. Curious caribou. Snooping centipedes.

"What's he making?"

"An animal?"

Giraffes peeking through leaves. Squirrels chattering gossip. Pausing. Wondering. Gibbering.

"A mountain?"

A sudden breeze, surprisingly warm, whistles through the leaves scattering dust from the lifeless form. And with the breath of fresh air comes the difference. Winging on the warm wind is his image. Laughter is laid in the sculpted cheeks. A reservoir of tears is stored in the soul. A sprinkling of twinkle for the eyes. Poetry for the spirit. Logic. Loyalty. Like leaves on an autumn breeze, they float and land and are absorbed. His gifts become a part of him.

His Majesty smiles at his image. "It is good."

The eyes open.

Oneness. Creator and created walking on the river bank. Laughter. Purity. Innocent joy. Life unending.

Then the tree.

The struggle. The snake. The lie. The enticement. Heart torn, lured. Soul drawn to pleasure, to independence, to importance. Inner agony. Whose will?

The choice. Death of innocence. Entrance of death. The fall.

Tear stains mingling with fruit-stains.

## II

The Quest.

"Abram, you will father a nation! And Abram—tell the people I love them."

"Moses, you will deliver my people! And Moses—tell the people I love them."

"Joshua, you will lead the chosen ones! And Joshua—tell the people I love them."

"David, you will reign over the people! And David—tell the people I love them."

"Jeremiah, you will bear tidings of bondage! But Jeremiah, remind my children, remind my children that I love them."

Altars. Sacrifices. Rebelling. Returning. Reacting. Repenting. Romance. Tablets. Judges. Pillars. Bloodshed. Wars. Kings. Giants. Law. Hezekiah. Nehemiah. Hosea… God watching, never turning, ever loving, ever yearning for the Garden again.

## III

Empty throne. Spirit descending. Hushed angels.

A girl…
a womb…
an egg.

The same Divine Artist again forms a body. This time his own. Fleshly divinity. Skin layered on spirit. Omnipotence with hair. Toenails. Knuckles. Molars. Kneecaps. Once again he walks with man. Yet the Garden is now thorny. Thorns that cut, thorns that poison, thorns that remain lodged, leaving bitter wounds. Disharmony. Sickness. Betrayal. Fear. Guilt.

The lions no longer pause. The clouds no longer hover. The birds scatter too quickly. Disharmony. Competition. Blindness.

And once again, a tree.

Once again the struggle. The snake. The enticement. Heart torn, lured. Once again the question, "Whose will?"

Then the choice. Tear stains mingle with bloodstains. Relationship restored. Bridge erected.

Once again he smiles. "It is good."

> For just as death came by means of a man, in the same way the rising from death comes by means of a man. For just as all men die because of their union to Adam, in the same way all will be raised to life because of their union to Christ.[1]

CHAPTER 14

# NO ACCIDENT

It has all the ingredients of a good sermon illustration.

It's emotional. It's dramatic. And it's a story that'll break your heart.

Heaven only knows how many times preachers have used it.

There's only one problem. It's not accurate.

Maybe you've heard it.

It's the story of an engineer who operated a drawbridge across a mighty river. With a control panel of levers and switches, he set into motion a monstrous set of gears that either lifted the bridge for the river traffic or closed it for the oncoming train.

One day he took his young son to work with him. The fascinated boy hurled question after question at his dad. It was not until the span had opened to allow the passage of a ship that the father noticed the questions had ceased and his son had left the room. He looked out the window of his control cabin and saw the young boy climbing on the teeth of the gears. As he hurried toward the machinery to get his son, he heard the whistle of an approaching train.

His pulse quickened. If he closed the bridge there would be no time to retrieve his son. He had to make a choice. Either his son would be killed or a trainload of innocent passengers would be killed. A horrible dilemma mandated a horrible decision. The engineer knew what he had to do. He reached for the lever.

A powerful story, isn't it? It's often used to describe the sacrifice of Christ. And it is not without its parallels. It's true that God could not save man without killing his son. The heart of God the Father did twist in grief as he slammed the gears of death down on Jesus. And it's sad, yet true, that the innocent have whizzed by the scene of the crime oblivious to the sacrifice that has just saved them from certain death.

But there is one inference in the story that's woefully in need of correction.

Read this quote from the first sermon ever preached about the cross and see if you can find the revealing phrase.

> Men of Israel, listen to this: Jesus of Nazareth was a man accredited by God to you by miracles, wonders and signs, which God did among you through him, as you yourselves know. This man was handed over to you by God's set purpose and foreknowledge; and you, with the help of wicked men, put him to death by nailing him to the cross.[1]

Did you see it? It's the solemn phrase in the paragraph. It's the statement that rings of courage, the one with roots that extend back to eternity. It is the phrase which, perhaps as much as any in the Bible, describes the real price God paid to adopt you.

Which phrase? "God's set purpose and foreknowledge." The Revised Standard Version calls it "the definite plan and foreknowledge of God." Today's English Version translates the phrase, "In accordance with his own plan." Regardless how you phrase it, the truth is ever so sobering: The cross was no accident.

Jesus' death was not the result of a panicking, cosmological engineer. The cross wasn't a tragic surprise. Calvary was not a knee-jerk response to a world plummeting towards destruction. It wasn't a patch-job or a stop-gap measure. The death of the Son of God was anything but an unexpected peril.

No, it was part of a plan. It was a calculated choice. "It was the LORD's will to crush him."[2] The cross was drawn into the original blueprint. It was written into the script. The moment the forbidden fruit touched the lips of Eve, the shadow of a cross appeared on the horizon. And between that moment and the moment the man with the mallet placed the spike against the wrist of God, a master plan was fulfilled.

What does that mean? It means Jesus planned his own sacrifice.

It means Jesus intentionally planted the tree from which his cross would be carved.

It means he willingly placed the iron ore in the heart of the earth from which the nails would be cast.

It means he voluntarily placed his Judas in the womb of a woman.

It means Christ was the one who set in motion the political machinery that would send Pilate to Jerusalem.

And it also means he didn't have to do it—but he did.

It was no accident—would that it had been! Even the cruelest of criminals is spared the agony of having his death sentence read to him before his life even begins.

But Jesus was born crucified. Whenever he became conscious of who he was, he also became conscious of what he had to do. The cross-shaped shadow could always be seen. And the screams of hell's imprisoned could always be heard.

This explains the glint of determination on his face as he turned to go to Jerusalem for the last time. He was on his death march.[3]

This explains the resoluteness in the words, "The reason my Father loves me is that I lay down my life—only to take it up again. No one takes it from me, but I lay it down of my own accord."[4]

It explains the enigmatic question, "Does this offend you? What if you see the Son of Man ascend to where he was before!"[5]

The cross explains...

Why he told the Pharisees that the "goal" of his life would be fulfilled only on the third day after his death.[6]

The mysterious appearance of Moses and Elijah on the Mount of Transfiguration to discuss his "departure."[7] They'd come to offer one last word of encouragement.

Why John the Baptist introduced Jesus to the crowds as the "Lamb of God, who takes away the sin of the world!"[8]

Maybe it's why he tore the grass out by the roots in Gethsemane. He knew the hell he'd endure for saying, "Thy will be done."

Maybe the cross was why he so loved children. They represented the very thing he would have to give: Life.

It adds gravity to his prophecies, "I lay down my life for the sheep."[9] "Jesus began to explain to his disciples that he must go to Jerusalem and suffer many things at the hands of elders, chief priests and teachers of the law, and that he must be killed and on the third day be raised to life."[10]

The reference to the rejected stone,[11] the anointing for burial,[12] the dismissal of Judas from the Last Supper:[13] All of these incidents take on a sobering dimension when the imminence of the cross is considered. Our Master lived a three-dimensional life. He had as clear a view of the future as he did of the present and the past.

This is why the ropes used to tie his hands and the soldiers used to lead him to the cross were unnecessary. They were incidental. Had they not been there, had there been no trial, no Pilate and no crowd, the very same crucifixion would have occurred. Had Jesus been forced to nail himself to the cross, he would have done it. For it was not the soldiers who killed him, nor the screams of the mob: It was his devotion to us.

So call it what you wish: An act of grace. A plan of redemption. A martyr's sacrifice. But whatever you call it, don't call it an accident. It was anything but that.

CHAPTER 15

# REDISCOVERING AMAZEMENT

*"I am with you always..."*
MATTHEW 28:20

From where I write I can see several miracles.

White-crested waves slap the beach with rhythmic regularity. One after the other the rising swells of salt water gain momentum, humping, rising, then standing to salute the beach before crashing onto the sand. How many billions of times has this simple mystery repeated itself since time began?

In the distance lies a miracle of colors—twins of blue. The ocean-blue of the Atlantic encounters the pale blue of the sky, separated only by the horizon, stretched like a taut wire between two poles.

Also within my eyesight are the two bookends of life. A young mother pushes a baby in a carriage, both recent participants with God in the miracle of birth. They pass a snowy-haired, stooped old gentleman seated on a bench, a victim of life's thief—age. (I wonder if he is aware of the curtain closing on his life.)

Behind them are three boys kicking a soccer ball on the beach. With effortless skill they coordinate countless muscles and reflexes, engage and disengage perfectly designed joints...all to do one task—move a ball in the sand.

Miracles. Divine miracles.

These are miracles because they are mysteries. Scientifically explainable? Yes. Reproducible? To a degree.

But still they are mysteries. Events that stretch beyond our understanding and find their origins in another realm. They are every bit as divine as divided seas, walking cripples, and empty tombs.

And they are as much a reminder of God's presence as were the walking lame, fleeing demons, and silenced storms. They are miracles. They are signs. They are testimonies. They are instantaneous incarnations. They remind us of the same truth: The unseen is now visible. The distant has drawn near. His Majesty has come to be seen. And he is in the most common of earth's corners.

In fact, it is the normality not the uniqueness of God's miracles that causes them to be so staggering. Rather than shocking the globe with an occasional demonstration of deity, God has opted to display his power daily. Proverbially. Pounding waves. Prism-cast colors. Birth, death, life. We are surrounded by miracles. God is throwing testimonies at us like fireworks, each one exploding, "God is! God is!"

The psalmist marveled at such holy handiwork. "Where can I go from your Spirit?" he questioned with delight. "Where can I flee from your presence? If I go up to the heavens, you are there; if I make my bed in the depths, you are there."[1]

We wonder, with so many miraculous testimonies around us, how we could escape God. But somehow we do. We live in an art gallery of divine creativity and yet are content to gaze only at the carpet.

Or what is pathetically worse, we demand *more.* More signs. More proof. More hat tricks. As if God were some vaudeville magician we could summon for a dollar.

How have we grown so deaf? How have we grown so immune to awesomeness? Why are we so reluctant to be staggered or thunderstruck?

Perhaps the frequency of the miracles blinds us to their beauty. After all, what spice is there in a springtime or a tree blossom? Don't the seasons come every year? Aren't there countless seashells just like this one?

Bored, we say Ho-hum and replace the remarkable with the regular, the unbelievable with the anticipated. Science and statistics wave their unmagic wand across the face of life, squelching the oohs and aahs and replacing them with formulas and figures.

Would you like to see Jesus? Do you dare be an eyewitness of His Majesty? Then rediscover amazement.

The next time you hear a baby laugh or see an ocean wave, take note. Pause and listen as His Majesty whispers ever so gently, "I'm here."

CHAPTER 16

# HOPE

It's one of the most compelling narratives in all of Scripture. So fascinating is the scene, in fact, that Luke opted to record it in detail. Two disciples are walking down the dusty road to the village of Emmaus. Their talk concerns the crucified Jesus. Their words come slowly, trudging in cadence with the dirge-like pace of their feet.

"I can hardly believe it. He's gone."

"What do we do now?"

"It's Peter's fault, he shouldn't have..."

Just then a stranger comes up from behind and says, "I'm sorry, but I couldn't help overhearing you. Who are you discussing?"

They stop and turn. Other travelers make their way around them as the three stand in silence. Finally one of them asks, "Where have you been the last few days? Haven't you heard about Jesus of Nazareth?" And he continues to tell what has happened.[1]

This scene fascinates me—two sincere disciples telling how the last nail has been driven in Israel's coffin. God, in disguise, listens patiently, his wounded hands buried deeply in his robe. He must have been touched at the faithfulness of this pair. Yet he also must have been a bit chagrined. He had just gone to hell and back to give heaven to earth, and these two were worried about the political situation of Israel.

"But we had hoped that he was the one who was going to redeem Israel."

*But we had hoped...* How often have you heard a phrase like that?

"We were hoping the doctor would release him."

"I had hoped to pass the exam."

"We had hoped the surgery would get all the tumor."

"I thought the job was in the bag."

Words painted gray with disappointment. What we wanted didn't come. What came, we didn't want. The result? Shattered hope. The foundation of our world trembles.

We trudge up the road to Emmaus dragging our sandals in the dust, wondering what we did to deserve such a plight. "What kind of God would let me down like this?"

And yet, so tear-filled are our eyes and so limited is our perspective that God could be the fellow walking next to us and we wouldn't know it.

You see, the problem with our two heavy-hearted friends was not a lack of faith, but a lack of vision. Their petitions were limited to what they could imagine—an earthly kingdom. Had God answered their prayer, had he granted their hope, the Seven-Day War would have started two thousand years earlier and Jesus would have spent the next forty years training his apostles to be cabinet members. You have to wonder if God's most merciful act is his refusal to answer some of our prayers.

We are not much different than burdened travelers, are we? We roll in the mud of self-pity in the very shadow of the cross. We piously ask for his will and then have the audacity to pout if everything doesn't go our way. If we would just remember the heavenly body that awaits us, we'd stop complaining that he hasn't healed this earthly one.

Our problem is not so much that God doesn't give us what we hope for as it is that we don't know the right thing for which to hope. (You may want to read that sentence again.)

Hope is not what you expect; it is what you would never dream. It is a wild, improbable tale with a pinch-me-I'm-dreaming ending. It's Abraham adjusting his bifocals so he can see not his grandson, but his son. It's Moses standing in the promised land not with Aaron or Miriam at his side, but with Elijah and the transfigured Christ. It's Zechariah left speechless at the sight of his wife Elizabeth, gray-headed and pregnant. And it is the two Emmaus-bound pilgrims reaching out to take a piece of bread only to see that the hands from which it is offered are pierced.

Hope is not a granted wish or a favor performed; no, it is far greater than that. It is a zany, unpredictable dependence on a God who loves to surprise us out of our socks and be there in the flesh to see our reaction.

CHAPTER 17

# ETERNAL INSTANTS

We played every game we knew. We ran up and down the hall. We played "find me" behind the couch. We bounced the beach ball off each other's heads. We wrestled, played tag, and danced. It was a big evening for Mom, Dad, and little Jenna. We were having so much fun that we ignored the bedtime hour and turned off the TV. And if the storm hadn't hit, who knows how late we would have played.

But the storm hit. Rain pattered, then tapped, then slapped against the windows. The winds roared in off the Atlantic and gushed through the nearby mountains with such force that all the power went off. The adjacent valley acted as a funnel, hosing wind and rain on the city.

We all went into the bedroom and laid on the bed. In the darkness we listened to the divine orchestra. Electricity danced in the sky like a conductor's baton summoning the deep kettle drums of thunder.

I sensed it as we were lying on the bed. It blew over me mixed with the sweet fragrance of fresh rain. My wife was lying silently at my side. Jenna was using my stomach for her pillow. She, too, was quiet. Our second child, only a month from birth, rested within the womb of her mother. They must have sensed it, for no one spoke. It entered our presence as if introduced by God himself. And no one dared stir for fear it leave prematurely.

What was it? An eternal instant.

An instant in time that had no time. A picture that froze in midframe, demanding to be savored. A minute that refused to die after sixty seconds. A moment that was lifted off the timeline and amplified into a forever so all the angels could witness its majesty.

An eternal instant.

A moment that reminds you of the treasures surrounding you. Your home. Your peace of mind. Your health. A moment that tenderly rebukes you for spending so much time on temporal preoccupations such as savings accounts, houses, and punctuality. A moment that can bring a mist to the manliest of eyes and perspective to the darkest life.

Eternal instants have dotted history.

It was an eternal instant when the Creator smiled and said, "It is good." It was a timeless moment when Abraham pleaded for mercy from the God of mercy, "But if there are just ten faithful." It was a moment without time when Noah pushed open the rain-soaked hatch and breathed in the clean air. And it was a moment in the "fullness of time" when a carpenter, some smelly shepherds, and an exhausted young mother stood in silent awe at the sight of the infant in the manger.

Eternal instants. You've had them. We all have.

Sharing a porch swing on a summer evening with your grandchild.

Seeing her face in the glow of a candle.

Putting your arm into your husband's as you stroll through the golden leaves and breathe the brisk autumn air.

Listening to your six-year-old thank God for everything from goldfish to Grandma.

Such moments are necessary because they remind us that everything is okay. The King is still on the throne and life is still worth living. Eternal instants remind us that love is still the greatest possession and the future is nothing to fear.

The next time an instant in your life begins to be eternal, let it. Put your head back on the pillow and soak it in. Resist the urge to cut it short. Don't interrupt the silence or shatter the solemnity. You are, in a very special way, on holy ground.

CHAPTER 18

# WHAT DO YOU SEE?

*"Anyone who has seen me has seen the Father."*
JOHN 14:9

Should a man see only popularity, he becomes a mirror, reflecting whatever needs to be reflected to gain acceptance. Though in vogue, he is vague. Though in style, he is stodgy. Personal convictions change with the seasons. Individual beliefs come in all colors, each for a different night of the week. He's a puppet on a thousand strings. He's a singer of a hundred songs, with no song of his own. His appearance changes to fit the setting so often that he forgets who he set out to be. He is everyone and no one.

Should a man see only power, he becomes a wolf—prowling, hunting, and stalking the elusive game. Recognition is his prey and people are his prizes. His quest is endless. There is always another world to conquer or another person to control. As a result, he who sees only power is degraded to an animal, an insatiable scavenger controlled not by a will from within but by lurings from without.

Should a man see only pleasure, he becomes a carnival thrill-seeker, alive only in bright lights, wild rides, and titillating entertainment. With lustful fever he races from ride to ride, satisfying his insatiable passion for sensations only long enough to look for another. Ferris wheels of romance. Haunted houses of eroticism. Hammer rides of danger and excitement. Long after the crowd is gone he can still be found on the carnival grounds rummaging through empty boxes of popcorn and sticky cones that held the cotton candy. He is driven by passion, willing to sell his soul if need be for one more rush, one more race of the pulse, one more sideshow that will take him away from the real world of promises broken and commitments to keep.

Seekers of popularity, power, and pleasure. The end result is the same: painful unfulfillment.

Only in seeing his Maker does a man truly become man. For in seeing his Creator man catches a glimpse of what he was intended to be. He who would see his God would then see the reason for death and the purpose of time. Destiny? Tomorrow? Truth? All are questions within the reach of the man who knows his source.

It is in seeing Jesus that man sees his Source.

PART TWO

# OUR IMITATION

*A student…*
*who is fully trained*
*will be like his teacher.*

LUKE 6:40

CHAPTER 19

# HE FORGOT

I was thanking the Father today for his mercy. I began listing the sins he'd forgiven. One by one I thanked God for forgiving my stumbles and tumbles. My motives were pure and my heart was thankful, but my understanding of God was wrong. It was when I used the word *remember* that it hit me.

"Remember the time I..." I was about to thank God for another act of mercy. But I stopped. Something was wrong. The word *remember* seemed displaced. It was an off-key note in a sonata, a misspelled word in a poem. It was a baseball game in December. It didn't fit. "Does he remember?"

Then *I* remembered. I remembered his words. "And I will remember their sins no more."[1]

Wow! Now, *that* is a remarkable promise.

God doesn't just forgive, he forgets. He erases the board. He destroys the evidence. He burns the microfilm. He clears the computer.

He doesn't remember my mistakes. For all the things he does do, this is one thing he refuses to do. He refuses to keep a list of my wrongs. When I ask for forgiveness he doesn't pull out a clipboard and say, "But I've already forgiven him for that five hundred and sixteen times."

He doesn't remember.

"As far as the east is from the west, so far has he removed our transgressions from us."[2]

"I will be merciful toward their iniquities."[3]

"Even if you are stained as red as crimson, I can make you white as wool!"[4]

No, he doesn't remember. But I do, you do. You still remember. You're like me. You still remember what you did before you changed. In the cellar of your heart lurk the ghosts of yesterday's sins. Sins you've confessed; errors of which you've repented; damage you've done your best to repair.

And though you're a different person, the ghosts still linger. Though you've locked the basement door, they still haunt you. They float to meet you, spooking your soul and robbing your joy. With wordless whispers they remind you of moments when you forgot whose child you were.

That horrid lie.

That business trip you took away from home, that took you so far away from home.

The time you exploded in anger.

Those years spent in the hollow of Satan's hand.

That day you were needed, but didn't respond.

That date.

That jealousy.

That habit.

Poltergeists from yesterday's pitfalls. Spiteful specters that slyly suggest, "Are you really forgiven? Sure, God forgets most of our mistakes, but do you think he could actually forget the time you..."

As a result, your spiritual walk has a slight limp. Oh, you're still faithful. You still do all the right things and say all the right words. But just when you begin to make strides, just when your wings begin to spread and you prepare to soar like an eagle, the ghost appears. It emerges from the swamps of your soul and causes you to question yourself.

"You can't teach a Bible class with your background."

"You, a missionary?"

"How dare you ask him to come to church. What if he finds out about the time you fell away?"

"Who are *you* to offer help?"

The ghost spews waspish words of accusation, deafening your ears to the promises of the cross. And it flaunts your failures in your face, blocking your vision of the Son and leaving you the shadow of a doubt.

Now, honestly. Do you think God sent that ghost? Do you think

God is the voice that reminds you of the putridness of your past? Do you think God was teasing when he said, "I will remember your sins no more?" Was he exaggerating when he said he would cast our sins as far as the east is from the west? Do you actually believe he would make a statement like "I will not hold their iniquities against them" and then rub our noses in them whenever we ask for help?

Of course you don't. You and I just need an occasional reminder of God's nature, his forgetful nature.

To love conditionally is against God's nature. Just as it's against your nature to eat trees and against mine to grow wings, it's against God's nature to remember forgiven sins.

You see, God is either the God of perfect grace…or he is not God. Grace forgets. Period. He who is perfect love cannot hold grudges. If he does, then he isn't perfect love. And if he isn't perfect love, you might as well put this book down and go fishing, because both of us are chasing fairy tales.

But I believe in his loving forgetfulness. And I believe he has a graciously terrible memory.

Think about this. If he didn't forget, how could we pray? How could we sing to him? How could we dare enter into his presence if the moment he saw us he remembered all our pitiful past? How could we enter his throne room wearing the rags of our selfishness and gluttony? We couldn't.

And we don't. Read this powerful passage from Paul's letter to the Galatians and watch your pulse rate. You're in for a thrill. "For as many of you as were baptized into Christ have *put on* Christ."[5]

You read it right. We have "put on" Christ. When God looks at us he doesn't see us; he sees Christ. We "wear" him. We are hidden in him; we are covered by him. As the song says, "Dressed in his righteousness alone, faultless to stand before the throne."

Presumptuous, you say? Sacrilegious? It would be if it were my idea. But it isn't; it's his. We are presumptuous not when we marvel at his grace, but when we reject it. And we're sacrilegious not when we claim his forgiveness, but when we allow the haunting sins of yesterday to convince us that God forgives but he doesn't forget.

Do yourself a favor. Purge your cellar. Exorcise your basement. Take the Roman nails of Calvary and board up the door.

And remember…he forgot.

CHAPTER 20

# FACING THE FACTS

I am writing in a hospital room.

I am sitting in one of those uncomfortable vinyl chairs that convert into an uncomfortable vinyl guest bed. Just a few feet from me sleeps my wife. She's minus one gallbladder. We've been here for four days (almost 100 hours). Denalyn is recovering well. But because of the medication she's sleepy most of the time, so I've had a good opportunity to do some observing. And I've come to a conclusion. And since she is asleep and the nurse doesn't seem too conversant, I think I'll write down my conclusion. Want to read it?

A hospital is a microcosm of the world.

Why? Let me explain.

On the surface, a hospital appears to be a great place. The sheets are clean and the staff is friendly. Nurses come and go with warm smiles. Doctors periodically appear wearing nice loafers, a tie, and a kind face. Friends and family visit bringing pretty plants and friendly words.

There's a curiously large number of smiles here. I've walked the halls and been greeted by the smiling Candy Stripers pushing the coffee cart. The gift shop downstairs is full of magazines with smiling people on the covers. The lady selling them smiled broadly at me when I bought one. The receptionist at the front desk smiles when you pass by.

Along with the smiles and the comfort is the escape hatch. The TV is placed near the ceiling and through it you can climb into the outside world. Just flip the switch and you are riding on the Love Boat or watching the Yankees game.

Smiles, efficiency, distraction. I've seen some resorts that don't offer this kind of treatment. My, you almost forget where you are.

In fact, were it not for the undisguiseable reminders, you would forget. But just when you relax—just when you begin to smile to yourself, just when you giggle at Bill Cosby—a siren reminds you. The scream of the patient next door reminds you. Paramedics rushing a stretcher toward the emergency room remind you.

And the reminder is sobering. This is a hospital. The sole function of this building is to bargain with death. The walls can't be white enough nor the staff polite enough to hide the stark reality of the bottom line: People come here to give all they have to postpone the inevitable.

We give it our best shot. We put up the best we have—the best technology, the best minds, the best equipment; and yet, at best we walk away with an extension, never a solution. And though we may walk or be wheeled out with smiles and waves of victory, down deep we know it is just a matter of time until the best we have won't be enough and the enemy will conquer.

So a hospital is a paradoxical place. A place where the reality is hidden, yet can't be hidden because the reality is too real.

You saw the same today in your world, didn't you? The script was the same; only the props were different. That's why I reached my conclusion—our world is identical to a hospital. Have you ever noticed the endless extremes to which a person will go to hide the realities of life?

Take age for example. Do you know anyone who has not aged? Do you know anyone who is younger today than when you met him? Aging is a universal condition. But the way we try to hide it, you would think it was a plague!

There are girdles which compact the middle-age spread for both sexes. There are hair transplants, wigs, toupees, and hair pieces. Dentures bring youth to the mouth, wrinkle cream brings youth to the face, and color in a bottle brings youth to the hair.

All to hide what everyone already knows—we're getting older.

Death is another lump in the carpet. We don't like it. (If you ever want to stall a conversation at a party just say, "How are you feeling about your approaching death?" It won't put much life into the conversation.)

I have a friend who has cancer. At present the cancer is in remission. Recently he had to go to the doctor for a physical. A nurse, apparently unaware of his condition, was asking him questions for his medical record. "Are you presently ill?"

"Well, yes. I have cancer."

She dropped her pencil and looked up at him. "Are you terminal?" she asked.

"Yes, aren't we all?"

You'd think we weren't, the way the subject is kept hush-hush.

We also try to disguise ourselves. It's wild. People from the country try to look like they're from the city and people from the city try to look like they're from the country. We change our accents, change our noses; we even try to change our names—all to avoid facing who we are.

But this obsession with fleeing the facts is as maddening as it is futile. For, as in the case of the hospital, the truth always surfaces. A siren sounds causing reality to shock us out of our sleep.

An old college roomie retires and you have to admit that if he is in the autumn of his life, you must be too.

You walk your daughter down the aisle. "When did she grow up?"

You wake up in an emergency room to the beeping of a machine and find wires suction-cupped to your chest.

Be the event pleasant or painful, the result is the same. Reality breaks through the papier-mâché mask and screams at you like a Marine drill sergeant. "You *are* getting old! You *are* going to die! You can't be someone you are not!"

The props are kicked away and you tumble head over feet, crashing onto the hard floor of the facts of life. You might as well turn off the TV and take off the new outfit. Reality has reared its head like the Loch Ness monster and you can no longer deny its existence.

The best thing for you to do now is pause and think. Take a good look at the facts. And while you're looking at them, it would be wise to take a good look at him. To those perched on the peak of Mount Perspective, His Majesty takes on special significance.

Jesus does his best work at such moments. Just when the truth about life sinks in, his truth starts to surface. He takes us by the hand and dares us not to sweep the facts under the rug but to confront them with him at our side.

Aging? A necessary process to pass on to a better world.

Death? Merely a brief passage, a tunnel.

Self? Designed and created for a purpose, purchased by God himself.

There, was that so bad?

Funerals, divorces, illnesses, and stays in the hospital—you can't lie about life at such times. Maybe that's why he's always present at such moments.

The next time you find yourself alone in a dark alley facing the undeniables of life, don't cover them with a blanket, or ignore them with a nervous grin. Don't turn up the TV and pretend they aren't there. Instead, stand still, whisper his name, and listen. He is nearer than you think.

CHAPTER 21

# LIGHT OF THE... STORAGE CLOSET?

A few nights ago a peculiar thing happened.

An electrical storm caused a blackout in our neighborhood. When the lights went out, I felt my way through the darkness into the storage closet where we keep the candles for nights like this. Through the glow of a lit match I looked up on the shelf where the candles were stored. There they were, already positioned in their stands, melted to various degrees by previous missions. I took my match and lit four of them.

How they illuminated the storage room! What had been a veil of blackness suddenly radiated with soft, golden light! I could see the freezer I had just bumped with my knee. And I could see my tools that needed to be straightened.

"How great it is to have light!" I said out loud, and then spoke to the candles. "If you do such a good job here in the storage closet, just wait till I get you out where you're really needed! I'll put one of you on the table so we can eat. I'll put one of you on my desk so I can read. I'll give one of you to Denalyn so she can cross-stitch. And I'll set you," I took down the largest one, "in the living room where you can light up the whole area." (I felt a bit foolish talking to candles—but what do you do when the lights go out?)

I was turning to leave with the large candle in my hand when I heard a voice, "Now, hold it right there."

I stopped. *Somebody's in here!* I thought. Then I relaxed. *It's just Denalyn, teasing me for talking to the candles.*

"OK, honey, cut the kidding," I said in the semidarkness. No answer.

*Hmm, maybe it was the wind.* I took another step.

"Hold it, I said!" There was that voice. My hands began to sweat.

"Who said that?"

"I did." The voice was near my hand.

"Who are you? What are you?"

"I'm a candle." I looked at the candle I was holding. It was burning a strong, golden flame. It was red and sat on a heavy wooden candle holder that had a firm handle.

I looked around once more to see if the voice could be coming from another source. "There's no one here but you, me, and the rest of us candles," the voice informed me.

I lifted up the candle to take a closer look. You won't believe what I saw. There was a tiny face in the wax. (I told you you wouldn't believe me.) Not just a wax face that someone had carved, but a moving, functioning, fleshlike face full of expression and life.

"Don't take me out of here!"

"What?"

"I said, don't take me out of this room."

"What do you mean? I have to take you out. You're a candle. Your job is to give light. It's dark out there. People are stubbing their toes and walking into walls. You have to come out and light up the place!"

"But you can't take me out. I'm not ready," the candle explained with pleading eyes. "I need more preparation."

I couldn't believe my ears. "More preparation?"

"Yeah, I've decided I need to research this job of light-giving so I won't go out and make a bunch of mistakes. You'd be surprised how distorted the glow of an untrained candle can be. So I'm doing some studying. I just finished a book on wind resistance. I'm in the middle of a great series of tapes on wick build-up and conservation—and I'm reading the new bestseller on flame display. Have you heard of it?"

"No," I answered.

"You might like it. It's called *Waxing Eloquently.*"

"That really sounds inter—" I caught myself. *What am I doing? I'm in here conversing with a candle while my wife and daughters are out there in the darkness!*

"All right then," I said. "You're not the only candle on the shelf. I'll blow you out and take the others!"

But just as I got my cheeks full of air, I heard other voices.

"We aren't going either!"

It was a conspiracy. I turned around and looked at the three other candles; each with flames dancing above a miniature face.

I was beyond feeling awkward about talking to candles. I was getting miffed.

"You are candles and your job is to light dark places!"

"Well, that may be what you think," said the candle on the far left—a long, thin fellow with a goatee and a British accent. "*You* may think we have to go, but I'm busy."

"Busy?"

"Yes, I'm meditating."

"What? A candle that meditates?"

"Yes. I'm meditating on the importance of light. It's really enlightening."

I decided to reason with them. "Listen, I appreciate what you guys are doing. I'm all for meditation time. And everyone needs to study and research; but for goodness' sake, you guys have been in here for weeks! Haven't you had enough time to get your wick on straight?"

"And you other two," I asked, "are you going to stay in here as well?"

A short, fat, purple candle with plump cheeks that reminded me of Santa Claus spoke up. "I'm waiting to get my life together. I'm not stable enough. I lose my temper easily. I guess you could say that I'm a hot-head."

The last candle had a female voice, very pleasant to the ear. "I'd like to help," she explained, "but lighting the darkness is not my gift."

All this was sounding too familiar. "Not your gift? What do you mean?"

"Well, I'm a singer. I sing to other candles to encourage them to burn more brightly." Without asking my permission, she began a rendition of "This Little Light of Mine." (I have to admit, she had a good voice.)

The other three joined in, filling the storage room with singing.

"Hey," I shouted above the music, "I don't mind if you sing while you work! In fact, we could use a little music out there!"

They didn't hear me. They were singing too loudly. I yelled louder.

"Come on, you guys. There's plenty of time for this later. We've got a crisis on our hands."

They wouldn't stop. I put the big candle on the shelf and took a step back and considered the absurdity of it all. Four perfectly healthy candles singing to each other about light but refusing to come out of the closet. I had all I could take. One by one I blew them out. They kept singing to the end. The last one to flicker was the female. I snuffed her out right in the "puff" part of "Won't let Satan puff me out."

I stuck my hands in my pocket and walked back out in the darkness. I bumped my knee on the same freezer. Then I bumped into my wife.

"Where are the candles?" she asked.

"They don't...they won't work. Where did you buy those candles anyway?"

"Oh, they're church candles. Remember the church that closed down across town? I bought them there."

I understood.

CHAPTER 22

# BLIND AMBITION

The scene is almost spooky: a tall, unfinished tower looming solitarily on a dusty plain. Its base is wide and strong but covered with weeds. Large stones originally intended for use in the tower lie forsaken on the ground. Buckets, hammers, and pulleys—all lie abandoned. The silhouette cast by the structure is lean and lonely.

Not too long ago, this tower was buzzing with activity. A bystander would have been impressed with the smooth-running construction of the world's first skyscraper. One group of workers stirred freshly made mortar. Another team pulled bricks out of the oven. A third group carried the bricks to the construction site while a fourth shouldered the load up a winding path to the top of the tower where it was firmly set in place.

It was a human anthill. Each worker knew his job and did it well.

Their dream was a tower. A tower that would be taller than anyone had ever dreamed. A tower that would punch through the clouds and scratch the heavens. And what was the purpose of the tower? To glorify God? No. To try to find God? No. To call people to look upward to God? Try again. To provide a heavenly haven of prayer? Still wrong.

The purpose of the work caused its eventual abortion. The method was right. The plan was effective. But the motive was wrong. Dead wrong. Read these minutes from the "Tower Planning Committee Meeting" and see what I mean:

"Come, let us build ourselves a city, and a tower with its top in the heavens, and [watch out] *let us make a name for ourselves.*"[1]

Why was the tower being built? Selfishness. Pure, 100 percent selfishness. The bricks were made of inflated egos and the mortar was made of pride. Men were giving sweat and blood for a pillar. Why? So that somebody's name could be remembered.

We have a name for that: blind ambition. Success at all cost. Becoming a legend in one's own time. Climbing the ladder to the top. King of the mountain. Top of the heap. "I did it my way."

We make heroes out of people who are ambitious. We hold them up as models for our kids and put their pictures on the covers of our magazines.

And rightly so. This world would be in sad shape without people who dream of touching the heavens. Ambition is that grit in the soul which creates disenchantment with the ordinary and puts the dare into dreams.

But left unchecked it becomes an insatiable addiction to power and prestige; a roaring hunger for achievement that devours people as a lion devours an animal, leaving behind only the skeletal remains of relationships.

The classic examples of nearsighted tower builders come to mind quickly. You'll recognize them, perhaps too well.

The husband who feeds his career with twelve-hour days, flight schedules, and apologies for being gone so much. "But it's just a matter of time, and I'll get my feet on the ground."

The social-conscious mother of three who never misses a chance to serve on a committee or attend a luncheon. "It's all for a good cause," she fools herself.

"I'll only need to do it this once," justifies the salesman as he lies about his product. Anything to get to the top of the tower.

Blind ambition. Distorted values.

The result? Rootless lives bouncing like tumbleweeds through ghost towns. Abandoned dreams. Crumbling homes. Windswept futures. All with one thing in common: a half-finished tower that stands as a stirring epitaph to those who follow.

God won't tolerate it. He didn't then and he won't now. He took the "Climb to Heaven Campaign" into his hands. With one sweep he painted the tower gray with confusion and sent workers babbling in all directions. He took man's greatest achievement and blew it into the winds like a child blows a dandelion.

Are you building any towers? Examine your motives. And remember the statement imprinted on the base of the windswept Tower of Babel: Blind ambition is a giant step away from God and one step closer to catastrophe.

CHAPTER 23

# WARNINGS

I was mad. Real mad. The kind of mad that makes your jaw ache. But I had no one to be mad at except myself.

I'd seen that silly light burning on the car panel for days. And for days I'd ignored it. Too busy. "I'll take the car to the mechanic tomorrow." But tomorrow never became today. The light continued to burn, vainly waving red flags before my blind eyes. Something was wrong, but I had too many things to do.

"Next time I'll pay attention," I mumbled to myself. The flashlight I was waving must have looked like a dancing firefly to the oncoming traffic. The situation was not pretty: a cold winter night, stranded on a lonely highway in rural Brazil with my daughter and pregnant wife.

My breath became smoke as I stood on the shoulder flagging cars. I promised myself I would never ignore a warning again.

Warnings. Red lights in life that signal us of impending danger. They exist in all parts of life. Sirens scream as a marriage starts to sour; alarms blare when a faith weakens; flares go up to alert us of morals being compromised.

They manifest themselves in a variety of ways: guilt, depression, rationalizations. A friend might confront. A Scripture might sting. A burden might prove too heavy. Regardless of how they may arrive, warnings come with the same purpose: To alert. To wake up.

Unfortunately, they are not always heeded. All of us have learned to cover our ears and shield our eyes at the right moment. It's amazing how adept we can be at keeping them out. Warnings can be as blunt as a sledgehammer and we still turn our heads and whistle them away. We have just enough of the rascal in us to believe we are the proverbial exception to the rule.

It's as if there were a miniature receptionist in our brain instructed to intercept all warnings and file them in appropriate files. Can you imagine the scene?

"Hello. Screening department. May I help you?"

"Yes. This is the safety spectrum. I'm calling to advise Mr. Lucado that he is driving too fast."

"I'm sorry. Mr. Lucado left instructions that that particular warning was for the 'other guy' who isn't as experienced on highways."

Or,

"Hello, Headquarters? This is the health department. Please advise Mr. Lucado that he is in desperate need of rest."

"I certainly will…tomorrow."

Or perhaps,

"This is Mr. Lucado's conscience calling."

"I'm sorry, Mr. Lucado left word that he is having his horizon expanded and doesn't plan to return your call."

Or,

"This is the Conviction Section. I need to arrange for Mr. Lucado to read the Book of James within the next twenty-four hours. There are a couple of things he needs to remember."

"Let me check his schedule…hmmm. The next time Mr. Lucado is free to read the Bible is next month. However, he does have several golf games scheduled. Is there any way you can talk to him on the golf course?"

Even,

"This is Mr. Lucado's faith calling to remind him—hello? Hello? That's strange, I've been disconnected."

Warnings flash about us unheeded while we doze in the canoe floating down the Niagara River.

We're often surprised at life's mishaps, but when pressed against the wall of honesty we have to admit that if we had just fired that silly receptionist and done something about those calls, we could have avoided many problems. We usually knew that trouble was just around the bend. Christians who have fallen away felt the fire waning long before it went out. Unwanted pregnancies or explosions of anger may appear to be the fruit of a moment's waywardness, but in reality, they're usually the result of a history of ignoring warnings about an impending fire.

Are you close to the falls? Are your senses numb? Are your eyes trained to turn and roll when they should pause and observe?

Then maybe you need to repair your warning detector. Tune it up with a few cautions from Scripture. Be careful about—

Sticking your nose in other people's business:

> Like one who seizes a dog by the ears is a passer-by who meddles in a quarrel not his own.[1]

One-night stands:

> For a prostitute will bring a man to poverty, and an adulteress may cost him his very life. Can a man hold fire against his chest and not be burned? Can he walk on hot coals and not blister his feet? So it is with the man who commits adultery with another's wife. He shall not go unpunished for this sin.[2]

Dust-covered Bibles:

> We must pay more careful attention, therefore, to what we have heard, so that we do not drift away.[3]

Secret scampering that you think will go unnoticed:

> Do not be deceived: God cannot be mocked. A man reaps what he sows.[4]

Poor selection of a mate:

> It is better to dwell in the wilderness, than with a contentious and angry woman.[5]

The poisoning effect of gossip:

> The words of a gossip are like choice morsels; they go down to a man's inmost parts.[6]

Careless choice of companions:

> Bad company corrupts good character.[7]

Denial of Christ:

> Whoever disowns me before men, I will disown him before my Father in heaven.[8]

The lack of parental discipline:

> Do not withhold correction from a child, for if you beat him with a rod, he will not die. You shall beat him with a rod, and deliver his soul from hell.[9]

And three warnings about ignoring warnings:

> Cease listening to instruction, my son, and you will stray from the words of knowledge.[10]
>
> Reproofs of instruction are the way of life.[11]
>
> Pride only breeds quarrels, but wisdom is found in those who take advice.[12]

Divine warnings. All inspired by God and tested by time. They're yours to do with as you wish. They are red lights on your dashboard. Heed them and safety is yours to enjoy. Ignore them and I'll be looking for you on the side of the road.

CHAPTER 24

# FATHER'S DAY: A TRIBUTE

Today is Father's Day. A day of cologne. A day of hugs, new neckties, long-distance telephone calls, and Hallmark cards.

Today is my first Father's Day without a father. For thirty-one years I had one. I had one of the best. But now he's gone. He's buried under an oak tree in a west Texas cemetery. Even though he's gone, his presence is very near—especially today.

It seems strange that he isn't here. I guess that's because he was never gone. He was always close by. Always available. Always present. His words were nothing novel. His achievements, though admirable, were nothing extraordinary.

But his presence was.

Like a warm fireplace in a large house, he was a source of comfort. Like a sturdy porch swing or a big-branched elm in the backyard, he could always be found and leaned upon.

During the turbulent years of my adolescence, Dad was one part of my life that was predictable. Girlfriends came and girlfriends went, but Dad was there.

Football season turned into baseball season and turned into football season again and Dad was always there. Summer vacation, Homecoming dates, algebra, first car, driveway basketball—they all had one thing in common: his presence.

And because he was there life went smoothly. The car always ran, the bills got paid, and the lawn stayed mowed. Because he was there the laughter was fresh and the future was secure. Because he was there my growing up was what God intended growing up to be; a storybook scamper through the magic and mystery of the world.

Because he was there we kids never worried about things like income tax, savings accounts, monthly bills or mortgages. Those were the things on Daddy's desk.

We have lots of family pictures without him. Not because he wasn't there, but because he was always behind the camera.

He made the decisions, broke up the fights, chuckled at Archie Bunker, read the paper every evening, and fixed breakfast on Sundays. He didn't do anything unusual. He only did what dads are supposed to do—be there.

He taught me how to shave and how to pray. He helped me memorize verses for Sunday school and taught me that wrong should be punished and that rightness has its own reward. He modeled the importance of getting up early and of staying out of debt. His life expressed the elusive balance between ambition and self-acceptance.

He comes to mind often. When I smell "Old Spice" after-shave, I think of him. When I see a bass boat I see his face. And occasionally, not too often, but occasionally when I hear a good joke (the kind Red Skelton would tell), I hear him chuckle. He had a copyright chuckle that always came with a wide grin and arched eyebrows.

Daddy never said a word to me about sex nor told me his life story. But I knew that if I ever wanted to know, he would tell me. All I had to do was ask. And I knew if I ever needed him, he'd be there.

Like a warm fireplace.

Maybe that's why this Father's Day is a bit chilly. The fire has gone out. The winds of age swallowed the last splendid flame, leaving only golden embers. But there is a strange thing about those embers, stir them a bit and a flame will dance. It will dance only briefly, but it will dance. And it will knock just enough chill out of the air to remind me that he is still—in a special way—very present.

CHAPTER 25

# FAMILY SEDANS OF THE FAITH

For an extraordinary pitcher he performed few extraordinary feats. Though a veteran of twenty-one seasons, in only one did he win more than twenty games. He never pitched a no-hitter and only once did he lead the league in any category (2.21 ERA, 1980).

Yet on June 21, 1986, Don Sutton rubbed pitching elbows with the true legends of baseball by becoming the thirtieth pitcher to win 300 games.

His analysis of his success is worth noting.

"A grinder and a mechanic" is what he calls himself. "I never considered myself flamboyant or exceptional. But all my life I've found a way to get the job done."

And get it done he did. Through two decades, six presidential terms, and four trades, he consistently did what pitchers are supposed to do: win games. With tunnel-vision devotion, he spent twenty-one seasons redefining greatness.

He has been called the "family sedan" of baseball's men on the mound.[1] The connotation is accurate. He certainly boasted none of the Ferrari style of a Denny McClane nor the Mercedes sparkle of a Sandy Koufax, but after they and their types were parked in museums or garages, Don Sutton was still there.

He reminds us of a quality that is a common denominator in any form of greatness—reliability.

It's the bread and butter characteristic of achievement. It's the shared ingredient behind retirement pens, Hall of Fame awards, and golden anniversaries. It is the quality that produces not momentary heroics but monumental lives.

The Bible has its share of family sedans. Consistent and predictable, these saints were spurred by a gut-level conviction that they had been called by no one less than God himself. As a result, their work wasn't affected by moods, cloudy days, or rocky trails. Their performance graph didn't rise and fall with roller-coaster irregularity. They weren't addicted to accolades or applause nor deterred by grumpy bosses or empty wallets. Rather than strive to be spectacular, they aspired to be accountable and dependable. And since their loyalty was not determined by their comfort, they were just as faithful in dark prisons as they were in spotlighted pulpits.

Reliable servants. They're the binding of the Bible. Their acts are rarely recited and their names are seldom mentioned. Yet were it not for their loyal devotion to God, many great events never would have occurred. Here are some examples.

Andrew wasn't a keynoter at the Pentecost crusade. He probably wasn't on the podium, on the schedule, or even on the planning committee. But if he hadn't been on his toes some years earlier, Peter the powerful preacher might have been nothing more than Peter the impetuous fish-catcher. Andrew, considering he was an apostle, is mentioned a surprisingly small number of times. Yet every time he is mentioned he's doing the same thing: introducing somebody to Jesus. No lights, no pulpits, no reviews, but not a bad epitaph.[2]

Epaphroditus would be on this list. "Epaphro-what-us?" you say. Just ask the apostle Paul. He'll give you the correct pronunciation. He'll also give quite a character reference.[3] To describe this fellow with the five-syllable name Paul used more succinct words like *brother, fellow worker, fellow soldier,* and *messenger.* You don't earn eulogies like these from appearing at an occasional youth rally or showing up at church picnics. These are compliments earned over years and tears. But Paul's finest praise of Epaphroditus was expressed in these words, "he almost died for the gospel." You can bet that Paul, who knew what it meant to die for a cause, didn't take sacrifice for granted. After writing the phrase, he must have leaned back against his prison wall and smiled at the mental picture of his old trail-buddy. Epaphroditus. The only thing longer than his name was his staying power.

Her hair is gray. Her skin is wrinkled. Perhaps her hand trembles as she touches the infant's face. But there is nothing senile about her words. "This is he. The Messiah." Anna should know. She'd been praying and fasting for this day for eight decades. Faithful servants have a way of knowing answered prayer when they see it, and a way of not giving up when they don't.

Re-liable. *Liable* means responsible. *Re* means over and over again.

I'm wondering if this book has found it's way into the hands of some contemporary saints of reliability. If such is the case I can't resist the chance to say two things.

The first?

Thank you.

Thank you senior saints for a generation of prayer and forest clearing.

Thank you teachers for the countless Sunday school lessons, prepared and delivered with tenderness.

Thank you missionaries for your bravery in sharing the timeless truth in a foreign tongue.

Thank you preachers. You thought we weren't listening, but we were. And your stubborn sowing of God's seed is bearing fruit you may never see this side of the great harvest.

Thanks to all of you who practice on Monday what you hear on Sunday. You spent selfless hours with orphans, at typewriters, in board meetings, on knees, in hospital wards, away from families, and on assembly lines. It is upon the back of your fidelity that the gospel rides.

Thank you for being the family sedans of society. You can be called on cold mornings and you'll deliver the goods. You can be sent over rough terrain and you'll make it on time. You can go miles without the pampering of a good polish or the luxury of a tune-up and you never complain. You get the job done.

I said I had two things to say. What is the second?

Keep pitching. Your Hall of Fame award is just around the corner.

CHAPTER 26

# INSENSITIVE SLURS

Insensitivity makes a wound that heals slowly. If someone hurts your feelings intentionally you know how to react. You know the source of the pain. But if someone accidentally bruises your soul, it's difficult to know how to respond.

Someone at work criticizes the new boss who also happens to be your dear friend. "Oh, I'm sorry—I forgot the two of you were so close."

A joke is told at a party about overweight people. You're overweight. You hear the joke. You smile politely while your heart sinks.

What was intended to be a reprimand for a decision or action becomes a personal attack. "You have a history of poor decisions, John."

Someone chooses to wash your dirty laundry in public. "Sue, is it true that you and Jim are separated?"

Insensitive comments. Thoughts that should have remained thoughts. Feelings which had no business being expressed. Opinions carelessly tossed like a grenade into a crowd.

And if you were to tell the one who threw these thoughtless darts about the pain they caused, his response would be "Oh, but I had no intention...I didn't realize you were so sensitive!" or "I forgot you were here."

In a way, the words are comforting, until you stop to think about them (which is not recommended). For when you start to think about insensitive slurs, you realize they come from an infamous family whose father has bred generations of pain. His name? Egotism. His children? Three sisters: Disregard, disrespect, and disappointment.

These three witches have combined to poison countless relationships and break innumerable hearts. Listed among their weapons are Satan's cruelest artillery: gossip, accusations, resentment, impatience, and on and on. And listed under the tide of *subterfuge* is this poison of insensitivity.

It's called subterfuge because it's so subtle. Just a slip of the tongue. Just a blank of memory. No one is at fault. No harm done.

Perhaps. And, perhaps not. For as the innocent attackers go on their way excusing themselves for things done without hurtful intention, a wounded soul is left in the dust, utterly confused. "If no one intended to hurt me, then why do I hurt so badly?"

God's Word has strong medicine for those who carelessly wag their tongues.

> The tongue also is a fire, a world of evil among the parts of the body. It corrupts the whole person, sets the whole course of his life on fire, and is itself set on fire by hell.[1]

> He who guards his mouth and his tongue keeps himself from calamity.[2]

> He who guards his lips guards his soul, but he who speaks rashly will come to ruin.[3]

> When words are many, sin is not absent, but he who holds his tongue is wise.[4]

The message is clear: He who dares to call himself God's ambassador is not afforded the luxury of idle words. Excuses such as "I didn't know you were here" or "I didn't realize this was so touchy" are shallow when they come from those who claim to be followers and imitators of the Great Physician. We have an added responsibility to guard our tongues.

These practical steps will purge careless words from your talk.

1. Never tell jokes that slander.
2. Never criticize in public unless you: have already expressed your disappointment with the other person in private, have

already taken someone with you to discuss the grievance with the person, and are absolutely convinced that public reprimand is necessary and will be helpful.

3. Never say anything about anyone in their absence that you wouldn't say in their presence.

Insensitive slurs may be accidental, but they are not excusable.

CHAPTER 27

# A SONG IN THE DARK

On any other day, I probably wouldn't have stopped. Like the majority of people on the busy avenue, I would hardly have noticed him standing there. But the very thing on my mind was the very reason he was there, so I stopped.

I'd just spent a portion of the morning preparing a lesson out of the ninth chapter of John, the chapter that contains the story about the man blind from birth. I'd finished lunch and was returning to my office when I saw him. He was singing. An aluminum cane was in his left hand; his right hand was extended and open, awaiting donations. He was blind.

After walking past him about five steps, I stopped and mumbled something to myself about the epitome of hypocrisy and went back in his direction. I put some change in his hand. "Thank you," he said and then offered me a common Brazilian salutation, "and may you have health." Ironic wish.

Once again I started on my way. Once again the morning study of John 9 stopped me. "Jesus saw a man, blind from birth." I paused and pondered. If Jesus were here he would *see* this man. I wasn't sure what that meant. But I was sure I hadn't done it. So I turned around again.

As if the giving of a donation entitled me to do so, I stopped beside a nearby car and observed. I challenged myself to see him. I would stay here until I saw more than a sightless indigent on a busy thoroughfare in downtown Rio de Janeiro.

I watched him sing. Some beggars grovel in a corner cultivating pity. Others unashamedly lay their children on blankets in the middle of the sidewalk thinking that only the hardest of hearts would ignore a dirty, naked infant asking for bread.

But this man did none of that. He stood. He stood tall. And he sang. Loudly. Even proudly. All of us had more reason to sing than he, but he was the one singing. Mainly, he sang folk songs. Once I thought he was singing a hymn, though I wasn't sure.

His husky voice was out of place amid the buzz of commerce. Like a small sparrow who found his way into a noisy factory, or a lost fawn on an interstate, his singing conjured an awkward marriage between progress and simplicity.

The passersby had various reactions. Some were curious and gazed unabashedly. Others were uncomfortable. They were quick to duck their heads or walk in a wider circle. "No reminders of harshness today, please." Most, however, hardly noticed him. Their thoughts were occupied, their agendas were full and he was…well, he was a blind beggar.

I was thankful he couldn't see the way they looked at him.

After a few minutes I went up to him again. "Have you had any lunch?" I asked. He stopped singing. He turned his head toward the sound of my voice and directed his face somewhere past my ear. His eye sockets were empty. He said he was hungry. I went to a nearby restaurant and bought him a sandwich and something cold to drink.

When I came back he was still singing and his hands were still empty. He was grateful for the food. We sat down on a nearby bench. Between bites he told me about himself. Twenty-eight years old. Single. Lives with his parents and seven brothers. "Were you born blind?"

"No, when I was young I had an accident." He didn't volunteer details and I didn't have the gall to request them.

Though we were almost the same age, we were light years apart. My three decades had been a summer vacation of family excursions, Sunday school, debate teams, football, and a search for the Mighty One. Growing up blind in the Third World surely offered none of these. My daily concern now involved people, thoughts, concepts, and communication. His day was stitched with concerns of survival: coins, handouts, and food. I'd go home to a nice apartment, a hot meal, and a good wife. I hated to think of the home he would encounter. I'd seen enough overcrowded huts on the hills of Rio to make a reasonable guess. And his reception...would there be anyone to make him feel special when he got home?

I came whisker-close to asking him, "Does it make you mad that I'm not you?" "Do you ever lie awake at night wondering why the hand you were dealt was so different from the one given a million or so others born thirty years ago?"

I wore a shirt and tie and some new shoes. His shoes had holes and his coat was oversized and bulky. His pants gaped open from a rip in the knee.

And still he sang. Though a sightless, penniless hobo, he still found a song and sang it courageously. (I wondered which room in his heart that song came from.)

At worst, I figured, he sang from desperation. His song was all he had. Even when no one gave any coins, he still had his song. Yet he seemed too peaceful to be singing out of self-preservation.

Or perhaps he sang from ignorance. Maybe he didn't know what he never had.

No, I decided the motivation that fit his demeanor was the one you'd least expect. He was singing from contentment. Somehow this eyeless pauper had discovered a candle called satisfaction and it glowed in his dark world. Someone had told him, or maybe he'd told himself, that tomorrow's joy is fathered by today's acceptance. Acceptance of what, at least for the moment, you cannot alter.

I looked up at the Niagara of faces that flowed past us. Grim. Professional. Some determined. Some disguised. But none were singing, not even silently. What if each face were a billboard that announced the true state of its owner's heart? How many would say "Desperate! Business on the rocks!" or "Broken: In Need of Repair," or "Faithless, Frantic, and Fearful"? Quite a few.

The irony was painfully amusing. This blind man could be the most peaceful fellow on the street. No diploma, no awards, and no future—at least in the aggressive sense of the word. But I wondered how many in that urban stampede would trade their boardrooms and blue suits in a second for a chance to drink at this young man's well.

"Faith is the bird that sings while it is yet dark."

Before I helped my friend back to his position on the street, I tried to verbalize my empathy. "Life is hard, isn't it?" A slight smile. He again turned his face toward the direction of my voice and started to respond, then paused and said, "I'd better get back to work."

For almost a block, I could hear him singing. And in my mind's eye I could still see him. But the man I now saw was a different one than the one to whom I'd given a few coins. Though the man I now saw was still sightless, he was remarkably insightful. And though I was the one with eyes, it was he who gave me a new vision.

CHAPTER 28

# IN THE MUD OF JABBOK

He was the riverboat gambler of the patriarchs. A master of sleight of hand and fancy footwork. He had gained a seamy reputation of getting what he wanted by hook or crook—or both.

Twice he dealt hidden cards to his dull-witted brother Esau in order to climb the family tree. He once pulled the wool over the eyes of his own father, a trick especially dirty since his father's eyes were rather dim, and the wool he pulled insured him a gift he would never have received otherwise.

He later conned his father-in-law out of his best livestock and, when no one was looking, he took the kids and the cattle and skedaddled.

Yes, Jacob had a salty reputation, deservedly so. For him the ends always justified the means. His cleverness was outranked only by his audacity. His conscience was calloused just enough to let him sleep and his feet were just fast enough to keep him one step ahead of the consequences.

That is, until he reached a river called Jabbok.[1] At Jabbok his own cunning caught up with him.

Jacob was camped near the river Jabbok when word reached him that big, hairy Esau was coming to see him. It had been twenty years since Jacob had tricked his brother. More than enough time, Jacob realized, for Esau to stir up a boiling pot of revenge. Jacob was in trouble. This time he had no more tricks up his sleeve. He was finally forced to face up to himself and to God.

To Jacob's credit, he didn't run away from the problem. One has to wonder why. Maybe he was sick of running. Or maybe he was tired of looking at the shady character he saw every morning in the mirror. Or maybe he simply knew that he'd dealt from the bottom of the deck one too many times. Whatever the motivation, it was enough to cause him to come out of the shadows, cross Jabbok Creek alone, and face the facts.

The word *Jabbok* in Hebrew means "wrestle," and wrestle is what Jacob did. He wrestled with his past: all the white lies, scheming, and scandalizing. He wrestled with his situation: a spider trapped in his own web of deceit and craftiness. But more than anything, he wrestled with God.

He wrestled with the same God who had descended the ladder at Bethel to assure Jacob he wasn't alone (although he deserved to be). He met the same God who had earlier guaranteed Jacob that he would never break his promise (though one could hardly fault God if he did). He confronted the same God who had reminded Jacob that the land prepared for him was still his. (Proof again that God blesses us *in spite* of our lives and not *because of* our lives.)

Jacob wrestled with God the entire night. On the banks of Jabbok he rolled in the mud of his mistakes. He met God face to face, sick of his past and in desperate need of a fresh start. And because Jacob wanted it so badly, God honored his determination. God gave him a new name and a new promise. But he also gave a wrenched hip as a reminder of that mysterious night at the river.

Jacob wasn't the only man in the Bible to wrestle with self and God because of past antics. David did after his rendezvous with Bathsheba. Samson wrestled, blind and bald after Delilah's seduction. Elijah was at his own Jabbok when he heard the "still, small voice." Peter wrestled with his guilt with echoes of a crowing cock still ringing in his ears.

And I imagine that most of us have spent some time on the river banks as well. Our scandalous deeds have a way of finding us. Want some examples? Consider these scenes.

> The unfaithful husband standing at the table with a note from his wife in his hands, "I couldn't take it anymore. I've taken the kids with me."

The twenty-year-old single in the doctor's office. The words are still fresh on her mind, "The test was positive. You are pregnant."

The businessman squirming in the IRS office. "Your audit shows that you took some loopholes that weren't yours to take."

The red-faced student who got caught red-handed copying the test answers of someone else. "We'll have to notify your parents."

All of us at one time or another come face to face with our past. And it's always an awkward encounter. When our sins catch up with us we can do one of two things: run or wrestle.

Many choose to run. They brush it off with a shrug of rationalization. "I was a victim of circumstances." Or, "It was his fault." Or, "There are many who do worse things." The problem with this escape is that it's no escape at all. It's only a shallow camouflage. No matter how many layers of make-up you put over a black eye, underneath it is still black. And down deep it still hurts.

Jacob finally figured that out. As a result, his example is one worthy of imitation. The best way to deal with our past is to hitch up our pants, roll up our sleeves, and face it head on. No more buck-passing or scapegoating. No more glossing over or covering up. No more games. We need a confrontation with our Master.

We too should cross the creek alone and struggle with God over ourselves. We too should stand eyeball to eyeball with him and be reminded that left alone we fail. We too should unmask our stained hearts and grimy souls and be honest with the One who knows our most secret sins.

The result could be refreshing. We know it was for Jacob. After his encounter with God, Jacob was a new man. He crossed the river in the dawn of a new day and faced Esau with newly found courage.

Each step he took, however, was a painful one. His stiff hip was a reminder of the lesson he had learned at Jabbok: Shady dealings bring pain. Mark it down: Play today and tomorrow you'll pay.

And for you who wonder if you've played too long to change, take courage from Jacob's legacy. No man is too bad for God. To transform a riverboat gambler into a man of faith would be no easy task. But for God, it was all in a night's work.

CHAPTER 29

# A LITTLE BIT OF HANGIN'

*"Lord...let me know how fleeting my life is!"*
PSALM 39:4

Abraham Lincoln once listened to the pleas of the mother of a soldier who'd been sentenced to hang for treason. She begged the president to grant a pardon. Lincoln agreed. Yet, he's reported to have left the lady with the following words: "Still, I wish we could teach him a lesson. I wish we could give him just a little bit of hangin'."

I think I know what the old rail-splitter had in mind. Yesterday, I got a little bit of hangin'.

We were having Sunday lunch at the home of a fellow missionary family. It was after the meal, and I was in the kitchen while Denalyn and our friends, Paul and Debbie, were talking in the living room. Their three-year-old daughter Beth Ann was playing with our two-year-old Jenna in the front yard. All of a sudden Beth Ann rushed in with a look of panic on her face. "Jenna is in the pool!"

Paul was the first to arrive at the poolside. He went straight into the water. Denalyn was next to arrive. By the time I arrived, Paul had lifted her up out of the water to the extended hands of her mother. Jenna was simultaneously choking, crying, and coughing. She vomited a bellyful of water. I held her as she cried. Denalyn began to weep. I began to sweat.

For the rest of the day I couldn't hold her enough, nor could we thank little Beth Ann enough (we took her out for ice cream). I still can't thank God enough.

It was only a matter of minutes, maybe seconds. We almost lost her. The thought was numbing and convicting.

It was a little bit of hangin'.

The stool was kicked out from under my feet and the rope jerked around my neck just long enough to remind me of what really matters. It was a divine slap, a gracious knock on the head, a severe mercy. Because of it I came face to face with one of the underground's slyest agents—the agent of familiarity.

His commission from the black throne room is clear, and fatal: "Take nothing from your victim; cause him only to take everything for granted."

He'd been on my trail for years and I never knew it. But I know it now. I've come to recognize his tactics and detect his presence. And I'm doing my best to keep him out. His aim is deadly. His goal is nothing less than to take what is most precious to us and make it appear most common.

To say that this agent of familiarity breeds contempt is to let him off easy. Contempt is just one of his offspring. He also sires broken hearts, wasted hours, and an insatiable desire for more. He's an expert in robbing the sparkle and replacing it with the drab. He invented the yawn and put the hum in the humdrum. And his strategy is deceptive.

He won't steal your salvation; he'll just make you forget what it was like to be lost. You'll grow accustomed to prayer and thereby not pray. Worship will become commonplace and study optional. With the passing of time he'll infiltrate your heart with boredom and cover the cross with dust so you'll be "safely" out of reach of change. Score one for the agent of familiarity.

Nor will he steal your home from you; he'll do something far worse. He'll paint it with a familiar coat of drabness.

He'll replace evening gowns with bathrobes, nights on the town with evenings in the recliner, and romance with routine. He'll scatter the dust of yesterday over the wedding pictures in the hallway until they become a memory of another couple in another time.

He won't take your children, he'll just make you too busy to notice them. His whispers to procrastinate are seductive. There is always next summer to coach the team, next month to go to the lake, and next week to teach Johnny how to pray. He'll make you forget that the faces around your table will soon be at tables of their own. Hence, books will go unread, games will go unplayed, hearts will go unnurtured, and opportunities will go ignored. All because the poison of the ordinary has deadened your senses to the magic of the moment.

Before you know it, the little face that brought tears to your eyes in the delivery room has become—perish the thought—common. A common kid sitting in the back seat of your van as you whiz down the fast lane of life. Unless something changes, unless someone wakes you up, that common kid will become a common stranger.

A little bit of hangin' might do us all a bit of good.

On a shelf above my desk is a picture of two little girls. They're holding hands and standing in front of a swimming pool, the same pool from which the younger of the two had been pulled only minutes before. I put the picture where I would see it daily so I would remember what God doesn't want me to forget.

And you can bet this time I'm going to remember. I don't want any more hangin'. Not even a little bit.

CHAPTER 30

# CARMELITA

The hot air hung thickly in the small cemetery chapel. Those who had fans used them to stir the stillness. It was crowded. The few chairs that had been set out were quickly taken. I found an empty corner off to one side and stood quietly, observing my first Brazilian funeral.

On a stand in the midst of the chapel rested the coffin and body of a woman who had been killed the day before in a car accident. Her name was Dona Neusa. I knew her because she was the mother of one of our first converts, Cesar Coutinho. Beside the casket stood Cesar, his sister, other relatives, and someone very special by the name of Carmelita.

She was a tall woman with dark, almost black skin. On this day her dress was simple and her face solemn. She stared earnestly at the casket with deep-set brown eyes. There was something noble about the way she stood beside the body. She didn't weep openly as did the rest. Nor did she seek comfort from the other mourners. She just stood there, curiously quiet.

The night before, I had accompanied Cesar on the delicate task of telling Carmelita that Dona Neusa had been killed. As we drove, he explained to me how Carmelita had been adopted into their family.

Over twenty years earlier, Cesar's family had visited a small town in the interior of Brazil. There they encountered Carmelita, a seven-year-old orphan living with poverty-stricken relatives. Her mother had been a prostitute. She never knew her father. Upon seeing the child, Dona Neusa was touched. She knew that unless someone intervened, little Carmelita was doomed to a life with no love or attention. Because of

Dona Neusa's compassion, Cesar and his family returned home with a new family member.

As I stood in the funeral chapel and looked at Carmelita's face, I tried to imagine the emotions she was feeling. How her life had changed. I wondered if her mind was reliving that childhood memory of climbing into a car and driving away with a strange family. One moment she had been without love, a home, or a future; the next moment she had all three.

My thoughts were interrupted by the noise of shuffling feet. The funeral was over and people were leaving the chapel for the burial. Because of my position in the extreme corner of the building, I was the last to leave. Or at least so I thought. As I was walking out I heard a soft voice behind me. I turned and saw Carmelita weeping silently at the side of the coffin. Moved, I stood in the chapel doorway and witnessed this touching *adieu.* Carmelita was alone for the last time with her adopted mother. There was an earnestness in her eyes. It was as if she had one final task to perform. She didn't wail, nor did she scream with grief. She simply leaned over the casket and caressed it tenderly as if it were the face of her mother. With silent teardrops splashing on the polished wood she said repeatedly, *"Obrigada, obrigada"* ("Thank you, thank you").

A final farewell of gratitude.

Driving home that day, I thought how we, in many ways, are like Carmelita. We too were frightened orphans. We too were without tenderness or acceptance. And we too were rescued by a compassionate visitor, a generous parent who offered us a home and a name.

Our response should be exactly that of Carmelita, a stirring response of heartfelt gratitude for our deliverance. When no one else would even give us the time of day the Son of God gave us the time of our life!

We, too, should stand in the quiet company of him who saved us, and weep tears of gratitude and offer words of thankfulness. For it is not our bodies that have been rescued, but our souls.

CHAPTER 31

# SEEING THE SUMMIT

This book was written at night. Not at dusk, nor in the evening, but at night. Past the bedtime hours. After the guests left. When the house was silent. While my wife was sleeping, I would slip into my storage closet converted into an office, greet my midnight mistress (my computer), and write. With the unceasing din of the city streets below and the soothing hum of the floor fan at my side, I enjoyed a nightly encounter with Light.

I'm not nocturnal by nature. Many nights a war was waged between my drowsiness and creativity. No, I'm not a late-nighter. But I'm a father and I'm a missionary and I found that the demands from those two tasks subsided about the hour when most people say "Good night." (I tried the early morning hours, which for some reason seemed more righteous—but the tow truck I needed to pull me out of bed couldn't make it up the stairs.)

Tonight appears to be my last rendezvous with this manuscript. *God Came Near* has gone through the necessary stages of feeding and grooming and is almost ready to be taken to market. Which, as you might expect, is a reason both for rejoicing and sadness. I'll miss this companion of the night. I don't mind telling you that more than once the impact of my late-hour ponderings took me out of my swivel chair and put me on my knees in thankfulness. We serve a wonderful God!

I recently read an insightful story that would serve as a good reminder for us both as we prepare to part ways. The story is about a group of climbers who set out to scale a large mountain in Europe. The view boasted a breathtaking peak of snowcapped rocks. On clear days the crested point reigned as king on the horizon. Its white tip jutted into the blue sky inviting admiration and offering inspiration.

On days like this the hikers made the greatest progress. The peak stood above them like a compelling goal. Eyes were called upward. The walk was brisk. The cooperation was unselfish. Though many, they climbed as one, all looking to the same summit.

Yet on some days the peak of the mountain was hidden from view. The cloud covering would eclipse the crisp blueness with a drab, gray ceiling and block the vision of the mountaintop. On these days the climb became arduous. Eyes were downward and thoughts inward. The goal was forgotten. Tempers were short. Weariness was an uninvited companion. Complaints stung like thorns on the trail.

We're like that, aren't we? As long as we can see our dream, as long as our goal is within eyesight, there is no mountain we can't climb or summit we can't scale. But take away our vision, block our view of the trail's end, and the result is as discouraging as the journey.

Think about it. Hide the Nazarene who calls to us from the mountaintop and see what happens.

Listen to the groans of the climbers as they stop and sit by the side of the path. Why continue if there is no relief in sight? Pilgrims with no vision of the promised land become proprietors of their own land. They set up camp. They exchange hiking boots for loafers and trade in their staff for a new recliner.

Instead of looking upward at him, they look inward at themselves and outward at each other. The result? Cabin fever. Quarreling families. Restless leaders. Fence-building. Staked-off territory. No trespassing! signs are hung on hearts and homes. Spats turn into fights as myopic groups turn to glare at each other's weaknesses instead of turning to worship their common Strength.

Mark it down. We are what we see. If we see only ourselves, our tombstones will have the same epitaph Paul used to describe enemies of Christ: "Their god is their own appetite, they glory in their shame, and this world is the limit of their horizon."[1] Humans were never meant to dwell in the stale fog of the lowlands with no vision of their Creator.

That's why God came near. To be seen.

And that's why those who saw him were never the same. "We saw his glory" exclaimed one follower.[2] "We were eyewitnesses of his majesty," whispered a martyr.[3] They saw the peak. They breathed the fresh air of the high country. They caught a glimpse of the pinnacle. And they refused to quit climbing until they reached the top. They wanted to see Jesus.

I began this book with some definitions: Christianity, in its purest form, is nothing more than seeing Jesus. Christian service, in its purest form, is nothing more than imitating him who we see. To see His Majesty and to imitate him, that is the sum of Christianity.

This is why those who see him today are never the same again. Remember Bob Edens? He's the one I told you about in the introduction who lived fifty-one years without seeing anything at all until complicated surgery gave him eyesight. Something else he said is worth noting.

"Grass was something I had to get used to…I always thought it was just fuzz. But to see each individual green stalk, and to see the hair on my arm growing like trees, and birds flying through the air…it's like starting a whole new life."

Getting vision can be like that. Especially getting a vision of your Maker. It can be like starting a whole new life. It can be like a new birth. In fact, the One who inspired this book said that new beginnings and good eyesight are inseparable. "Unless a man is born again, he cannot see the kingdom of God."[4]

God came near. If he is who he says he is, there is no truth more worthy of your time.

Think about that. Now, if you don't mind, I think I'll get some sleep.

# Study Guide

CHAPTER 1

# THE ARRIVAL

1. *God goes to those who have time to hear him—so on this cloudless night he went to simple shepherds.*

A. If the Messiah had been born in our time, to what group do you think the angels would have made the announcement? Who do you suppose would have taken time to listen?

B. Read Luke 2:8–20 to see the shepherds' reaction to the announcement. How did they respond? Why do you think God chose them to receive the good news?

C. Read Luke 7:18–30 to see how others reacted to the news that the Messiah had come. How did Jesus respond when they asked if he was the Messiah? What was the response of the crowds? What was the response of the Pharisees and the experts in the law? Why do you think each group responded as it did?

D. In what ways do you hear God? How often do you set aside time just to listen to him? When does God "have your ear"?

2. *Those who missed His Majesty's arrival that night missed it not because of evil acts or malice; no, they missed it because they simply weren't looking. Little has changed in the last two thousand years, has it?*

A. How do you respond to Max's statement that little has changed in the last two thousand years? Do you think people are more or less receptive now? Why do you think so many people "miss his arrival"?

B. Read Proverbs 8:17 and John 14:21. What is promised to those who seek God?

C. According to Hebrews 11:6 and Hebrews 7:22–25, what is required of those who seek God? What is promised to them?

D. In what ways do you look for God? Where do you most often find him? In his Word? In prayer? In song? Manifested in his followers?

CHAPTER 2

# "JUST A MOMENT..."

1. *There is something about keeping him [Jesus] divine that keeps him distant, packaged, predictable. But don't do it. For heaven's sake, don't. Let him be as human as he intended to be. Let him into the mire and muck of our world. For only if we let him in can he pull us out.*

A. Does it make you uncomfortable to think of Jesus in fully human terms? Why?

B. What does Max mean by "only if we let him in can he pull us out"? Do you agree? If Jesus had been able to save us without becoming human, how would that influence your attitude toward him as your Savior?

C. In the following passages, what aspects of Jesus seem very "human": Luke 24:36–43; Mark 4:35–40; John 11:1–36; Mark 14:32–40? Do those passages make him seem more real to you? How does the awareness of his humanity affect your relationship with him?

D. Read Psalm 103:8–18; Hebrews 2:14–18; and Hebrews 4:14–16. What reassurances do they give us that the Lord understands us and cares for us?

E. If you keep in mind both Jesus' divinity and humanity, how does that affect your ability to handle trials? How does it affect your ability to handle temptations? How does it affect your prayers?

2. *The world will see another instantaneous transformation. You see, in becoming man, God made it possible for man to see God. When Jesus went home he left the back door open.*

A. What is meant by "when Jesus went home he left the back door open"?

B. Read John 14:1–14. What kind of home is Jesus preparing? For whom?

C. Read Exodus 33:12–23 and 34:29–35. What happened when Moses asked to see God face to face? What effect did God's presence have on Moses?

D. According to Matthew 5:8; Hebrews 12:14; and Revelation 21:22–22:5, who will see the face of God?

E. What do you think of when you think about Jesus' return? What kind of emotions does it stir? Why? If you knew that Jesus' return was imminent, what priorities would you have? How would you spend your time?

C H A P T E R 3

# ABSURDITY IN THE FLESH

1. *After a nation of chosen ones had stripped him naked and ripped his incarnated flesh, he still died for them. And even today, after billions have chosen to prostitute themselves before the pimps of power, fame, and wealth, he still waits for them. It is inexplicable. It doesn't have a drop of logic nor a thread of rationality. And yet, it is that very irrationality that gives the gospel its greatest defense. For only God could love like that.*

A. Have you ever felt that the story of Jesus is absurd? Do you ever talk with people who challenge the authenticity of the story? How do you answer them?

B. How do these passages describe the love of God: Romans 5:6–8; Titus 3:3–8; Romans 8:13–17, 31–39?

C. According to 1 John 4:7–21, if we truly understand God's love for us, what is our response to him? What is our response to others? How does it affect our attitude toward the judgment day? What emotion cannot coexist with God's love in us?

D. When have you felt God's love most strongly? In what ways do you express God's love to others? How do you express your love to God?

2. *God became earth's mockery to save his children. How absurd to think that such nobility would go to such poverty to share such a treasure with such*

*thankless souls. But he did. In fact, the only thing more absurd than the gift is our stubborn unwillingness to receive it.*

A. How do we receive God's gift of salvation? Why do you think people don't accept God's gift of salvation?

B. Look up the following passages which describe people rejecting salvation: Luke 14:15–24; Romans 9:30–32; 1 Corinthians 1:18–31. According to these passages, what attitudes prevent people from accepting God's gift?

C. According to these passages, what are some of the attitudes and actions that characterize those who do accept God's salvation: Philippians 3:7–11; 2 Corinthians 7:10; Ephesians 2:8–9; James 1:19–27?

D. What attitude or action is the biggest challenge to your salvation?

CHAPTER 4

# MARY'S PRAYER

1. *Rest well, tiny hands. For though you belong to a king you will touch no satin, own no gold. You will grasp no pen, guide no brush. No, your tiny hands are reserved for works more precious: to touch a leper's wounds, to wipe a widow's weary tear, to claw the ground of Gethsemane.*

A. What petitions to God do you make on behalf of your children?

B. Think about some of the ways Jesus used his hands here on earth. What do these passages tell us about his nature: Mark 1:40–42; Matthew 14:28–31; Matthew 9:18–26; Matthew 19:13–15; Mark 8:22–26; Luke 4:40; Luke 24:36–39? Was it necessary for Jesus to touch people in order to heal them? Why do you think he chose to touch them?

C. What instructions did Jesus leave us in Matthew 25:31–46 about showing compassion and helping those in need? What are the consequences of ignoring these commands?

D. Today it is easy to help people from a distance without ever having to deal with them face to face. What is lost without that personal contact? Why do we shy away from personal contact? What face to face involvement are you willing to have to carry out Jesus' commands?

2. *And little heart...holy heart...pumping the blood of life through the universe: How many times will we break you?*

A. When you sin and break the Lord's commands, what reaction do you see Jesus having? Anger? Disgust? Frustration? Disappointment? Condemnation? "I knew it all along"? Do you imagine it breaking his heart?

B. Look at these passages that describe God's mercy and compassion and forgiving spirit: Exodus 34:4–7; Isaiah 55:6–7; Jeremiah 9:23–24; Micah 7:18–19; Ephesians 2:1–10. How does God respond when we are truly repentant? What are the most revealing and significant words in each passage?

C. According to 2 Corinthians 1:3–7, in what way do we share in the sufferings of Christ? If we share in his sufferings, how do we also share in his comfort? How do we then share his comfort with others?

D. How would you chart the progression from being a sinner that breaks the heart of Jesus to being a person capable of ministering to others?

CHAPTER 5

# LIMB-CLIMBER OR BRANCH-SITTER

1. *Joseph knew that the only thing worse than a venture into the unknown was the thought of denying his Master.*

A. What difficulties lay ahead for Joseph by venturing with God into the unknown? What risks did he have to take?

B. Although little is said about Joseph, note how he responded in each of these events: Matthew 1:18–24; Luke 2:21–24; Matthew 2:13–15; Matthew 2:19–23; Luke 2:41–48. How would you now characterize Joseph? How would you describe his belief in God?

C. In what ways does God call us today to venture into the unknown?

2. *Have you been called to go out on a limb for God? You can bet it won't be easy. Limb-climbing has never been easy.*

A. When have you felt that God was asking you to go out on a limb for him? How did you respond? What was the result?

B. Look at some others that God called to go out on a limb. What risk did God ask these people to take: Abraham (Genesis 22:1–19); Moses (Exodus 3:1–4:18); Gideon (Judges 7); the widow at Zarephath (1 Kings 17:7–24); the rich young ruler (Luke 18:18–30)? How did each respond? How did God respond to their willingness or unwillingness to go out on a limb for his sake?

C. For you, which of these "limbs" would have required the greatest faith?

D. From these examples, what principles can you derive about God's response to our going out on a limb for him?

E. Is God calling you now to go out on a limb? How do you plan to respond?

CHAPTER 6

# TWENTY-FIVE QUESTIONS FOR MARY

1. What have you wondered about Jesus' years growing up? What questions would you like to ask Mary?

2. What other questions would you like to ask Jesus?

3. Read John 1:1–14. How does John describe Jesus' existence prior to his being born to Mary?

4. Read Philippians 2:5–11. What was Jesus' attitude about coming to earth as a human? In what way should our attitude "be the same as that of Christ Jesus"?

5. If you could talk with one person from the Bible, other than Jesus, who would it be? Why? What questions would you ask?

6. Do you envision heaven as an opportunity to spend time talking with Jesus and Moses and Paul and people you have loved on earth? How does that make you feel about going to heaven?

Chapter 7

# Christmas Night

1. *The magical dust of Christmas glittered on the cheeks of humanity ever so briefly, reminding us of what is worth having and what we were intended to be.*

A. What kind of Christmas traditions did you have growing up? What kind of traditions are you establishing in your own family?

B. What are your priorities at Christmas time? Does Christmas time bring out the best or the worst in you?

C. In reality, what are the only things that matter? What would these passages say are the most important things in life: Deuteronomy 10:12–13; Ecclesiastes 12:13–14; Matthew 22:34–40; James 1:25–27?

D. What are your priorities for the next week? the next month? the next year?

2. *If he can do so much with such timid prayers lamely offered in December, how much more could he do if we thought of him every day?*

A. Do we limit God's ability to act? If so, how?

B. What images did Jesus use to describe the importance of commitment in these passages: Matthew 6:19–24; Mark 9:42–50; Matthew 13:1–23; Matthew 25:14–30?

C. What do the Scriptures say about consistency in and commitment to prayer? Read 1 Thessalonians 5:16–18; Ephesians 6:18; James 5:13–16; Luke 11:5–13; Luke 18:1–8.

D. In what way could you increase people's awareness of Christ throughout the year?

CHAPTER 8

# OUT OF THE CARPENTRY SHOP

1. *You see, he didn't have to go. He had a choice. He could have stayed. He could have kept his mouth shut. He could have ignored the call or at least postponed it.*

A. Did Jesus have a choice? Do you think he made that choice once or numerous times? Do you think he ever doubted that humanity was worth the price he was going to pay?

B. What do the following passages reveal about not only Jesus' willingness but his determination to die for our sins: John 10:11–18; Matthew 26:36–54; John 18:4–11; Philippians 2:6–8; Hebrews 7:23–27?

C. On a piece of paper, in one column list everything Jesus chose to give up for your sake. In a second column, list everything he has asked you to give up for his sake.

2. *He saw your face aglow the hour you first knew him. He saw your face in shame the hour you first fell. The same face that looked back at you from this morning's mirror, looked at him. And it was enough to kill him. He left because of you.*

A. Is it difficult to conceive of Jesus seeing you and hearing you centuries before you were born? Is it difficult to realize that even now he sees and understands everything about you? How do you make Jesus a present reality in your life?

B. To better understand how well Jesus knows each of us, read the following passages: Psalm 139:1–18; Matthew 10:29–31; Hebrews 4:13. What insights do they give?

C. Read one of the Gospel accounts of Jesus' arrest, trial and crucifixion (e.g. Matthew 26:3–27:61). Can you imagine someone choosing to suffer that pain and abuse specifically for you? Can you imagine God choosing to do so? Why did God choose to die for you?

D. How would it alter your life if a friend died for you? How does it alter your life to realize that Jesus died for you?

CHAPTER 9

# "JUST CALL ME JESUS"

1. *There was not one person who considered him too holy, too divine, or too celestial to touch. There was not one person who was reluctant to approach him for fear of being rejected.*

A. For what reasons did people approach Jesus? What were people's reactions to him?

B. How did Jesus treat the outcasts of society? The moral outcasts (John 8:1–11)? The social outcasts (Mark 2:13–17)? The physical and spiritual outcasts (Matthew 8:1–4; Mark 5:1–20)?

C. How did Jesus treat those who rejected him? Judas (Matthew 26:47–50)? Peter (Mark 14:66–72; 16:1–7)? the rich, young ruler (Mark 10:17–27)? What is the most surprising element of each instance?

D. For whom were Jesus' harshest words reserved (Matthew 23; John 2:12–16)? Why did Jesus condemn them?

E. How Christlike and approachable are you? to your children? your mate? your coworkers? strangers that you meet daily? those less fortunate than you? those who are "lower on the social ladder"? What could you do to make yourself more approachable?

2. *Remember. It is man who creates the distance. It is Jesus who builds the bridge.*

A. What causes people to move away from Jesus? Times of tragedy and difficulty? Times of success? Apathy? Why?

B. Based on the teachings in these passages, in what ways does Jesus build the bridge to us: Romans 8:5–17, 26; 1 John 5:14–15; John 5:24; Psalm 145:13b–20; Romans 5:6–8?

C. What images did Jesus use to show his concern for us? Look at these passages for some examples: Matthew 23:37; Luke 15:1–32; Isaiah 40:11. For you, which of these most powerfully illustrates his love for people?

D. Do you believe you are closer to or farther from Jesus than you were a year ago? In what ways would you like to move closer to him?

CHAPTER 10

# WOMEN OF WINTER

1. *Those who scramble in at quitting time get the same wage as those who beat the morning whistle. I guess that's what makes grace, grace.*

A. Have you known of someone who came to Jesus in the "winter" of his or her life? Or someone who came with seemingly little to offer in Jesus' kingdom? What impact did this person have?

B. Look at the "rest of the story" of these three women in Luke 7:11–17; John 4:1–42; and Luke 8:43–47. What impact did they and these events have on the people around them?

C. What circumstances or characteristics in these people did Jesus use to further his kingdom?

D. What "winter people" do you know? What circumstances or characteristics in them could God use to touch their hearts and the hearts of those around them?

2. *No, no one would have blamed Jesus for ignoring the three women. To have turned his head would have been much easier, less controversial, and not nearly as risky. But God, who made them, couldn't do that. And we, who follow him, can't either.*

A. When are you tempted to turn your head rather than deal with a "risky" person? For you, what elements of society require more risk than you are willing to take? How willing is your church to get involved with the controversial elements of society?

B. After reading Matthew 10:28–42, how would you define "risk" from God's perspective? What are we to fear? What are we not to fear?

C. If you had only Luke 14:7–14 to go by, how would you describe Jesus' "social ladder"?

D. What three ingredients would be essential for your church to become more involved with the "winter people" of society?

CHAPTER 11

# WHEN GOD SIGHED

1. *I'd thought of God as one who commands. I'd thought of God as one who weeps. I'd thought of God as one who calls forth the dead or created the universe with a command...but a God who sighs?*

A. How do you most often picture God? Can you envision God sighing? What might prompt God to sigh? What emotions does that imply?

B. Mark 7:34 describes it as a "deep sigh." Why do you think Jesus sighed? What lesson is there for us in Jesus' response?

C. Compare this incident to the one in Mark 8:11–13. Why do you think Jesus sighed when the Pharisees questioned him? How might Jesus' feelings have differed from the previous incident?

D. Read Romans 8:22–27 and 2 Corinthians 5:2–4 where Paul describes our groaning for heaven. What is conveyed by "groaning" in these passages?

E. Would you describe yourself as a person who "groans" for heaven? Why or why not? What perspective on life does it imply?

2. *So, I found a place for the word [sigh]. You might think it strange, but I placed it beside the word* comfort, *for in an indirect way, God's pain is our comfort. And in the agony of Jesus lies our hope.... That holy sigh assures us*

*that God still groans for his people. He groans for the day when all sighs will cease, when what was intended to be will be.*

A. What does Max mean by "God's pain is our comfort"? In what way is that a true statement?

B. Read John 17:1–26. What was God's design for our relationship with Jesus? for our relationship with each other? What was "intended to be"? How does God comfort us until the "day that all sighs will cease"? Why is unity so important?

C. Spend some time reading psalms that speak of the comfort God provides, such as Psalm 23, Psalm 34, and Psalm 46. In what ways does God comfort us?

D. In what ways do you see believers unified? In what areas do we need to strive for greater unity?

CHAPTER 12

# THE QUESTION FOR THE CANYON'S EDGE

1. *Only God can deal with our ultimate dilemma—death. And only the God of the Bible has dared to stand on the canyon's edge and offer an answer. He has to be God in the face of death. If not, he is not God anywhere.*

A. What does Max mean by "He has to be God in the face of death. If not, he is not God anywhere"? What is the answer to death that God offers? How did he offer the answer?

B. Read 1 Corinthians 15:12–28 and restate in your own words Paul's argument concerning death and resurrection.

C. How would you answer someone who questions that Jesus rose from the dead and that there is life after death?

2. *Do you believe that a young, penniless itinerant is larger than your death? Do you truly believe that death is nothing more than an entrance ramp to a new highway?*

A. Max describes death as an entrance ramp. What other helpful comparisons can you make to explain what death is like?

B. What insights do these passages give into the relationship of death to life: Luke 20:34–38; John 11:25–26; Romans 8:10–11?

C. What would you say to someone facing death that would help the person see God's answer?

CHAPTER 13

# A TALE OF TWO TREES

1. *The struggle. The snake. The lie. The enticement. Heart torn, lured. Soul drawn to pleasure, to independence, to importance. Inner agony. Whose will?*

A. Read Genesis 2:15–17 and 3:1–24. What temptations were present? What choices were made by Adam? by Eve? Whose will controlled the choices?

B. To what extent are those same temptations still prevalent today? To which ones are we most susceptible?

C. Based on Adam's and Eve's example, what makes us susceptible to temptation and to self-will?

2. *Once again the struggle. The snake. The enticement. Heart torn, lured. Once again the question, "Whose will?"*

A. Read Matthew 26:1–75. What enticements were present at this struggle? for Judas? for Peter? for Jesus?

B. To what extent are these temptations strong today?

C. How did Jesus show submission to God's will at the Passover meal? in Gethsemane? at his arrest? before the high priest and the Sanhedrin?

D. From Jesus' example, what principles can you deduce for resisting temptation and for submitting to God's will?

CHAPTER 14

# NO ACCIDENT

1. *Jesus was born crucified. Whenever he became conscious of who he was, he also became conscious of what he had to do.*

A. Do you ever wish you could know your future? What if that future held a painful death in an effort to save another person's life? Would you want to know ahead of time? Would you try to alter the course of events?

B. As Jesus anticipates his imminent death in Matthew 16:21–23; Luke 9:51; Luke 13:31–32; and John 10:17–18, what attitudes about his coming death does he reveal? How did he respond to those who tried to alter his course?

C. Is there a goal in your life that you pursue with single-minded devotion? Should there be such a goal? What would it be? How would it change your daily life to pursue it with total devotion?

2. *Had Jesus been forced to nail himself to the cross, he would have done it. For it was not the soldiers who killed him, nor the screams of the mob—it was his devotion to us.*

A. How would you rank the following according to their responsibility for his death: Judas, the mob, the religious leaders, the Roman authorities, and the soldiers? Is there anyone else you would add to the list?

B. According to these passages who was responsible for Jesus' death: Romans 5:8; Ephesians 2:1–5; 1 John 4:9–10?

C. According to Psalm 145:20; Ephesians 3:17–19; and John 14:23, what happens when we realize Jesus' devotion to us and respond with love for him?

D. As Jesus' death was an act of will on his part, how are our lives to be an act of will? What is the result when we don't make conscious choices to live for Jesus? What controls our lives?

C H A P T E R 15

# REDISCOVERING AMAZEMENT

1. *We wonder, with so many miraculous testimonies around us, how we could escape God. But somehow we do.... Or what is pathetically worse, we demand more. More signs. More proof. More hat tricks. As if God were some vaudeville magician we could summon for a dollar.*

A. Do you ever wish you could have witnessed the miracles Jesus performed on earth? Do you think it would increase your faith? Do you ever wish that God would perform a specific miracle for you now so that it would be easier to believe?

B. How did seeing Jesus' miracles affect people's faith? What different responses were there when Jesus raised Lazarus from the dead (John 11:38–53)?

C. Read these examples of people who asked for miracles: Matthew 12:38–39; Matthew 16:1–4; Acts 8:9–23. What was wrong with their motive in each case?

D. According to John 2:11; Acts 2:22; and John 20:30–31, what was God's purpose in miracles?

E. Upon what should our belief in Jesus be based?

2. *Would you like to see Jesus? Do you dare be an eyewitness of His Majesty? Then rediscover amazement.*

A. What event has most strongly impressed you with the majesty of God? For you, what setting most strongly reveals God's presence—the mountains, the ocean, a starry night, a rainbow?

B. Read some of the passages that describe God's miracles and majesty, such as Job 9:4–10; Job 38, 39; and Psalm 104. How do they affect your image of God? Based on these passages, what words would you use to describe God?

C. Read Job 42:1–6. What was Job's response to God's description of his power? In what way is your response similar? different?

CHAPTER 16

# HOPE

1. *Our problem is not so much that God doesn't give us what we hope for as it is that we don't know the right thing for which to hope.*

A. Give an instance in which God failed to answer a prayer, for which you were later grateful.

B. Read 2 Samuel 7. What did David hope to do? What were his motives? What was God's answer to David? How did David respond to God's answer?

C. Read the accounts in Matthew 20:20–28 and Mark 10:35–45 of the request made by James and John and their mother. What did they hope for? What appears to have been their motive? In what way were they hoping for the wrong thing?

D. From these two examples and the others in the chapter, what principles can you determine about the things for which we should hope and pray? What should be our response when God answers us differently than we have hoped?

2. *Hope is not a granted wish or a favor performed; no, it is far greater than that. It is a zany, unpredictable dependence on a God who loves to surprise us out of our socks and be there in the flesh to see our reaction.*

A. Have you ever been surprised by a far greater answer to your prayer than you could have anticipated? Give an example.

B. "Hope," as it is used in the New Testament, is not wishful thinking but confident expectation. It is not desire but dependence. Read the following passages substituting "confident expectation" for "hope" each place it appears: Romans 15:4; Titus 1:1–3; Titus 3:3–8; Hebrews 6:13–20; Hebrews 10:19–25 and Hebrews 11:1. How does that affect the impact of these verses? In your opinion, which verse does it make the strongest?

C. What do you "confidently expect" from God? Beyond what reason dictates, in what ways do you absolutely, unquestioningly depend on God?

CHAPTER 17

# ETERNAL INSTANTS

1. *An eternal instant. A moment that reminds you of the treasures surrounding you. Your home. Your peace of mind. Your health.*

A. Describe an "eternal instant" you experienced. What were the circumstances? What was the impact?

B. According to the following passages, what are some of the treasures we have on earth: Psalm 127:3–5; Psalm 128:1–6; Proverbs 31:10–12; Proverbs 19:14?

C. According to these examples, while Jesus was on earth, what did he do to stay focused on what was important: Matthew 14:22–23; Mark 1:35; Luke 5:15–16; Luke 9:18?

D. In what way does our lifestyle work against "eternal instants"? What could we do to create more opportunities for these special moments? What could you do this week with your family—earthly or spiritual—that would remind you of what a blessing family is?

2. *Eternal instants remind us that love is still the greatest possession and the future is nothing to fear.*

A. Do you agree that love is the greatest possession? If so, how would you justify that statement? If not, what is the greatest possession?

B. What makes the future seem fearful? Do you expect the next ten years to be more difficult than the last ten? Do you look toward the turn of the century with anticipation or anxiety?

C. Read Psalm 103; 2 Timothy 2:11–13; and Hebrews 10:19–25. Who can face the future with confidence?
D. According to these passages, why can we feel secure about the future: Psalm 27:1–5; Psalm 121; Isaiah 54:10?

E. How would you explain to a new Christian what is meant by "perfect love drives out fear" (1 John 4:18)?

CHAPTER 18

# WHAT DO YOU SEE?

1. *Seekers of popularity, power, and pleasure. The end result is the same: painful unfulfillment.*

A. What examples can you give of people who have sought popularity, power, and pleasure only to find emptiness and pain?

B. What did each of the following people seek: Absalom (2 Samuel 15:1–17; 2 Samuel 18:1–18); the Jewish leaders (John 12:37–50); Moses (Hebrews 11:23–28); the Corinthians (1 Corinthians 5:1–13; 6:9–20)? What was the result in each case?

C. What wisdom does Proverbs offer in these passages regarding popularity, power, and pleasure: 21:17; 11:7; 13:20; 18:24; 19:6; 21:22; 25:6–7; 25:27?

D. What proverb would you write regarding popularity, power, or pleasure? By contrast, what has brought you the most fulfillment in life?

2. *Destiny? Tomorrow? Truth? All are questions within the reach of the man who knows his source. It is in seeing Jesus that man sees his Source.*

A. For the person who knows Jesus as his source, what are the answers to "What is my destiny?" "What does tomorrow hold?" and "What is truth?"

B. Read the following passages to see how Jesus answered these same questions: Destiny: Matthew 25:31–46; Tomorrow: Matthew 6:25–34; Truth: John 3:3–21; John 5:24–30; John 6:53–58; John 8:51; John 14:12. How would you restate his answer to each question?

C. What answers are there for the person who does not see Jesus as his source? Read John 3:18–20 and 1 John 5:10–12.

D. How would you direct someone to see Jesus as the source for life's answers?

C H A P T E R 19

# HE FORGOT

1. *For all the things he [God] does do, this is one thing he refuses to do. He refuses to keep a list of my wrongs.*

A. What good can come from remembering our sins? At what point does it become harmful to remember our sins?

B. The Bible uses several images to depict God's forgiveness of our sins. Which of these helps you most to visualize that God truly forgets: Psalm 103:12; Isaiah 1:18; Isaiah 43:25; Psalm 32:1; Isaiah 44:22?

C. Read Psalm 32, which is a psalm of praise for God's forgiveness. What insights does it give into the effect of unconfessed sin? into God's response to the penitent heart?

D. On a piece of paper, write down a sin that you have had difficulty forgiving in yourself. Then erase your writing or burn the paper. When you are tempted to agonize over that sin again, remember that it has been destroyed by God and by you.

2. *We are presumptuous not when we marvel at his grace, but when we reject it.*

A. Why do you think people reject God's grace in forgiving sins? Why do people continue to feel guilty even after asking God's forgiveness?

B. Because we are clothed with Christ, how may we approach God's throne in prayer, according to these passages: Ephesians 3:8–12; Hebrews 4:14–16; Hebrews 10:19–23?

C. If we truly understand God's grace toward us, what is our natural response, according to Hebrews 10:24–25?

D. Based on the lesson, what do you want to remember better? What do you want to forget more easily?

CHAPTER 20

# FACING THE FACTS

1. *Have you ever noticed the endless extremes to which a person will go to hide the realities of life?*

A. What examples do you see of society's desire to hide or escape the realities of life, such as aging, death, and self? Do you see the trend increasing? If so, in what ways? What reality do you think people have the hardest time facing?

B. What is God's perspective on aging, as seen in these passages: Job 12:12; Proverbs 16:31; Isaiah 46:4; Titus 2:3–5?

C. What is God's perspective on us as his creation, as seen in these passages: Psalm 8:3–8; Psalm 139:1–18?

D. How are the older members viewed in your church? What contributions do they make to the church? to the community? Are they isolated from the mainstream of the church, or are they active participants and leaders in the church's programs? What vital roles are they filling?

2. *Funerals, divorces, illnesses, and stays in the hospital—you can't lie about life at such times. Maybe that's why he's always present at such moments.*

A. In the face of a serious illness or the death of a loved one, what was important to you? What was unimportant? What was comforting to you? What truths about life were especially clear?

B. What insight do these passages provide about God's perspective on death: Psalm 116:15; Romans 14:7–8; 1 Corinthians 15:50–58; Revelation 14:13?

C. What passage of Scripture is the most comforting to you when you consider the reality of death?

D. What would you want said about you at your funeral?

CHAPTER 21

# LIGHT OF THE... STORAGE CLOSET?

1. *"I'm not ready," the candle explained with pleading eyes. "I need more preparation."*

A. How much preparation is needed to be an effective "light" for Christ? When is too little preparation dangerous? In what way is excessive preparation dangerous? At what point does the desire for more preparation become an excuse for hiding one's light?

B. What can be learned from Acts 18:24–28; Hebrews 5:11–6:3; and James 1:22–25 about balancing preparation with action?

C. In what area are you best prepared to serve? In what ways could you use that preparation more fully?

2. *The last candle had a female voice, very pleasant to the ear. "I'd like to help," she explained, "but lighting the darkness is not my gift."*

A. How can we determine what our gifts are?

B. What do 1 Corinthians 12:1–11 and Romans 12:3–8 reveal about spiritual gifts?

C. What should our response be when we are asked to serve in an area that we don't consider our strength? Is it wisdom or selfishness not to serve in areas where we believe we aren't "gifted"? Why?

3. *"Where did you buy those candles anyway?" "Oh, they're church candles. Remember the church that closed down across town? I bought them there."*

A. What is the meaning of Max's story about the candles? What problems within churches is he pointing out? To what extent do you see those problems surfacing among Christians?

CHAPTER 22

# BLIND AMBITION

1. *Ambition is that grit in the soul which creates disenchantment with the ordinary and puts the dare into dreams.*

A. For you, what historical or contemporary person best exemplifies positive ambition—one who dared to dream?

B. Look at the following examples of people who dared to dream: Joshua (Numbers 13:1–14:9; 27:12–23); David (1 Samuel 17:1–54); and the Canaanite woman (Matthew 15:21–28). In each case, why do you believe they were successful in achieving their dreams?

C. What is your greatest ambition at this point in your life? What motivates that ambition?

2. *Blind ambition is a giant step away from God and one step closer to catastrophe.*

A. What modern examples can you give of blind ambition even within churches? How can we distinguish between a sincere desire to be a leader in the church and blind ambition?

B. There are several examples of men in the Bible who desired to "build" for the Lord—the men at Babel (Genesis 11:1–9); David (2 Samuel 7); and Peter (Matthew 17:1–8). In each case, why did God thwart their plans?

C. How does Psalm 127:1 relate to these examples?

D. What questions would you ask yourself to check that your ambitions are rightly motivated?

CHAPTER 23

# WARNINGS

1. *Warnings can be as blunt as a sledgehammer and we still turn our heads and whistle them away.*

A. Give an example of a time when you ignored a warning and paid the price for it.

B. In addition to the passages Max mentions, what warnings does Proverbs offer about laziness (10:4–5; 12:11, 24); stinginess (11:24–26, 28; 19:17); and self-control (12:16, 23; 20:25; 21:23)?

C. In looking through Proverbs, what other warnings do you see occurring frequently?

D. Are there warning lights that you have been ignoring? about your health? your relationships with family or friends? your relationship with God?

E. If you were to write a proverb of warning for people today, what would you warn them about?

2. *We're often surprised at life's mishaps, but when pressed against the wall of honesty we have to admit that...we could have avoided many problems.*

A. Do you agree that we could avoid many of the mishaps in our lives? What kinds of mishaps are preventable? Why are we reluctant to admit that there have been warning signs?

B. Perhaps one of the best known examples of a person ignoring a warning is the story of Peter's denial of Jesus. Read the account in Matthew 26:31–46, 69–75 or in one of the other Gospels. How did Peter respond to Jesus' warning? Why? What made him deny Jesus even after being warned?

C. What lessons can we learn from Peter's experience that would help us heed the warnings we are given?

CHAPTER 24

# FATHER'S DAY: A TRIBUTE

1. *It seems strange that he isn't here. I guess that's because he was never gone. He was always close by. Always available.*

A. What images come to mind when you think of your dad? What words would you use to describe him as a father?

B. What God-given role are fathers to play in the lives of their children? What do these passages reveal: Deuteronomy 6:4–9; Psalm 78:1–8; Proverbs 3:11–12; Proverbs 13:24; Proverbs 22:6; Ephesians 6:4; 1 Timothy 3:1–5; 1 Timothy 5:8?

C. In order to fulfill those responsibilities, what three factors would be most critical?

D. What positive influences did your dad have on your life? If he is still alive, how could you express your appreciation to him for those things? If he isn't, to whom could you pass on those blessings?

2. *He is still…in a special way, very present.*

A. If you have lost a parent or some other close family member, in what way is that person still very present with you?

B. What does your family do to keep the loved one's memory alive? What makes those memories joyous rather than sad?

C. Why do you suppose God describes himself as our father? What fatherly characteristics do you see in these passages: Isaiah 64:8; Matthew 7:11; Matthew 10:29–31; 2 Thessalonians 2:16–17?

D. How does your faith affect your acceptance of the death of a loved one?

CHAPTER 25

# FAMILY SEDANS OF THE FAITH

1. *Reliability is the quality that produces not momentary heroics but monumental lives.*

A. Which has more appeal to us—to be considered heroic or reliable? Why? To what extent does Christianity call us to be heroic? To what extent does Christianity call us to be reliable?

B. Even though little is said about Andrew, what do you learn about him in each of these instances: John 1:35–42; 6:1–11; 12:20–22?

C. Anna is mentioned only in Luke 2:36–38, yet those verses sum up the eighty years of her life. In what ways was she remarkably reliable?

D. How would you rate your own reliability? How reliable are you in bringing others to Christ, like Andrew? How reliable are you in prayer, like Anna?

2. *I'm wondering if this book has found its way into the hands of some contemporary saints of reliability. If such is the case I can't resist the chance to say two things. The first? Thank you.*

A. Within your own church what examples do you see of people who are models of reliability in their service to God? Where is their work generally done—"on stage" or "behind the scenes"? How are lives affected by their reliability?

B. Another word for "reliable" can be "faithful." How does Matthew 24:45–51 describe the faithful and unfaithful servants? What will be their end?

C. The faithfulness of God is a familiar theme throughout the Bible. Read Psalm 117. In what ways will God be faithful forever?

D. What could you do to thank or honor the "family sedans" within your church and to encourage others to be even more reliable?

CHAPTER 26

# INSENSITIVE SLURS

1. *If someone hurts your feelings intentionally you know how to react. You know the source of the pain. But if someone accidentally bruises your soul, it's difficult to know how to respond.*

A. How do you respond if someone intentionally attacks you or your family or your friends? How do you respond if someone accidentally hurts you? Do you acknowledge it or ignore it? Can you slough it off or does the pain linger?

B. What wisdom do the following verses provide in responding to insults, intentional or not: Proverbs 19:11; Ecclesiastes 7:21–22; Luke 11:4; Luke 17:3–4; and 1 Corinthians 4:12–13?

C. To what extent does it matter if the attacker asks for forgiveness? How are we to respond if he asks for forgiveness? If he doesn't?

2. *He who dares to call himself God's ambassador is not afforded the luxury of idle words.*

A. Give an example of an instance in which you accidentally hurt someone by what you said.

B. Read Matthew 12:33–37. What is meant by "careless" words? What does this passage mean?

C. Read Proverbs 10:1–32. What contrasts are there between the words of the wicked and the words of the righteous?

D. What is the best advice you can give for using our words to God's glory?

CHAPTER 27

# A SONG IN THE DARK

1. *The passersby had various reactions. Some were curious and gazed unabashedly. Others were uncomfortable.... Most, however, hardly noticed him.*

A. In which category do you fall? When confronted with someone like the blind beggar, are you curious, uncomfortable, or generally oblivious? Why?

B. Are you reluctant to get involved, to get too close to the situation? Why or why not?

C. What was Jesus' response anytime people tried to shield him from others in need? How did he respond to the blind man (Mark 10:46–52); the children (Mark 10:13–16); the Canaanite woman (Matthew 15:21–28); Lazarus (John 11:1–16)? Why did Jesus' followers try to keep these people from him?

D. What can be done individually and as a church not to "pass by" those in need?

2. *Someone had told him, or maybe he'd told himself, that tomorrow's joy is fathered by today's acceptance. Acceptance of what, at least for the moment, you cannot alter.*

A. Where is the right balance between accepting difficult circumstances and striving to improve them?

B. A striking example in the Bible of a person accepting what he could not change was Paul. Read 2 Corinthians 12:7–10. Why was Paul given the thorn in the flesh? How easily did he accept it? How did he use it for good?

C. Paul wrote to the Philippians apparently after he had been given the thorn in the flesh. What do we learn from Philippians 4:10–13 about his attitude of acceptance? What made Paul able to accept adversity?

D. What does Philippians 4:4–9 teach us about how to find joy even in difficult circumstances?

Chapter 28

# In the Mud of Jabbok

1. *The best way to deal with our past is to hitch up our pants, roll up our sleeves, and face it head on.*

A. What happens when we try to ignore the past? What does Max mean by facing it "head on"? How is that different from dwelling on the past?

B. Read Genesis 32:1–33:3. Why did Jacob fear meeting Esau again? How did Jacob face the situation head on?

C. How can we wrestle with God in dealing with our past? In what way might we also carry a limp?

2. *And for you who wonder if you've played too long to change, take courage from Jacob's legacy. No man is too bad for God.*

A. Have you ever talked with someone who believed he or she had lived too bad a life to be accepted by God? What did you say to them?

B. To get a picture of Jacob, the "riverboat gambler," read Genesis 27:1–45. What character traits does he exhibit?

C. Yet, at the end of his life, what promise does God make to Jacob in Genesis 46:2–4? What blessings came through the descendants of Jacob?

D. What passages would you recommend to someone who is struggling with God's ability and willingness to forgive? Consider Isaiah 55:6–7; 1 Timothy 1:13–16; and 1 John 2:1–2.

E. Read Psalm 78, which describes Israel's relationship with God. How many examples does it give of God's provision for Israel despite their rejection of him? In one sentence, what is the message of this psalm?

CHAPTER 29

# A LITTLE BIT OF HANGIN'

1. *His aim is deadly. His goal is nothing less than to take what is most precious to us and make it appear most common.*

A. What things are easiest for us to take for granted? A mate? Children? Health? God's love? Our lives? The future? Our salvation?

B. Are those who have grown up believing in God at greater risk for taking their salvation for granted? In your experience, who seems most susceptible to becoming apathetic?

C. What happens when we take our salvation for granted and become mediocre? What warning was given to the church in Ephesus that had lost its original love for Christ (Revelation 2:2–5)? What warning was given to the church in Laodicea for being lukewarm (Revelation 3:14–22)?

D. How can we keep from taking for granted that which is precious? As Max put the picture of Jenna on his desk, what reminder of "the precious" could you put in front of yourself?

2. *The stool was kicked out from under my feet and the rope jerked around my neck just long enough to remind me of what really matters. It was a divine slap, a gracious knock on the head, a severe mercy.*

A. What is meant by a "severe mercy"? Have you ever experienced a "severe mercy," "a divine slap"? What happened? How did it change you?

B. In each of the following cases, how was a "divine slap" given: Jonah (Jonah 1–4); Zechariah (Luke 1:5–25, 57–80); Paul (2 Corinthians 12:7–10)? What benefit came from each?

C. How can we learn to respond to difficulties as severe mercies rather than letting difficulties defeat us?

# Carmelita

1. *We too were frightened orphans.... We too were rescued by a compassionate visitor, a generous parent who offered us a home and a name.*

A. In what ways does the statement above aptly describe what God has done for us?

B. To what is our relationship with God and Jesus compared in each of these passages: Isaiah 64:8; Psalm 95:6–7; 1 Peter 2:16; Romans 6:22; John 13:35? What different aspects of our relationship does each comparison point out?

C. How do these passages describe our relationship to God and to Jesus: Romans 8:6–17; 1 John 2:28–3:10; Matthew 7:7–12? What is unique about being God's very children? What is significant about the phrase "Abba, Father" in Romans 8:15?

D. In John 14:15–21, Jesus himself said he would not leave us as orphans. What did he promise those who love him?

E. Is it hard to conceive of having the God of the universe as your own father? When do you feel closest to your heavenly father?

2. *We, too, should stand in the quiet company of him who saved us, and weep tears of gratitude and offer words of thankfulness. For it is not our bodies that have been rescued, but our souls.*

A. Have you ever witnessed a dramatic rescue? How did you feel?

B. According to the following passages, what are some of the things from which God has rescued us: Psalm 72:12–14; Romans 7:24–25; Titus 3:3–8; Colossians 1:13–14? How do we feel when we realize the fate from which we have been rescued? Compare the intensity of our emotions in a physical rescue with those in a spiritual rescue.

C. Read Revelation 7:9–17 and Psalm 8. What emotions do they capture? Spend a month reading the Psalms to focus on gratitude and praise for your salvation.

CHAPTER 31

# SEEING THE SUMMIT

1. *Christianity, in its purest form, is nothing more than seeing Jesus.*

A. What hinders us from seeing Jesus? Are we not looking? In what ways is he too obscure? In what ways is he perhaps too familiar?

B. What promise is given to those who truly seek him? See Isaiah 55:6–7; Hebrews 11:6; Matthew 7:7–8.

C. Has *God Came Near* helped you to see Jesus more clearly? If so, in what way? What new impressions do you take with you?

2. *Christian service, in its purest form, is nothing more than imitating him who we see.*

A. If you could do only one thing to imitate Christ, what one thing would you choose to best depict Jesus to those who don't know him?

B. According to Ephesians 5:1–2, what will characterize those who imitate Christ? By looking at the greater context of Ephesians 4:17–5:21, what else will be true of those who imitate Christ?

C. What one area of your life could you work on this week to imitate Christ more closely?

*"To see His Majesty and to imitate him, that is the sum of Christianity."*
*May this book and this Bible study have helped you to see His Majesty more clearly and to imitate him more fully.*

Multnomah Publishers®

The publisher and author would love to hear your comments about this book. *Please contact us at:*
www.multnomah.net/lucado

# Notes

*Chapter 1*

1. Luke 1:33

*Chapter 2*

1. Mark 12:31
2. Mark 10:29
3. Matthew 5:44
4. Matthew 28:20
5. 1 Corinthians 15:51–52, NKJV

*Chapter 9*

1. Colossians 4:11
2. Acts 13:6
3. Matthew 27:17; William Barclay, *Jesus As They Saw Him* (Grand Rapids, Mich.: Wm. B. Eerdmans).
4. Matthew 1:21
5. Hebrews 4:15

*Chapter 10*

1. Luke 7:11–17
2. John 4:1–42
3. Luke 8:43–47

*Chapter 11*

1. Mark 7:31–35
2. Romans 8:22–27

*Chapter 13*

1. 1 Corinthians 15:21–22, TEV

*Chapter 14*

1. Acts 2:22–23

2. Isaiah 53:10
3. Luke 9:51
4. John 10:17–18
5. John 6:61–62
6. Luke 13:32
7. Luke 9:31
8. John 1:29
9. John 10:15
10. Matthew 16:21
11. Matthew 21:42
12. Mark 14:3–9
13. John 13:27–30

*Chapter 15*

1. Psalm 139:7–8

*Chapter 16*

1. Luke 24:13–24

*Chapter 19*

1. Hebrews 8:12, RSV
2. Psalm 103:12
3. Hebrews 8:12, RSV
4. Isaiah 1:18, TLB
5. Galatians 3:27, RSV (italics mine)

*Chapter 22*

1. Genesis 11:4, RSV (italics mine)

*Chapter 23*

1. Proverbs 26:17
2. Proverbs 6:26–29, TLB
3. Hebrews 2:1
4. Galatians 6:7
5. Proverbs 21:19, NKJV

6. Proverbs 26:22
7. 1 Corinthians 15:33
8. Matthew 10:33
9. Proverbs 23:13–14, NKJV
10. Proverbs 19:27, NKJV
11. Proverbs 6:23, NKJV
12. Proverbs 13:10

*Chapter 25*

1. *Inside Sports* (September 1986), 10.
2. John 1:42; 6:8–9; 12:21–22
3. Philippians 2:25–30; 4:18

*Chapter 26*

1. James 3:6
2. Proverbs 21:23
3. Proverbs 13:3
4. Proverbs 10:19

*Chapter 28*

1. Genesis 32

*Chapter 31*

1. Philippians 3:19, Phillips
2. John 1:14, Phillips
3. 2 Peter 1:16b, RSV
4. John 3:3

# More Encouraging Words from Max Lucado

## God Came Near: Chronicles of the Christ

This proven bestseller brings readers face-to-face with the awesome truth that God dwelt among us. He wants us to be eyewitnesses to His majesty, to see Him for ourselves, to know Him as friend.

**ISBN 1-57673-386-6**

**Available in Drive Time Audio™ ISBN 1-57673-532-X**

## Six Hours One Friday

They were the most critical hours in history. For during those six hours on that Friday, God embedded in the earth anchors sturdy enough to withstand any storm—even the ones Christians face today.

**ISBN 1-57673-601-6**

## The Gift for All People

*The Gift for All People* is a celebration of God's gift of salvation wrapped in a collection of inspirational stories. The concluding special story, written especially for this book, urges readers to give their lives to Jesus Christ and shows them how to do so.

**ISBN 1-57673-464-1**

## No Wonder They Call Him the Savior

This bestseller by beloved author Max Lucado focuses on Jesus and the vital importance of the Cross to the Christian faith and our daily lives.

**ISBN 1-57673-388-2**

**Available in Drive Time Audio™ ISBN 1-57673-533-8**

## And the Angels Were Silent

In one of Max Lucado's most insightful and moving books ever, he'll lead you from Friday's defeat to Sunday's victory. Like never before, believers and seekers alike will see Christ's passion, sense His power, and hear His promise.

**ISBN 1-57673-599-0**

**Available in Drive Time Audio™ ISBN 1-57673-732-2**

# Treasured Gift Editions from Max Lucado

**God Came Near: Chronicles of the Christ**

In this newly repackaged gift edition of a timeless bestseller, beloved author Max Lucado gently leads readers to glimpse the risen Lord in all his glory and feel His loving presence in their lives.

**ISBN 1-57673-723-3**

**The Final Week of Jesus**

These selections from Max Lucado's book *And the Angels Were Silent* are combined with full-color, pastel illustrations to bring home powerful truths. See Jesus' passion. And hear His promise.

**ISBN 1-088070-630-9**

**The Cross**

With dramatic photos and memorable selections from Max Lucado's treasured writings, this magnificent gift book celebrates the glory, the mystery, and the inescapable reality of the cross. Timeless photographic images depict the cross in spiritually moving ways...and cross-centered inspirational thoughts beautifully highlight God's ultimate sacrifice.

**ISBN 1-57673-920-1**

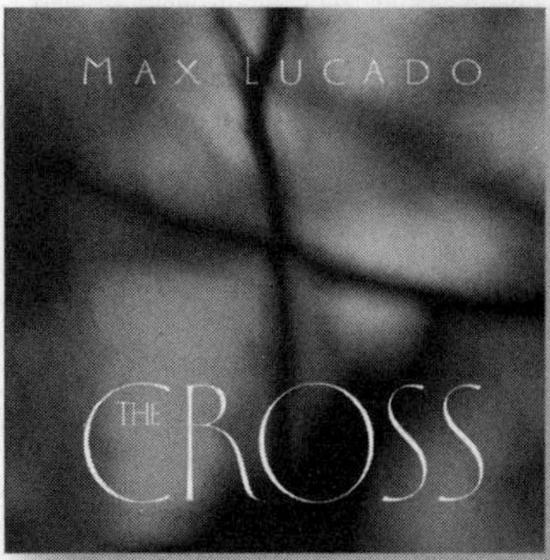


**No Wonder They Call Him the Savior**

Bestselling author Max Lucado invites readers to meet the blue-collar Jew—as never before—whose claim altered a world and whose promise has never been equaled.

**ISBN 1-57673-754-3**